THE MALE EGO

▸ ▸ ▸ ▸ ▸ ▸ ▸ ▸ ▸ ▸ ▸

THE MALE EGO

WILLARD GAYLIN, M.D.

VIKING

VIKING
Published by the Penguin Group
Viking Penguin, a division of Penguin Books USA Inc.,
375 Hudson Street, New York, New York 10014, U.S.A.
Penguin Books Ltd, 27 Wrights Lane, London W8 5TZ, England
Penguin Books Australia Ltd, Ringwood, Victoria, Australia
Penguin Books Canada Ltd, 10 Alcorn Avenue, Suite 300,
Toronto, Ontario, Canada M4V 3B2
Penguin Books (N.Z.) Ltd, 182–190 Wairau Road, Auckland 10, New Zealand

Penguin Books Ltd, Registered Offices:
Harmondsworth, Middlesex, England

First published in 1992 by Viking Penguin,
a division of Penguin Books USA Inc.

1 3 5 7 9 10 8 6 4 2

Grateful acknowledgment is made for permission to reprint the following copyrighted
works: Cavafy, C. P., "Monotony" and "The City," Keeley, Edmund and Sherrard,
Philip, trans., C. P. Cavafy: *Collected Poems*, ed. George Savidis. Copyright © 1975
by Edmund Keeley and Philip Sherrard. Reprinted by permission of Princeton University Press. E. E. Cummings, "Buffalo Bill's" is reprinted from *Tulips and Chimneys*
by E. E. Cummings, edited by George James Firmage, by permission of Liveright
Publishing Corporation. Copyright 1923, 1925 and renewed 1951, 1953 by E. E.
Cummings. Copyright © 1973 by the Trustees of the E. E. Cummings Trust. Copyright © 1973, 1976 by George James Firmage. James Dickey, excerpts from *Deliverance*
by James Dickey. Copyright © 1970 by James Dickey. Reprinted by permission of
Houghton Mifflin Co., and James Dickey and his agents, Raines & Raines, 71 Park
Avenue, New York, N.Y. 10016. All rights reserved. David Gilmore, excerpts from
Manhood in the Making: Cultural Concepts of Masculinity. Copyright © 1990 by Yale
University. Reprinted by permission of the publisher, Yale University Press. Gilbert
Herdt, excerpts from *Guardian of the Flutes: Idioms of Masculinity*, © 1984. Reprinted
by permission of the publisher, McGraw-Hill, Inc. James Joyce, excerpts from "Counterparts," from *Dubliners* by James Joyce. Copyright 1916 by B. W. Heubsch. Definitive text copyright © 1967 by the Estate of James Joyce. Used by permission of
Viking Penguin, a division of Penguin Books USA Inc. Norman Mailer, excerpts
from *Why Are We in Vietnam?* Copyright © 1967 by Norman Mailer. Reprinted by
permission of the author and the author's agents, Scott Meredith Literary Agency,
Inc., 845 Third Avenue, New York, New York 10022. Philip Shenon, excerpts from
"War Notebook," *The New York Times*, 19 February 1991, and "Irate Wife, Talky
Mistress, Shellshocked General," *The New York Times*, 1 August 1991. Copyright ©
1991 by The New York Times Company. Reprinted by permission.

LIBRARY OF CONGRESS CATALOGING IN PUBLICATION DATA
Gaylin, Willard.
The male ego / Willard Gaylin.
p.   cm.
Includes bibliographical references and index.
ISBN 0–670–83588–9
1. Masculinity (Psychology)   2. Men—Psychology.   I. Title.
BF692.5.G38 1992
155.6'32—dc20   91–45581

Printed in the United States of America
Set in Plantin Light   •   Designed by Ann Gold

Dedicated with love to:

David Heyward and Charlie Smith,
  who will live the male experience,

    and

Emily Heyward, Laura Smith, and Sarah Heyward,
  who must live with it

Buffalo Bill's
defunct
        who used to
        ride a watersmooth-silver
                                    stallion
and break onetwothreefourfive pigeonsjustlikethat
                                        Jesus

he was a handsome man
                    and what i want to know is
how do you like your blueeyed boy
Mister Death

                            —e. e. cummings

ACKNOWLEDGMENTS

As a man writing a book about the male experience, I have, with serendipity, been blessed with an absolutely essential ingredient: a coterie of wise, supportive, and constructively critical women.

My gratitude to all:
At the Hastings Center: Marna Howarth, Janet Bower, and Julie Rothstein
My editors and agent: Kathryn Court, Beena Kamlani, and Pam Bernstein
My home-grown editors (and daughters): Jody Heyward and Ellen Smith
And, as always, my life-long collaborator in life itself, my wife Betty.

—W. G.

CONTENTS

INTRODUCTION:
METHODS AND MADNESS

For two hundred thousand years or more, *Homo sapiens* relentlessly pursued his conquest of the earth. Armed with a physiology that alerted him to danger and an intelligence that outmaneuvered stronger and larger foes, he proceeded to establish his dominion over "the fish of the sea, and over the fowl of the air, and over every living thing that creepeth upon the earth." Equipped by nature with the hands of a master builder and the imagination of a scientist, he molded this planet to his own design and purposes. But something strange and unexpected has happened on this march to glory: two hundred years of modern civilization is undoing our evolution.

Our capacity to change the world permitted us to create an environment that is inimical with our physiology. Our bodies are directing us toward behavior that no longer serves our needs. We have created an artificial world in which we no longer work. It was for the most part men—having the power—who designed our culture. With a tragic irony it is that titan, the human male—despite what you may have heard— who is now becoming obsolete and unreliable.

Men and women are different. Those differences are not merely cultural artifacts. Culture must act on a genetic endowment that elicits different responses to the same stimulus from men and women. The intuitive male physiological responses are out of whack with the conditions of the culture he has created: they are driving him to solutions that are ineffective, mobilizing him for conflicts that are now defunct. If the female sensibility must be understood to repair past injustices, the male ego must now be understood to protect future survival.

It is with a certain amount of trepidation that I reenter the arena of gender role. My first research interest and first published papers were in the specific field of masculine identification: what it means to be a "man" and how we experience failures in manhood. And while I may have strayed far afield in more recent research and writings, identification (both masculine and feminine) has been a central concern and continuing interest in my day-to-day practice of psychoanalysis and psychiatry. Why then the trepidation?

The rebirth of interest in gender—what it means to be a woman as distinguished from what it means to be a man—has emerged with power, vigor, and insight out of the political and intellectual world of feminism. The majority of books on gender role published in the last twenty to thirty years have been written by women and about women. These women and their readers shared a deep skepticism—based on legitimate historical evidence—of male motives and judgments when discussing a woman's world, a woman's perceptions, and a woman's place. Male comments were suspect, unwanted and uninvited.

Since all observations about gender suggest by implication something about the other gender, few men dared step into this preserve. Those men who did step forward were apt to be either hostile and patronizing, or sycophantic groupies whose contributions were minimalized by their eagerness to ingratiate the newly established female authorities. Most male researchers were content to recognize the politics and fragility of the new field and stay away.

I remember an incident from those days when as a new young writer I was implored by two extraordinary countertrend women—my literary agent Marie Rodell, and my editor Beatrice Rosenfeld—to write a book on mother-daughter relationships. I particularly recall Marie urging me to "get on with it." I meekly suggested that either she or I was bonkers. How could she contemplate such a treacherous, doomed, and feckless venture? No man could write such a book. Nor would any woman accept it. Surely she recalled that in addition to being of the wrong sex, I was a member of a suspect profession. In those early days of feminism, not only were men's motives kept under strict surveillance, but the entire theory and practice of psychoanalysis was viewed as a sexist conspiracy.

I did acknowledge that no decent book had yet been written that did justice to the complexity and richness of what I perceived—and still affirm—to be the most profound of human relationships. I urged Marie to go ahead with one of her formidable women authors. No man, certainly not this terrified novice, could dare make pronouncements and survive with his reputation. On the contrary, she said, the mother-daughter relationship is so intense, so all-consuming, that no daughter having experienced it could ever sufficiently remove herself from her specific experience to adequately approach the generic problem; only a man could safely and objectively examine this most intense of relationships. She cited as authority that respected early feminist, Virginia Woolf: "There is a spot the size of a shilling at the back of the head which one can never see for oneself. It is one of the good offices that sex can discharge for sex—to describe that spot the size of a shilling at the back of the head."[1]

I certainly agreed with the reasoning of both Marie Rodell and Virginia Woolf. Nonetheless, I demurred. It may not have been the most courageous decision I have made, but I think it was a wise one. The fact that a woman writer would bring the biases of the feminine perception did not seem relevant. The same arguments, after all, had been accepted without much debate about the black experience. But is it true that only a woman can understand her own kind? What about the German Werner Jaeger, who wrote perhaps the most masterful statement on Greek civilization in his *Paidea*? What about the Frenchman de Tocqueville's comments on American life? Are Emma Bovary, Anna Karenina, or Cousin Bette less authentic because they emerged full-blown like Minerva from the heads of their male creators? No more authentic characters exist unless they are George Eliot's Casaubon or Jane Austen's Darcy.

Now, over thirty years have passed, and the feminist writers have illuminated the dilemmas of women with great brilliance (although that book on the mother-daughter experience remains to be written). Gender differences have become important and respectable. One effect has been to invite the same careful attention to explorations of the male experience, and in great part thanks to the feminist writers, I find myself once again returning to the area of gender role. Approaching the concept of male gender at this stage of my career and life, I am inclined to view things differently from my more technical earlier efforts. I now have thirty years of experience in treating people with identity and gender problems, and have myself passed through most, if not all, of the rites of passage of a modern Western man.

Yet this is still not a field cleared of land mines, and some of them are worth flagging. In the academic community, the messenger who presents unfashionable ideas threatening the status quo is effectively "knocked off" by ignoring his troublesome arguments and attacking instead his methods. This is particularly the case in the social sciences, where data are soft, methods of observation imprecise, quantification problematical, and subjectivity to a certain degree inevitable. (My good friends in the "hard" sciences insist that precisely the same is true there, but never mind.)

Social scientists have shamefully neglected the major problems of our time: sexism, racism, prejudice and bias, street violence, drug addiction, deterioration of the family, and war. When I recently surveyed the literature on bias and prejudice, I found some interesting articles on anti-Semitism and a few on racial bias, but nothing of significance on the nature of bias per se—on the concept of scapegoating in general. The last significant article was a forty-year-old treatise on prejudice, written by Gordon Allport.

Such neglect on the part of the intellectual community is not exactly a mystery. One problem is the thankless nature of approaching such work. When Kardiner and Ovesey did their basic and pioneering work on racism,[2] they were attacked as Fascists. At a time when it was not yet fashionable, they declared that blacks were indeed different from whites, that they carried the "mark of oppression," and that it was the price that had been paid for the so-called "separate but equal" doctrine. When Glazer and Moynihan wrote their warnings about the deterioration of the black family, they too were vilified.[3] The intellectual community did not come to their defense. Even if their ideas were incorrect, the liberal intellectual community should have supported the nature of such research. Instead, their motives were questioned and their integrity impugned.

Five aspects of my thesis in this book will predictably be challenged in attempts to avoid confronting my unfashionable conclusions: one, the bias inherent to my frame of reference; two, the limits of psychoanalytic observation; three, the tyranny of genetic determinism; four, the effects of polarization; and five, the dangers of generalization.

THE BIAS INHERENT IN MY FRAME OF REFERENCE

I approach human nature, perception, and behavior from the standpoint of medicine, psychiatry, and psychoanalysis, the disciplines in which I was trained. While trying to avoid the jargon, I will nonetheless use the framework of these disciplines and inevitably their values—or biases, depending on your point of view.

Scientific language is absolutely essential for communication among professionals. It seems as natural for a psychoanalyst to talk of "cathecting an object" and "regression to a fixation point" as it is for a philosopher to talk about "deontology" and "utilitarian calculus." In the social sciences, however, professional language can be used as a smoke screen to obscure vacuity or as a gloss to cover the mundane. I once insisted that a class of psychoanalytic students translate into every-day language any article from a then mandatory psychoanalytic journal. Stripped of the camouflage, a great percentage of the articles began to read like this: "Here is Dick, Dick is a boy. See Dick. Dick is frightened. See Dick run."

But while I can discard the language, I cannot detach myself from the basic assumptions of my profession (e.g., all behavior is dynamic and related to the past) or its research methodology—in the case of psychoanalysis, in-depth observation of relatively small populations. All professional analyses of human nature and human behavior are based on a combination of observations and insights. The frame of reference, however, will vastly modify the nature of conclusions drawn. A so-phisticated observer will understand that different conclusions are not necessarily alternative ones, or do not necessarily exist along a spectrum of right and wrong. The cellular biologist will have different things to say about the nature of a plant than an ecologist or, for that matter, a gardener. They are emphasizing different aspects. What can be under-stood about a rose under microscope is no "truer" than what is under-stood by smelling it. A CAT scan is not a more scientifically accurate view of Grandpa than the portrait of him that hangs above the mantel. It is important, however, to know in advance the perspective and frame of reference of the individual theoretician.

What, then, are the basic assumptions of psychoanalysis? Well, noth-ing so refined or fancy as "penis envy," "castration anxiety," or "Oe-dipus complex." These are sidebars. Basic Freud is more profound and revolutionary.

• Behavior, Freud said, is motivated. That is, it moves always with purpose, and toward a goal. It is never just random. There is an explanation for any action in terms of some anticipation, emotion, or desire—some purpose that may or may not be fully apparent even to the driven individual.

• Behavior must also be seen as dynamic. No single action is the product of any single cause. Think of a giant game of Bladderball, where hundreds of students may be pushing the ball from hundreds of different angles and the ball remains still. That does not mean there are no forces in motion. It simply means that they are balanced. If the ball moves slightly to the northeast, it is not necessarily that someone in the southwest has pushed it there; the balance of forces—of hundreds of forces—has led to that result.

• Behavior must be understood in a developmental context. Nothing that happens today can be understood as a thing in itself, but rather as one in a continuum or sequence of events from the past leading to a specific goal in the future. To read today's events without having understood the events that have preceded them is to ignore the essential truth of what is happening. The present is captive to the past.

• Further, Freud postulated that we are mostly unaware of the determinants of our behavior. Much of behavior is determined not in the conscious sphere but in the "unconscious." We are as likely to feel or do something for unconscious reasons as for the conscious rationale we construct to explain our actions, but which in the end may only be rationalizations after the fact.

• Finally, psychoanalysis exposes its roots in German philosophical idealism. Freud assumed the existence of a "real" world, but saw it as irrelevant in explaining everyday actions of human beings. It is what we *perceive* to be true that causes us either joy or despair. Our self-image, a profound element in shaping our perceptions and our behavior, is always more dependent on what we think we are, what we once were, or for that matter, what we were once considered to be, than on what we may actually be.

THE LIMITS OF PSYCHOANALYTIC OBSERVATION

First, one obvious and profound strength of psychoanalytic observation is that a psychoanalyst deals with an individual for two to five hours a week for three, five, seven, or an even longer number of years. During that time he will come to know his patient in a way that few other researchers can ever know their subjects. Given the pressures of pain and mental illness, the patient exposes himself to the psychoanalyst to a degree and depth beyond what he was prepared to reveal to any other human being, including himself. A psychoanalyst therefore can be expected to have the most profound evaluation of any given individual.

On the other hand, because of the intensity of the method, the psychoanalyst is limited in the *number* of patients he will see. It is true that Harvey discovered the principle of circulation of the blood by pressing one thumb (his) against one pulse (his own); basic generalizations about the human being can be made by extrapolation from one careful set of analyses. Nonetheless, generalizations about specific behavior traits or diseases that are not universal allow for major errors when drawn from inadequate sampling. If, for example, one is researching compulsive gambling or travel phobias, it is the rare analyst who can have treated in psychoanalysis more than twenty to fifty of these patients in a lifetime. He must then make generalizations about large populations from a small sample, and in so doing runs the risk inherent in such generalizing.

All methods have their limitations. Data gathering that depends on questionnaires allows for surveys of enormous populations. It is notoriously vulnerable, however, in that a person is as likely to lie on a questionnaire as to tell the truth. What motivation does he have for exposing himself to a total stranger? When asked a question about his feelings, a person is as likely to answer what he thinks the questioner wants him to feel, what he thinks intelligent people feel, what he thinks he ought to feel, and even what he thinks he feels. None of which necessarily indicate his true feelings.

The cultural anthropologist devotes himself to the community at large with specific references to some few individuals. Yet he, too, is subject to bias. He is a foreigner in a foreign place. He introduces the artifact of his strange presence in the group, and he invites all the posturing and secrecy that might be presented to a foreigner. Language difficulties can confound us to a ludicrous point, and as a result we may face charges—after the fact—such as have recently surfaced, for example, in relation to some of the pioneering work of Margaret Mead, as to whether she was interpreting her populations correctly, or whether they were "conning" her and feeding her the mythology they thought she wanted to hear. To a psychoanalyst, even a patient's lies reveal something of the truth about him.

The anthropologist, no more than the psychoanalyst, is never a value-free instrument. I think of the sorry example drawn from an otherwise admirable book which surveyed manhood in cultures around the world. The book is almost compulsive in its attempt at "objectivity." Yet, in an offhand manner, the author casually refers to the "secular, assimilated Jewish-American culture" (which he has not studied) as one of the rare cultures "in which women virtually dominate men."[4] This odd, sweeping generalization—uncited, undocumented, and undefended— is out of keeping with the otherwise precise tenor of the book. One must presume it represents some painful personal experience of the author. At least that is the undocumented assumption of this psychoanalyst.

The case study is the traditional research tool of psychoanalysts. Let me say a few words about psychoanalytic use of case histories with particular reference to their omission in my writings. One of the most powerful tools of a psychoanalyst is the detailed case history. It compensates in its detail for the lack of a broad data base previously described. All of Freudian theory was essentially developed on the basis of five case histories. Freud, in his most creative days, was starved for patients, and used his self-analysis and this limited number of cases to elaborate all of his major theories which underlie current Freudian psychology.

In that tradition, most modern psychoanalytic writers still use detailed case histories. There remains a problem, however. For its fullest flavor, the case history should not be too modified. Each detail altered for purposes of anonymity both reduces the integrity of the story and allows for embroidery that might serve the biases of the writer. Even when a case history is modified sufficiently so that the general public cannot identify the individual—he is a lawyer instead of a physician, born in Chicago instead of Cleveland, short instead of tall—the individual patient is likely to recognize himself. I have never felt free to utilize a case history in any of my writings.

I do use anecdotes from many of my cases. I will describe dreams and introduce incidents from therapeutic sessions to give specificity to generalized theories. This I view as different from the actual life story of an individual. I am uncomfortable with the latter. It borders on a betrayal of confidentiality and a sacrifice of the interests of the patient in the interest of the "truth," or worse, the therapist. I have chosen to use literature to substitute for the longer story, which offers a different kind of verification from the short anecdote. You may say that literature is not "true," but I have generally found more truth in great literature than in history. In this book I have used Stephen Crane's *The Red Badge of Courage* and a cluster of three books on wilderness and hunting: William Faulkner's "The Bear," James Dickey's *Deliverance,* and Norman Mailer's *Why Are We in Vietnam?* From these four books, I draw supporting evidence for conclusions I have reached from my practice and research. These books represent my "case histories."

There is one area of research in which the psychoanalyst has an enormous advantage, where he can combine the depth of his work with the breadth and security of a large research population: when he is dealing with gender problems. This affords us the best of both worlds; we are likely to have something close to 50 percent of our population of one gender, and we spend extravagantly long periods of time with each of them. Gender generalizations therefore are particularly broad-based and should have a greater reliability than any other observations from a psychoanalyst.

THE TYRANNY OF GENETIC DETERMINISM

Who is not sick of the incessant discussion of genetic determinism versus developmental influence; nature versus nurture; constitution versus culture? Under whatever name, it has been a nagging and persistent bore. It should not be so. At least not when dealing with the human being, given the peculiar nature of human nature. We have in recent times woefully ignored genetic contributions to human behavior for fear of falling into the neo-Darwinian trap epitomized by Nazi assumptions about racial superiority. Anyone with an ounce of brains—anyone with a modicum of knowledge of science and genetics—knows that we must acknowledge genetic aspects in human behavior. We are protected from neo-Darwinism by our awareness of how readily modifiable are the genetic substrata in matters of personality and behavior.

Like all animals, we have genetic determinants that can influence our behavior as well as our development. But unlike any other animal, almost everything that is genetically influenced in *Homo sapiens* relative to behavior—as distinguished from eye color, diseases, body type, and the like—is soft-wired. There is nothing in lower animals equivalent to the freedom of will of the human being. There is no lower animal, not even the highest lower animal, the chimpanzee, that can liberate itself from the tyranny and destiny of instinct. "Instinct," Kant has said, "is that voice of God that is obeyed by all animals."[5]

But we human beings are free to disobey almost everything. As Rousseau said: "Nature commands every animal and the creature obeys.

Man feels the same impetus, but he realizes that he is free to acquiesce or resist. . . . A beast cannot deviate from the rule that is prescribed to it even when it would be advantageous for it to do so, and a man deviates from it often to his detriment."[6]

We educate and condition our children and ourselves for good and for bad, in directions that amaze, delight, and yes, often appall us. The modifiability of the human being is the feature that most distinguishes it from all other creatures, and makes us as different from a chimpanzee as a chimpanzee is from a worm. We need not be afraid of genetics. It only whispers to us; it only suggests to us. And we are free—and have always been free, and always will be free—to ignore most of its directives.

If we desire a model of maleness that emphasizes gentility, passivity, and is non-confrontational, it does not matter that androgens drive aggression. Culture and conditioning and the setting of models can dispense with these directives—although we may pay a price. We can design more aggressive women and less aggressive men, we can change the primary caretaker of the infant and let the male parent be "Mom." We are free to share in our design with our Creator.

One should not be frightened of genetics. Genetics tells us what the potential is and what the initiating pathways are. We must know these in order to be able to choose to modify them. Such modification is not always that difficult. The price of modification, on the other hand, is complex and contains the possibilities of both stunning success and disaster. To deny the genetic roots of certain differences in behavior between male and female is unnecessary foolishness. For the most part, we can modify genetic directives for human behavior. Where we cannot, we may be happier for the diversity. We are as free to shout "Away with the difference!" as to exclaim "Vive la différence!" We are free to choose.

THE EFFECTS OF POLARIZATION

Another caution: avoid thinking in terms of polarities or opposites. If I state that men are X, I am not suggesting that women are non-X. What do I mean by that? Love, for example, is not the opposite of hate. It has more in common with hate than with many other things. Similarly, masculine is not the opposite of feminine, nor man the opposite of woman.

In constructing a picture of maleness, of male identity, of the male ego, there will be features readily recognizable as attributes of femininity, femaleness, and the female ego. What defines each gender is the special amalgam of traits; the arrangement and the priorities of the values and attributes ascribed to each; the cultural values we decide to use as standards of excellence.

Denying polarity does not mean subscribing to a "spectrum" between femininity and masculinity, though it is an interesting idea. What I am saying is something different. Eggs, flour, and water brought together in different proportions can produce two things as antithetical as a crêpe and a soufflé. Not only that, but the measure of elegance of these two foods constructed of similar ingredients would be defined in almost opposite terms—the thinness of the crêpe or the height of the soufflé. Lightness, on the other hand, is a common virtue of both. The carbon in coal is identical to the carbon in diamonds. A lump of coal is definitely not a gemstone, yet were I describing what is essential to coal, I would be including features that the diamond possesses. Simply because our culture has tended to define "masculine" in opposition to "feminine" does not mean that as intelligent observers we need go along. What man shares with woman is all the profound, idiosyncratic behavior that defines humankind as a glorious discontinuity in the animal kingdom, something halfway between the beasts and God, something "a little lower than the Angels," as the Psalmist would have it.

THE DANGERS OF GENERALIZATION

A word about generalization and its risks, particularly in terms of human character traits and behavior. Here, rather than attempting my own defense, I will use the words of that consummate and poetic observer of human nature, Primo Levi.

> I agree with you: it is dangerous, wrong, to speak about the "Germans," or any other people, as of a single undifferentiated entity, and include all individuals in one judgment. And yet I don't think I would deny that there exists a spirit of each people (otherwise it would not be a people), a *Deutsch-tum*, an *Italianita*, an *Hispanidead:* they are the sums of traditions, customs, history, language, and culture. Whoever does not feel within himself this spirit, which is national in the best sense of the word, not only does not belong to his own people but is not part of human civilization. Therefore, while I consider insensate the syllogism, "All Italians are passionate; you are Italian; therefore you are passionate," I do however believe it legitimate, within certain limits, to expect from Italians taken as a whole, or from Germans, etc., one specific, collective behavior rather than another. There will certainly be individual exceptions, but a prudent, probabilistic forecast is in my opinion possible. . . .[7]

All of my generalizations about men allow for men who are unlike the generalized, as there are Italians and Swedes who defy their cultural stereotypes. Nonetheless, the generalization is necessary and constructive in that it describes the wide segment of the bell-shaped curve from which we draw all of our generalized assumptions. The exceptions are acknowledged and respected.

Finally, in describing the basic elements of masculinity, I am establishing the pillars that support a basic concept of manhood. On those pillars pediments and embellishments will be found to account for the variability, not just of individuals but of distinct subgroups. The specific and special nature of black men, gay men, handicapped men, the very rich and the very poor, await another author or another place.

PART I

▶▶▶▶▶▶▶▶▶▶

DEFINING MANHOOD

1 ▸ REDEFINING MANHOOD: THE TASK AHEAD

We humans have come a long way in the last ten thousand years or so: out of the caves and into the sunlight; out of the natural habitats of the jungles and into the artificial cities of our own creation. In the course of that journey we have changed our environment—and changed ourselves. No other species could have made this odyssey. All other animal species, from the amoeba up through the chimpanzee, are essentially born complete, destined to become that which they must become. Designed totally by nature to a predetermined course, each animal replicates the history of the generation that preceded it with a predictability that is constant and inflexible, awaiting only a major mutation every few hundred thousand years or so that might lead, not to its own change, but to a different species entirely. Only human beings command nature. Only we reshape our lives to our own designs. We do so for the better *and* for the worse.

Our biology has taken us far. But part of that biological nature is now discordant with the culture we have created.

Feelings are the fine instruments which shape decision-making in an animal cursed and blessed with intelligence, and the freedom which is its corollary. They are signals directing us toward goodness, safety, pleasure, and group survival.

4

Feelings can, like every other aspect of our humanity, be corrupted from their original purposes. As hunger drove the primitive man to the nurture required for life, gluttony can drive modern man to the obesity that destroys. So, too, with feelings. Jealousy, which serves the struggle for survival, can deteriorate into the envy which draws defeat even from victory. We can be overwhelmed by inappropriate guilt, anxiety, shame and the like.

Male anger is a prime example of an obsolete emotion—of biology gone astray. Our anger mechanism was designed to protect us from predators, human and animal, which threatened our existence in the primitive jungles from which we evolved. Male biology is geared to protect us from physical assaults that no longer exist. It prepares us for a world we have long since ceased to occupy. In so doing, our biology sends us false messages that waste our energies and distract our concentration from the real threats of modern existence.

For two hundred thousand years or more our human ancestors survived the assault of the predators that stalked and threatened them. They did so by using their strength and their wits. The male animal was given primary responsibility for the group and the female for the protection of the individual. Unlike the simpler animals, when human beings were frightened, their intelligence guided them to new methods of flight and cover. Their intelligence devised instruments of destruction that could kill animals for which they were no match physically.

Even in the period before our creative nature brought us to the discovery of weapons of attack and defense, we were not helpless. We had a physiology designed for survival. Fear and anger mobilized our bodies for fight or flight. The mechanisms of anger made sure that when we were attacked, we were at our fittest. Blood was properly distributed, the appropriate muscles tensed, endocrines and sphincters adjusted to enhance and ensure the maximum effort. But what maximum effort of sinew or muscle is necessary these days? What threats are solved by a clean and direct physical assault? As we approach the twenty-first century, man the warrior is receiving signals from a physiology that is more likely to undo him than to save him. Allow your macho pride, your instinctual need to assert your masculine presence, to take precedence over your prudence, and you are likely to get stabbed by the thug who simply wants your wallet and your watch. Take a warrior stance in relationship to your boss, and you will be fired. Assert your male dominance to those who work for you and are dependent on you, and they will gradually destroy you by the small persistent stings of passive aggression.

Male aggression served our evolution in the early days. Some commentators insist that it still does. The social theorist Ernest Becker claims that "These aggressions are still 'in the service of the organism' because they represent a reaction to feeling cheated, duped, stripped naked, undermined. A person . . . reacts to assert himself, to show and feel that he is someone to reckon with. Anger generally has this function for the person and is a way of setting things in balance once again."[1]

Yet I fail to see how aggression remains in the service of survival when it so often produces a negative result. A man may have a momentary flush of victory, of getting his own back, but it cannot be considered to be in the service of *survival* to lose one's job or life simply to satisfy one's ego or vanity.

The psychiatrist David Hamburg, answering Becker, supports my position: "Any mechanism [once adaptive] . . . may become largely maladaptive when there are drastic changes in environmental conditions. . . . Some of the mechanisms which evolved during the millions of years of amazing primate and human evolution are less useful than they once were."[2]

Since a good deal of anger in modern life arises from events that are essentially trivial, although symbolically profound, we are constantly over-responding. Our bodies are preparing us for life or death struggles that exist only in our unconscious and in our physiology.

Man the warrior is passé, except for those rare professions and those rare times in our history when wars have been necessary to secure our survival. Even war and its rationale raise questions: was the threat real or illusory? When a population that feels impotent and unsure of its worth is mobilized by a leader who shares those feelings of inadequacy, but who is in a position to act on them, the result can threaten the survival of us all.

We have come through a frightening period in which a disproportionate number of the world's leaders have proved to be men trapped in their own power struggles. Hitler, Stalin, or Mussolini, strutting in uniform and acting out paranoid fantasies, are, of course, frightening. But the danger exists beyond these flagrant examples. With the emergence of the political memoirs and biographies of respected world leaders who dominated the power structure of recent times comes a disturbing sense of how much pathology was contained beneath the public stance. The actions of Lyndon B. Johnson and Richard M. Nixon, to name but two, raise questions of whether or to what degree a man in position of leadership is capable of separating his personal feelings of pride, anxiety, intimidation, anger, and humiliation from the national purpose.

So much for man the warrior. What about man the provider? He, too, must adapt to new conditions. Work is no longer singularly masculine and most work is no longer a source of joy. Work has been reduced to a necessary burden that is rarely a source of male pride.

A similar argument can be made in the sexual arena, where man the procreator can no longer take comfort in having fulfilled his role by producing numerous offspring. Numerous offspring help no one these days. With an overpopulated globe, restraint in this area becomes a virtue. Beyond that, the biological revolution is taking us to the point where a man, i.e., a specific man, is no longer needed for procreation itself. A sperm bank will do very satisfactorily.

Down through the centuries, across cultures, the essence of manhood has been defined by fulfilling these three biologically guided roles: protector (warrior); provider (hunter); and procreator (sire). These were the models against which we were measured. These were the standards on which we built our pride. Now these three props that supported the male ego are being dangerously undermined.

What can we do, beyond recognizing that we are trapped in a vestigial and maladaptive emotional system that has become obsolete? I can tell you some of the things that will not help. It will not help for us to take a weekend off: join in the woods together, strip naked to the waist, paint our bodies with mystical signs, pound drums, and rage to the moon. It will not help to get huggy and feely with another sweaty man as we cry on each other's beards over the fact that our daddies never loved us. We do not have to "locate" the primitive man within us. He is only too evident in our behavior. We must remove or mitigate cave-man psychology *and* caveman physiology.

One intriguing option in this golden age of scientific advances might be direct physiological intervention. Either through pharmacological or genetic methods yet to be developed, we have the capacities to assist our physiology in catching up with our psycho-social reality. We have already done so in limited areas. The introduction of Beta-blockers in the treatment of hypertension and coronary artery disease permits a man to experience rage and frustration while blocking the physiological responses that transmit those feelings into chemical agents for raising blood pressure, increasing heart rate, and the other autonomic responses to distress.

The objection most often offered to a pharmacological and physio-logical approach is a naive and mystical warning against tampering with Mother Nature. Many intelligent people display a stubborn and often illogical resistance to the concept of modifying our nature. To them it seems disrespectful of the forces that created us and, as such, fright-ening. It reduces our special quality. The idea of consciously modifying or adapting ourselves seems to trivialize the nature of the self.

But we constantly thwart nature for our purposes. After all, we modify behavior of plants; we control the genes of lower animals; we adapt *things* to our uses—the latest example being the replacement of worn-out body parts with "spares" from others (both living and dead) or artificial parts. Beyond such high technology we significantly change our nature by changing our culture. We live in climates "unsuitable" for our species. We cultivate lands not meant to support crops. We change our diets, immunize ourselves against diseases, cure ourselves with medicines, and kill ourselves with drugs. For good and bad, we have been sharing in our design for years; we have not always done so to specifications.

I do, however, see serious problems in a pharmacological and physiological approach, even if we overcome our biases about change itself. There is the whole question of the direction of the change. Whose values will prevail? On what data will we base these judgments? How will we weigh the merits of competing values? There is advantage in variability, and danger in undertaking a homogeneous universal design.

I am frightened by how we might engineer improvement, who will be the deciders of that improvement, and how we will measure the consequences. Lessons from the past have indicated that "improvements" can often be fatal. But we are approaching a watershed. I see an erosion of gratification and satisfaction in the life we have now created for ourselves without intentional design. We should apply our logic and our reason to the problem of redefining manhood, as we have to other problems, but we must be cautious and modest in our approach.

Women have been attempting to redefine their role for some time now. It would be refreshing were we to learn from their early mistakes instead of repeating them. We will not correct the problems of male identity by assuming a "feminine" identity, any more than women will find their solution in assuming the painful if different duties assigned to the male gender. Yet this is precisely the lunacy we seem to be adopting. Hollywood—still the best whacko index around—indulged in an absolute orgy of such gender-bendery in the summer of 1991. We were introduced to a kinder, gentler male hero. True, William Hurt had to have his throat torn open to effect the transition from male chauvinist pig to snooky-ookums. Harrison Ford, being a harder case, required a bullet through his brains to "feminize" him.

The quintessential transition occurred in that touching story of parental love, *Terminator II*. Here a fourteen-year-old boy learns tenderness, caring, and affection from Arnold Schwarzenegger, a robot designed as a killer. He clings to the steel-reinforced bosom (pectorals) of the machine, since his real-life mother is the "new woman"—all muscle and ugliness. She is Sylvester Stallone in drag, with the foulest mouth this side of a Marine barracks. Tough, mean, vicious, she is too busy toting a 100-pound cannon to give hugs to her son. Hugs, you realize, are what boys "need" and now don't get from their daddies. Is this what we really want: Dad as June Cleaver and Mom as Rambo?

The real answer lies not in role reversal but in the gradual mitigation of the sharp distinctions between the two sexes. Some distinctions between gender roles will inevitably remain, unless we are prepared to abandon the concept of the family as traditionally structured. We are free to do that—we are in effect already allowing it to happen. The unknown risks following from such a radical intervention in the nature of child rearing will not be inconsiderable.

Something more modest would seem sensible. We should look to the attributes that underlie the traditional roles of protector, provider, and procreator, and find means of relocating them to different, more viable areas. Behavior is rarely controlled by simple genetic or chemical devices, and modifying complex behavior is best handled through the psychological and sociological methods of persuasion, seduction, education, or, indeed, coercion. Because one no longer has to hunt to become a provider does not mean that the need for beneficence and the pride in caretaking cannot be nurtured in men in other forms. We must explore alternative routes to manhood, and support them with the same respect and rewards now given to traditional masculine traits. In so doing, we will start the process that is the only means for changing male aspirations. Gender identity is built on models and identifications, which then become the primary means for changing the nature of the emerging self.

To change the child, one must change the parent. We change our children in a number of subtle ways that fall into two categories. The first can be considered cognitive, or more precisely, behavioral. We *tell* the male child what we want him to do. We do more than that. Parents encourage the little boy toward certain behaviors and away from others by rewards or disapprovals, not just in their statements but in their faces and manner. Since the child sees his survival as dependent on this approval, the withholding of love or affection, or invocation of an anger, shame, or disappointment in his parent is as coercive a directive to the child as the gun in the hand of the mugger is to his victim. This is what we call "education." The borders between education and coercion are always blurred; bypassing a child's autonomy in the service of character and goodness is perfectly legitimate. Not only is it legitimate; it is by far the most effective means of "educating" the child.[3]

The child also learns behavior in big blocks by incorporating various identities during his lifetime. The child's identification with the parent is so obvious and apparent a device that we may take it for granted. The fusion is so automatic that, like the air around us, it is difficult to perceive. A little boy "behaves" as his father wants him to behave out of fear of his father, love of his father, or a need to ingratiate and be loved by the father. But that same little boy also behaves like his father—even if that may not be the way his father wants him to behave—out of a strong and almost mechanistic mimicry. Beyond mimicry is another device even more powerful: identification. Identification involves what we in psychoanalysis with our penchant for ugly terms have called "introjection." That means that a boy "swallows up his father" as he sees him, and establishes him within himself as an ideal, as a fused part of his own identity. It is a "wholesale" adoption of the parent's conduct, manners, and values.

A son resembles his father because of genetics, because of the conditioning I have just described, but also because he *is* in part his father. His internalized image of his father will be a basic building block out of which his identity will be constructed. He will also incorporate images of his mother, older siblings, and many "significant others" to form the final self. But when we are dealing with the question of maleness, man as man, the incorporation of the father or an equivalent masculine figure is central. We are likely to be unaware of the degree to which we contain that man, loved or despised, within us. To find yourself, with age, recognizing your father's face in the mirror is one thing. But to find yourself relating to your children with the irrationalities that you resented in your own father is, to say the least, unsettling.

Gender identity is built on conditioning, modeling, and identification. To change the boy, one must change the men around him—and one must have men around him. No small task these days.

If we can, through consciousness raising and the devices of self-education, change ourselves, we can alter the roles we play in the lives of our children and eventually change those children. Such efforts may not have the "magic" of the male-bonding weekend in the woods, but a number of weekends in the woods with our sons can be one step in restoring pride in the masculine role. And the "woods" need not be woods; museums will serve as well.

We must find ways to liberate masculine pride. The virtues inherent in the traditional definition of manhood are hardly obsolete. Courage, steadfastness, responsibility, duty, fortitude, generosity, and beneficence are character traits that seem in woefully short supply today. We must reassign the activities and the arenas in which these virtues are learned and applied. The price of our gender stereotyping in the past has been to take the traditional *liebe und arbeit*—love and work—of classical psychoanalysis and assign one to men and the other to women. As a result, everyone has suffered. This is not a battle of the sexes. To reassign work to women and love to men would be the height of inanity. The rush to "quickie" solutions is itself a dangerous masculine conceit—another indication of the obsolete machismo we must replace. The Gordian knot will not be severed with one swipe of the blade; forget the phallic image of the sword of Alexander. What is necessary is a gradual and general blurring of gender roles—with the eventual emergence of a man and a woman still different but equally respectworthy.

It is no help to "rediscover" the primal man within us. That primal man is only too available. He is a dangerous anachronism. Instead, we have to redefine our manhood, relocate the sources of man's pride. It is not an easy task, but not impossible, either—not for a species that went to the moon and aspires to the stars. We must start by understanding the male ego. What is it? What nurtures it? And what threatens it?

2 ▸ WHAT DO WE MEAN BY "EGO"?

The male ego—that fragile, vulnerable, but potent product of our male-dominant society—is a poorly understood phenomenon. We know more about women. Feeling that the nature of the female ego had long been distorted or ignored, feminist writers over the past thirty years have undertaken a careful evaluation of female sensibilities. They assumed that we had attended better to the questions of manhood. We had not. Both sexes simply accepted their assigned roles, without defining them or evaluating either whether they were inevitable—they are not—or whether they were optimal—which they certainly are not.

Feminists have focused on the inequity of the role assignment. They are aware that women have been deprived by the arbitrary definitions of "a woman's proper role." The erroneous assumption was then drawn by some that female deprivation has been compensated for by male privilege. The truth is that gender definitions burden and deprive *both* genders, albeit in different ways. The male experience must be examined with the same sensitivity that has been applied to the female experience.

To understand the terrors and travails of men in our society, one must examine the male ego through which these experiences are filtered and judged. "Ego" is not an easy term to define. In common parlance, it is used in at least two quite different although related ways. In the broadest sense, the ego is the self, or one's sense of oneself. In normal parlance, however, we are most likely to use "ego" when referring to those specific aspects of the self that deal with vanity or, less commonly, pride. We say that Ted is "egotistical," meaning self-centered; Brian has an "inflated ego," suggesting conceit and smugness; Tom is on an "ego trip"—an inelegant addition to the vernacular, but nonetheless describing clearly an attitude whose primary function is to reassure himself of his importance, heft, or significance. The ego trip is a necessary excursion in a culture like ours that tends to be abrasive and diminishing to most egos, male or female.

On the other hand, when we say that something is "good for one's ego," it does not imply criticism: it simply refers to something that makes one feel good about oneself, that helps one to function well. A hair transplant may be described both ways: pejoratively as an ego trip, or recommended as being good for Murray's ego. These are two separate judgments, which would lead to two different opinions about the advisability of this procedure.

The ambiguities relating to the differing definitions of the word "pride" lie behind these two seemingly contradictory ways of judging activities that serve ego needs. Pride is listed as the first of the Seven Deadly Sins, since in a Christian religion that honors humility, it suggests arrogance; but in the modern-day religion of psychoanalysis, pride is a virtue. Self-pride is considered a primary goal of treatment, along with self-respect, self-esteem, and self-confidence, all ingredients of pride. Pride underlines our dignity, our sense of special worth.

When we suffer a blow to our ego, we feel we have been diminished, made less important or less trustworthy in our own eyes. But even more important, we feel that our very sense of self has been shaken. This, then, leads us back to that first and more profound meaning of the word "ego," with which I am primarily concerned: the sense of self.

Psychoanalysts used ego in a multiplicity of ways. Freud had difficulty in defining the ego. It was that component of the human being that was conscious, that seemed to control behavior and that had direct dealing with the real world or the external environment. In classical Freudian theory, ego was one of three components of the mind. It was distinguished from the "id," which represented the unconscious, primitive, and fundamental drive mechanisms of the individual, and the "superego," which could be crudely and roughly compared to the conscience of the individual.

Later, one finds the term being used in different ways, including: the identity of the individual; the executive or functioning abilities of the individual; the perceiving and sensing person; and finally, in modern usage, the self which may include all of the preceding.

Psychoanalysts have now come round to accepting the ego as the self, or, as the dictionary defines it, "the total, essential, or particular being of one person; the individual." Ego includes those qualities that distinguish one man from another, his personality, his character, his individuality, his identifications. Paradoxically, it also defines what binds one person to another in common identity.

Who are you? Your answer may be: I am a human being, a man, a physician, a husband, a father, a son, a brother, an American, an Episcopalian, a Bostonian, a black from a Jamaican background, a liberal Democrat, a paraplegic, a forty-six-year-old amateur musician and philatelist. All of the above, and on and on. And still I would not necessarily know who you "are." Could I respect you? Would I like you? Should I trust you?

You may not know who you are, either. Those who share your life may actually know you better than you do yourself. They see you in action. Your behavior and your general conduct will determine the identity ascribed to you by others, and rightly so. You are in great part what you do—not what you mean to do, not what you would like to do, not what you think you do. Hitler was Hitler, independent of any latent tenderness within him and notwithstanding any humanistic purpose to which he himself might have attributed his behavior. You may believe most people are aware of what they do, and understand their own purposes and effects on others. Don't bet the farm on it. While the capacity for insight differs from one individual to another, no one ever got poor by overestimating the potential of any human being for self-deception. Yet your own perceptions, misguided as they may be, are also components of the ego.

Somewhere there is—as complicated and multi-faceted as it may be—an essential self. This self is the executive that directs your behavior and actions, and it is what informs every perception that you have. These perceptions in turn will determine your conduct and your actions. You may not understand or know this self, but it will determine the degree to which you understand and know all other things. It is the perceiving, aspiring, suffering, joyous, agonized, jealous, despairing, or exultant channel through which all of life's experiences are driven and given meaning. This sense of self is smuggled into every activity and every relationship we are part of. Don't worry if you cannot define it; the most important things in life generally resist definition.

The "discovery" of one's self, as an epiphany, tends to occur in novels and theater rather more frequently than in life. The Victorians, with their wonderful way with words, said that the last thing a fish is likely to discover is water, and so it is with us and our selves. Nonetheless, that self defines our view of the world at large and whether our place in it justifies our existence. A distorted sense of self can take the elements of heaven and make a living hell for us.

Ultimately, it makes pathetically little difference to you what you "really" are. It even makes little difference how the world judges you, unless you are prepared to buy that image and allow it to penetrate and modify your sense of self. A depressed patient will be only further depressed by the reassurances of his loved ones that he is worthy and lovable. His sense that he has even "deceived" them is likely to intensify his self-loathing and drive him toward suicide.

Studies of human development are in great part explorations of how the "you" becomes different from the "others" that surround you. The developing self, building upon genetic and biological clues and suggestions, will be shaped by the general culture—you will take on the characteristics of a modern American male. These traits will be modified by the specific environmental influences of your family. A middle-class, white American male growing up in Cleveland, Ohio, will share common traits with his fellow "Buckeyes" that will generally distinguish his behavior from a typical Sambia warrior of the Eastern Highlands of Papua New Guinea—and from the typical bourgeois Frenchman growing up in Lyons. He also will share some personality traits with members of other cultures—they are all human beings—and he will differ from members of his own culture, fine-tooled by the nature of the specific and differing life experiences within that culture.

All animals have genetically built into them all the behaviors necessary for their survival. Environmental experience is necessary to allow these genetic traits to emerge—the baby seal must be nurtured and suckled by his mother to survive, but just as she is driven by her genes to suckle, he is driven by his genes to suck. The mother leopard must take her cub out on its first hunting expeditions to train and indoctrinate it, but the need to hunt, the desire to hunt, the wherewithal and the wiles of the hunt, are all there waiting to emerge.

Only the human being must be taught to be the adult he will become. This explains the extraordinary variability of the human being. Penguins don't just look alike to us, penguins *are* alike. They may vary somewhat in size, shape, and aggressiveness, but even that will be conditioned by their genes. Only we human beings shape boys into men or girls into women according to models that are often as arbitrary and destructive as they are competent and satisfying.

Like rubber tires, hickory baseball bats, and silver sporting trophies, the human male is in great part a man- (and woman)-made "product." Using certain intrinsic endowments of natural substances, he fashions them to his own design for his own purposes. Consider the peculiar ritual with which the typical man in our culture begins his day. He takes a finely honed piece of stainless steel—manufactured by himself for this specific purpose—and meticulously scrapes it across the surface of his face, removing all vestiges of the beard which nature intended to emerge.

To paraphrase the Talmud, if God had intended man to be smooth-shaven (the Talmudic example was naturally circumcision), why would he not have made him that way in the first place? The answer is that man, alone among the animals, is created incomplete, and endowed with the power and privilege of sharing with his Creator in his own design. Granted, what is inherent in the human being is much more complex than a simple substance of rubber, wood, or silver; and even granted it is less mutable than our liberal imagination would choose to believe it to be, we still do shape and design ourselves to our own ends.[1]

We are taught not only how to grow up, but even what "grown-up" means. Acceptable grown-up behavior is defined in ridiculously different ways in different cultures. We must learn the definitions of our culture as we learn our native tongue.

This does not deny the impact of instinctual directives forcing us in one direction or another; but our extraordinary modifiability is yet another biological characteristic that is unique to our species. As a result, our variability is staggering. And our need to learn how to behave properly—whatever that means—is inevitable.

I vividly recall an incident from my early days of psychotherapy. A young woman came into her session angry, hurt, and confused, insisting that I be the arbiter between her and her husband. What happened was so typical as to be a cliché. Her eight-year-old son had come home from school with a bloody nose. The concerned mother asked him what had happened, and in tears, the boy said a bigger boy in his class had provoked a fight and punched him. The mother asked what he did then, and he said he cried and walked away. The mother, attempting to support her son, said that was the mature thing to do, suggesting that fighting never solved any problems and that it was a sign of strength to refuse to allow himself to be dragged down to a "brute" level.

The second part of the anecdote is only too predictable. The father came home, was told the same story, and the son received an entirely different answer. The father said, "Don't you *ever* walk away from a fight! People who pick fights are bullies. Your walking away is a sign of weakness and will encourage him to pick on you again. I know it hurts to be punched, and no one likes pain, but next time if someone hits you, you punch back as hard as you can and let them know you're someone to be reckoned with." And the father went on, "You may suffer the pain of a few bruises, but you won't suffer the pain and humiliation of feeling a wimp or coward."

In the peculiar irony of our day, the role of moralist is often foisted upon the psychiatrist. The mother had not asked me what was the "morally correct" thing to do but what was the "healthy" thing to do. I explained to her that to my knowledge neither of these responses to a sock in the nose was healthier or sicker than the other, but that each approach would produce a different kind of adult.

This type of early social conditioning explains in part the "hereditary" nature of personality. It deals equally well with the question of why little French boys tend to be so "Gallic," whereas Swedish boys insist on behaving like Swedes. More important for our purposes, it is a key to understanding how men are taught to behave like "men." Reward and punish. Encourage and discourage. In a thousand different incidents that constitute a thousand different learning experiences, a pattern of predictable and characteristic behavior will emerge.

A sense of self is built through conscious and unconscious pieces of conditioned behavior, conscious and unconscious emulation, and also through identification, which proceeds in a purely unconscious fashion. A man may find himself consciously or unconsciously, wittingly or unwittingly, behaving like his father. He walks like him, talks with his inflections, and may begin to behave toward others as his father does, even if he loathes the way his father behaves. That we do this, despite our will, often leads us to confusion and chagrin; but most of what drives behavior and compels choice will have been established much earlier by less voluntary and rational methods than emulation and imitation. Modeling is nothing compared to the power of the automatic identification that goes on willy-nilly, even while the child assumes he is rejecting the parental authority and image.

Identification occurs even when a son behaves precisely in opposition to the model of his father. Here we would call the father a "negative model." It does not matter whether we do something because our father did it or because we refuse to behave as our father did. Both these determinants of behavior maintain our father at the center. It is his model and his ideals that are determining our behavior, either in compliance or defiance. Defiance is a form of dependency. True independence means doing things you believe in, whether your father did them or not.

In a circular fashion our sense of self will determine our behavior, and our behavior will also affect our sense of self. In his poignant and painfully honest journals, John Cheever confronts this disparity between his rational judgment and his gut feeling. Despite a passion for women and a heterosexual way of life, he is plagued with homosexual fantasies:

> Why do I blame myself for this? Homosexuality seems to be a commonplace in our time—no less alarming than drunkenness and adultery—but my anxiety on the matter is very deep and seems incurable. I suffer, from time to time, a painful need for male tenderness, but I cannot perform with a man without wrecking my self-esteem. What, then, is my self-esteem? It seems composed of imponderables—shifty things. It is, at its worst, I suppose, a deep wish to placate Muzzy and Dazzy. It is, at its best, a sense of fitness that approaches ecstasy—the sense of life as a privilege, the earth as something splendid to walk on.[2]

In these complicated ways we design not only our own sense of self but the way others will perceive us. The views we have of ourselves will be recognizable to those around us and accepted as truth by many. We hang identifying signs around our neck—"irresistible," "undesirable," "failure," "powerhouse," "sissy"—and, surprisingly, people are likely to accept these signs whether they are "true" or not. They will begin to treat us according to our expectations. In this way, a false sense of self will eventually become our reality. We have to visualize ourselves as a success or as a leader in order to become one. Our ego sets the boundaries and the limits of our achievement.

A brilliant and talented man I know was the younger of two brothers, separated by only fifteen months. They were both highly successful men in different fields, and both, according to my standards at least, natural athletes. Nonetheless, the man I knew was considered the "jock" by the family and his elder brother the "brain." The standards in this family were high in both areas, as were discriminatory judgments of ability. My friend told the following story, versions of which I would hear repeated over and over again in my practice.

He was raised in a small town and had become a successful, nationally recognized scientist. On returning home after a thirty-year absence he was delighted to find the same druggist at the soda fountain he had known as a boy. After serving him an ice cream soda, the druggist turned to him quizzically and said, "You're one of the Jones boys, aren't you?" "Yes, I am," he replied. "Which one are you, the smart one or the athlete?" "The athlete," my friend answered, without a moment's hesitation. So he had been identified as a child.

In terms of national recognition, he had actually surpassed his brother. But since he and "everybody else" knew his brother was the smart one, his success was obviously a deception, a sham and a fraud. Because of this early identification, this brilliant man was plagued by recurrent dreams of exposure as a fraud, fearing that luck and deception someday would fade and all would be revealed. During analysis he recognized the derivation of these dreams. Although they were mitigated by the process, in times of stress he would still have occasional dreams of being exposed as a fraud.

This particular man was driven to hard work in part because he "knew" he wasn't all that smart; discipline, energy, and drive would have to substitute. Many men carry with them a "lazy boy" image while working eighty hours a week, juggling two or three major careers. Many more are physically handsome, yet view themselves as unattractive because their father or brother was assigned that role. The unreliability of family reporting and comparison is so great that years ago, in violation of all the then inflexible rules of psychoanalysis, I began to encourage my patients to bring in snapshots of themselves at various ages with their siblings, parents, and significant members of the household. The disparity between the photos and the perceptions was shocking. Rarely was the family "beauty" significantly more beautiful than other members of the family. Pathetically, rarely was the family beauty even a beauty. One thin young man saw himself as "a fat boy" in remission, or on parole, from an obesity that might be called back at any moment. It turned out that he had only been fat during one short three-year period of his childhood. A skinny boy until about eight, he became pudgy until eleven, and then outgrew the pudginess. Nonetheless, that three-year period left its mark.

I have treated extremely courageous men who see themselves as cowards and deprecate their courage as merely a defense against their anxiety at being exposed or recognized as a coward—as though courage is ever anything more than the ability to overcome one's fear. Or, if it is, as though the courageous act is lessened by the unconscious motivation. It seems clear that if courage came naturally, almost by definition, it would no longer be courage.

Through various models and multiple mechanisms we establish a sense of self which is carried with us into all of our perceptions and all of our activities, and beyond that, will actually determine what we do and how well we will succeed. Obviously, identity involves more than gender identity. But in males, gender identity—the idea of being a man—dominates the sense of self as a person to a greater degree than it does in women. More of a man's pride system is channeled through a stereotype of manhood than a woman's is through the concept of "womanhood."

This distinction between male and female can be seen as leaving the man more vulnerable than the woman. Her sense of identity, worth, and purpose can be nurtured and supported in many ways—through her attachments, her achievements in work and other areas, and in the multiple roles she will play. But men will interpret almost everything in terms of their manhood.

The debates on the formation of identity are as vitriolic and as numerous as the continuing conflicts on learning and development. Nonetheless, a certain consensus is beginning to emerge in the field of psychiatry. Male identity seems almost universally shaped by the following scenario:

The human infant forms a primary bond and attachment with his mother and a primary identification with her. Development, then, proceeds through multiple stages which I will only suggest here. The infant learns to cling and attach to this sustaining and nurturing parent, the mother, and lives in a state of approximate symbiosis—parasitism might actually be more accurate. The child, male or female, forms his primary identification with the mother. Eventually, borrowing strength from that loving parent, he will find the courage to bear separation and begin the process of self-confidence and pride that leads to an independent self.

But perverse creatures that we are, we must form a new kind of identification in this intermediary state. We learn to "become like" the parent of our own gender. Here is where the two genders separate dramatically.

A girl never has to undo her primary attachment and identification as a woman. In other words, she may separate her sense of "self" from that of her mother, but even while doing so she continues her identification—as a woman—with this female parent.

The poor boy must follow a more complicated path. He must, like the girl, detach himself in order to reach maturity and independence. At the same time, however, he must begin to form another sense of gender identity. He must learn to be a man, and in so doing he must reject his earlier identity with his mother, which will now be seen as "feminine" and, for reasons that will later become clear, extraordinarily threatening.

Cultures so dissimilar as to seem totally unrelated, on examination prove to use variations on the same identical themes when it comes to "making a man." The Sambia tribesmen of Papua New Guinea are superbly described in Gilbert Herdt's book, *Guardians of the Flutes:* "Men are manly and they must be that way. Warfare demands it, hunting requires it, women expect it. This is the Sambian view: it is the consuming impetus of masculine ritual."[3]

In New Guinea, assaults from neighboring villages are commonplace; rape and abduction are the rule. These men work and fight with their muscles, aided only by tools of the simplest kind. Physical force and vigilance are unadulterated by modern technologies. Herdt continues,

Without a sophisticated technology, guns or steel armaments or electronic barriers—Sambia cannot hide from their foes or life's constant dangers. A man's only certain protection against this world is his own unbending masculinity. For Sambia, far more than for ourselves, manliness is viewed as an individual achievement. Both nature and nurture are crucial for attaining manhood as Sambians see it. Nature provides male genitals and potentials, but by itself the male body cannot stimulate the spark necessary for masculine development or cold-blooded courage.[4]

Where does the environmental influence come in? It is introduced, according to the Sambia, by the strong and essential ties between mother and son in the early days. These necessary ties produce pollutants and contaminants. The son is fed "womanly" food, like milk and yams. He is nursed, and the spirit of the feminine enters his body through this milk. Later, horrible rituals will be demanded of the boy to purge him of all residual maternal feeding.

To make a Sambian warrior, the males in Sambian society begin to spend more time with their sons at four or five years of age. The purpose is clear. A wedge must be driven between mother and son in order to masculinize the boy.

> A boy's body is perceived as an open vessel highly susceptible to environmental influence. Mother is the primary influence: father is a weak second. Nothing innate to male biology seems to resist or repel the feminizing effects of women. Girls are not at risk; they simply succumb to their mother's influence and the drives of their natural biology. They become feminine like their mothers. Boys must be separated from women. Still, separation, in itself, is not sufficient for attaining adult masculine competence. Boys must be wiped clean of female contaminants—and by characteristically painful means. Pain and trauma thus become a sign of the hard won path to manhood required by the ritual cult. . . . Through successive initiations, steps must be taken that maintain the precious growing bud of manliness in the boy, since he (like men), forever remains vulnerable to feminine contaminations and hence, regression to a premasculinized state of being, and death. Against this danger a defence is needed; masculine rituals and taboos, forced on boys, provide just that.[5]

In other words, in Sambia culture, just like ours, a boy must not be feminine, and to avoid being feminine demands severing the cord between mother and son. We do not have their rituals, yet we have the same struggle. In both cultures, a primary goal is to eliminate the "Mama's boy" that is inevitably there in every man. The argument may be presented that lacking the rituals, the struggle is more intense. The Sambia boy, after surviving scarification, torture, bleeding, enforced fellatio with older men, and other initiation rites, is publicly acclaimed a man. We have precious few such public signs of manhood in our culture, but we have the same objectives of separating a boy from his early identification to prepare him for identification as a man with men.

Distinguished feminists, Nancy Chodorow in particular,[6] have now joined the psychoanalytic argument that there is a disjuncture, a discontinuity, a struggle, necessary for the male child that is not necessary for the girl child. After puberty a woman's self-definition is the same as that before puberty. She is a woman—like her mother—and she will be a woman at the heart of her identity all her life.

A boy has a different problem. He must now establish his masculinity, but all of those earlier identifications with the mother are persistently present within him. They are never completely outgrown. In his search for manhood, any "feminine" character traits and aspirations will be interpreted as being womanly and therefore threatening. To prove himself a man, a boy must first prove himself *not a woman*. His definition of self is always comparative and contrary. It is in opposition to something—but something that is inescapably within him. He will forever feel threatened in his gut, in his essential identity, by anything that reminds him of feminine behavior and the early feminine identification from which he can never fully escape.

Chodorow says that "A boy, in order to feel himself adequately masculine, must distinguish and differentiate himself from others in a way that girls need not—must characterize himself as someone apart. Moreover, he defines masculinity negatively as that which is not feminine and—or connected to women, rather than positively."[7]

The little boy must somehow incorporate a new male image that is often in opposition to the earliest identification with the mother. He must separate his sense of self from that internalized mother which he has incorporated just as profoundly as has his sister. To assist in achieving this end, he will be "worked on" by the instruments of his culture that are invested in his achieving manhood.

This concept of manhood as something that must be attained, something that must be earned, something that is precious and fragile, something that must be defended, is distinct from the basic concept of femininity. Current anthropological research sees this need to "make a man" as an almost universal phenomenon rediscovered in each new and diverse culture that has been explored.

A man is at his most vulnerable when his manhood is questioned. A threat to his manhood goes beyond even his survival. Since, in the symbolic world he lives in, almost anything may be interpreted as a challenge to male pride, awful and terrifying acts may result from seemingly trivial affronts. To mitigate the consequences, to diminish the volatility that is an inherent aspect of a fragile male ego, we must understand the metaphors which dominate a man's existence. We must understand what it means to be a "real man."

3 ▸ "REAL MEN" AND "MAMAS' BOYS"

We say about Joe that he is a "real man," and we instantly understand all that suggests. For good or for bad, it is an expression that generates immediate recognition. The meaning may change somewhat in different cultures; the methods of becoming a real man are certainly different— we are not expected to go out and kill a lion single-handed in the streets of New York; here we have more difficult initiations—but for the most part it is amazing how little cultural variation exists in the understanding of the term. A "real man" is strong, sexy, courageous, stoic, beneficent, modest, independent. He is not whiny, weak, clinging, emotional, vain, girlish—he is not a "Mama's boy." He must fulfill the conditions necessary for the three components of manhood—protector, provider, and procreator. He must have all the attributes of the long-lost roles of warrior and hunter, and the continuing role of procreator.

In contrast we rarely say about a woman that she is a "real woman." We are more likely to say she is a "real lady." But that is not the same. The term "real lady" evokes a cultural stereotype, one aspect and only one aspect (and in these days not necessarily the most admired aspect) of womanhood. There are many women who would not want to be described as a "real lady." It might seem prissy or priggish or sexist.

There is not a man to my knowledge who would not want to be described as a "real man."

Consider this "news" article from *The New York Times*, which appeared under the heading "Real Food for a Real Man":

> These Army generals do like to talk tough. Maj. Gen. Paul Funk, commander of the Third Armored Division, had this to say in describing himself to an American pool reporter: "I don't eat salad. I eat beef and wear wool."[1]

What is such a non sequitur doing in an internationally famous newspaper? Granted, this was at the height of the Gulf War, when precious little news was available. On the face of it, if someone from an alien culture were to analyze each element in this statement, it would be totally bewildering. Why would a general, in describing himself to reporters who are concerned about the progress of a war, think to mention his food preferences or the fiber from which his clothes are made?

The average reader needs no explanation. He fully understands the quotation, knows why it is there, and is amused. An alien would look for some coded message. But where masculinity is concerned, there are no alien cultures on earth; the most diverse cultures set the conditions of manhood in almost identical terms. Every reader knows the encoded message: "I am a real man." And the importance then becomes apparent. It is critical that a man who commands the lives of other men and women in a field of battle be strong, powerful—a "real man." Someday there will be women commanding forces at war. Yet, I do not know whether a woman—even if a field general—would ever make a statement like that.

By contrast, take this paragraph from a recent bestseller by a linguistics scholar. While writing about the essential differences in verbal communication between men and women, she gratuitously inserts an anecdote about herself:

As a woman who has achieved a high level of status in my profession, I grapple with this contradiction daily. When I go to academic conferences, I often meet colleagues from other universities who know me only by my scholarly publications and reputation. Not infrequently, new acquaintances say that they are surprised that I am so nice or so feminine. "You're not what I expected," I have repeatedly been told. "You're not aggressive at all." Others have remarked, "I thought you'd be cold," or "hard" or "competitive." When I press them about why they expected that of me, I am told, "I just figured that any woman who is as successful as you would have to be that way."[2]

I cannot imagine our Gulf War general relating the point, for example, that people are surprised that a world-famous warrior "like me" could be so "charming, handsome, and sexy." It is not that men are any less narcissistic than women, it is that part of the macho image is that while carrying a big stick one must speak softly about it. Gary Cooper dare not be seen glancing at his image in a mirror on the way to his face-off at high noon. The vanities of each gender determine even the accepted means for defining or denying vanity.

In discussing the male ego, I will inevitably describe many events and perceptions that female readers will recognize as being part of their experience. These experiences will not, however, be integrated into the "self" in the same way. The same incidents and ordeals will be perceived differently by men and women, and will have significantly different metaphorical or symbolic meanings. Men must avoid all the threatening implications of femalelike behavior.

The essential goal in becoming a real man is to liberate one's self from the previous feminine identification with the mother. To be a real man we must stop being a "Mama's boy," since a crucial stage in male development defined in the previous chapter demands abandoning the primary identification with the mother.

From prepubescence on, a boy will be struggling to prove that he is a real man. A barrage of words or finger and hand signs will be aimed at the boy as a challenge to his manhood that must be answered in kind, or be ignored with shame and humiliation. He will be called a "Mama's boy," a "fag," or their equivalents. The term "Mama's boy" tends to be reserved for younger males, although at times it can be and is used later in life. More likely, with maturity, such slurs will tend to become, like "sissy," submerged into the homosexual imagery. Still, we do use vulgar equivalents of "Mama's boy" to taunt men to action. Someone is a sissy, a wimp, gutless, lily-livered, has no balls, and the like.

But don't we say of Susan that she is "her Daddy's girl"? Yes, we do, and nothing better illuminates the difference between identities in the two genders than that expression. Notice that we say "*her* Daddy's girl." The generic term, "a Daddy's girl," is meaningless. It offers no fixed connotations whatsoever. It does not tell us whether she is gentle, aggressive, aesthetic, athletic, eats salad or red meat. It simply means that she is a favorite of her father and will do anything to please him. What will please him will vary with the father and his expectations of his daughter. When we say of a woman, she is "her Daddy's girl," we can only understand her if we know her Daddy.

In other words, "Daddy's girl" is a specific phrase, illuminating a relationship between *one* father and *his* daughter, and is understandable only in terms of knowing both the father and the daughter; whereas "Mama's boy" is a generic cliché that always has the same specific meaning, which we all understand only too well.

Nature helps us, of course. Biological directives are vastly different between the genders. Twenty years ago, it was fashionable to assume that all observed gender differences were the products of specific cultural pressure. It was a ridiculous assumption, but it was thought politically essential to help in the liberation of women from a male-dominant society.

The experience of generations of mothers that boys are "born" different from girls was dismissed as irrelevant. Hundreds of years of obvious distinctions in play between little boys and little girls were also dismissed because such data did not conform to the accepted policy necessary for the revolution at hand. Only recently, when a small number of feminist observers using a minuscule number of cases "pronounced" that little girls were indeed different from little boys, was the social scientific imprimatur given to what the less educated and less sophisticated knew all along. We can now listen to mothers and accept their wisdom.

This need for documentation from a pseudo-scientific authority is one of the pathetic traditions of academia. The age of equality, inflamed by the fashionable Marxist concept of a tabula rasa—children born indistinguishable one from the other—asserted that environment was all. The insistence that children were born identical was contrary to all knowledge. It was fed by the anxiety that seeing any genetic differences among people would suggest qualitative judgments and open the way for an "aristocratic" view of human beings. When this ideology was carried to all of nature, the results were a disaster.

The same anxieties pervaded discussions of gender role. It was argued that little boys played predominantly with cars and trucks because they were "given" cars and trucks. Little girls liked dolls and doll play because "it was forced on them." Every mother knew differently and every mother knew better. Only when a generation of determined feminists started raising their own children—and, if anything, the girls were given the cars and the boys were given the dolls—was the power of genetic directive made apparent. Now "science" is catching up, if just barely.

Conventional wisdom in academia insisted that while sexual identity (knowing that you are a boy rather than a girl) emerged early, gender differences (masculine and feminine attitudes and behavior) only emerged at about age five! In fact, recent research has shown an early, aggressive identification with gender in boys that seems not to exist in little girls.

Barbara Lloyd and her colleagues observed and interviewed children from eighteen months to four years of age. They concluded that "Even at this early age, girls and boys use toys differently. Boys avoid feminine toys and employ masculine toys to mark their membership of a gender category, while girls do not use toys to mark their gender identities."[3] When the teachers tried to break down stereotypical behavior and maintain groups divided equally between girls and boys, their efforts were undermined by the resistance of the boys, and only the boys, who insisted on forming all-boy groups. Lloyd concludes:

> Our discussions with teachers revealed a genuine desire to provide greater scope for girls and boys to gain access to experience unfettered by conventional gender restrictions. Despite this, the rigidity with which older children adhere to gender prescriptions . . . suggests that girls and boys inhabit different social worlds and follow distinct developmental pathways. I believe that this deep separation of femininity and masculinity reflect the naturalization of gender and a conceptual collapse of the distinction between sex and gender.[4]

Nature does supply the genetic directives that will eventually aid in the inevitably necessary separation from the primary maternal identification. Boys are born with different attributes and tendencies from girls. These genetic differences are dramatic and apparent even in that stage of male development when boys are primarily attached to their mothers. Even when they are Mama's boys, they are *boys*. Boys are born with a potential for a larger body mass. Their verbal skills seem retarded until a later age of development. They are less analytical. They are born that way—kinetic, aggressive, with large motor skills early dominant—ready to be shaped into the form of a man, with a capital M. Still, in all, those directives are soft-wired and can be attenuated or even reversed; but we would be prudent to acknowledge honestly their existence and differences.

We see genetic differences not only in what games boys play, but also in how they play them. Very early little girls become conversational

.nicative. Games are elaborated that closely follow life ex-
vhether it is tea parties, playing dolls, or mimicking mothers
.1ow doctors and lawyers. Their activities are centered on re-
ıp and conversation. In contrast is the inevitable boring pro-
gression of boys' play, from cars and trucks to dinosaurs to space ships
and war games, a commonplace in hundreds of thousands of households
across the United States.

Of course, little boys can enjoy cooking and arts and crafts, but even
the way in which they approach these activities is likely to be different.
First of all, they are so rule-oriented that the rules are often more
important than the game. Recently my seven-year-old grandson, being
deprived of a more fitting and exciting companion (his twelve-year-old
male cousin), was reduced to asking whether I would play Battle Beast
with him. He had gone through the entire household and I was, alas,
his last hope. I had seen him play this game endlessly with his cousin
and dreaded the encounter.

I did not know the rules, but I knew enough to know there were
rules. I said, "Let's get started." He insisted that we couldn't get started
until we "got set up." Whereupon he dumped out of a bucket some
eighty almost indistinguishable battle figures, made of flexible plastic,
each carrying a tiny "weapon." "Let's start choosing," he said. Inno-
cently I grabbed for one little purple object, but he stopped me with
disdain. First we had to take all of the weapons out of the figures' hands.
That doubled the size of our pile.

Carefully we took turns selecting a battle creature until the pile was
diminished. Every time I took one, he explained who the creature was,
often adding, "Wow, that's a good one," telling me the characteristics—why this one was capable of flying, that one turning into fire, etc.
Finally we had our armies assembled but still were not permitted to
begin. We then had to select a special weapon to insert into their hand.
"Oh, my God," I thought, "another hour." Each choice was carefully
calculated and executed by him; nor would he ever allow me to grab
the first weapon. In fairness, he would explain why it was not a good

one for the creature I had picked and why I might be leaving myself vulnerable.

I never did get to the game. We were interrupted, blessedly, by a call to dinner. I have been told by the mothers of these two boys that the set-up generally takes longer than the game.

In contrast, it was with joy that I often eavesdropped on games between my seven-year-old and nine-year-old granddaughters, also cousins. In a few spare minutes of their play I learned more about them, more about their fathers and mothers, and the trials and tribulations of their everyday life, than I had from their parents.

These activities are all biologically driven. Not, of course, the elements of the game—a fascination with cars and trucks can hardly be genetically driven—but the *way* they are played. We are now allowed to accept the evidence of our experience and can acknowledge the roots of masculinity in the early drives of young boys. If we decide it is essential to live in a less aggressive society, we can begin to reward conciliatory behavior in boys while discouraging blatant aggressiveness. We must remember that even though gender differences are not primarily cultural artifacts, they can be influenced by culture to some degree. However, the evidence is clear that aggression is often driven by androgens (the male hormone): brute power is the privilege of the larger and stronger male creature; therefore guile and politicking must be substituted by the weaker-muscled sex.

In many ways this better prepares women for modern life than male biology does. We do not live in a world in which power is measured by grip, height, or size of biceps, but by position, accomplishment, intellectual achievement, and the like. The early lessons the little boys learn about becoming men may tragically become the spears on which their self-respect will be impaled in modern adult life. But the lesson of those early days persists, and men will be trapped testing themselves on an obsolete power basis throughout their lives, if only in symbolic language and metaphorical actions. We must mitigate this sense of manhood not just for the sake of the women who have been its victims but for the men themselves who, in different ways, were equally victimized.

Boys, just as girls, originally seek approval in the eyes of their mothers; but as they grow older, this all changes. Men become men in the eyes of other men, since masculinity is defined in terms of competition, power, and achievement. Ironically, women too for the most part will become women in the eyes of men, although they are spared the exclusivity of this one path.

I do not mean to suggest that mastery and achievement are not important to a woman and that failure in these areas cannot be humiliating and devastating. But given the cultural conditions that we still live with, work failures do not attack her at her core—as a woman. Women are victims of gender stereotyping and pay an extraordinary price for this in our culture. While a woman may often know better, she inevitably buys into much of the system—none of us are resistant to the bias of our culture. Still, a woman's stereotype is rooted in diverse areas. A man's pride and self-respect are brutally and exclusively equated with his manhood. Everything is funneled into this one channel—power, status, position in the world around him. All are seen in terms of his being a "real man."

A woman, in caring for her child, does not think about the fact that she is being a "real woman." She is unconsciously supported by the sense of herself as a nurturer. Such behavior is its own reward: it need not be converted into gender or genital meaning. But a man in our culture will judge himself almost exclusively in phallic terms. Since he no longer kills lions and hunts for food, it is through the symbolic world of material accretion and status that he establishes that he's got it—"it" being, to use the vernacular, "a large, swinging dick."

A man's personhood *is* his manhood. They are difficult, if not impossible, to separate. A man's sense of pride is always tied to the larger environment of other men. It is a competitive, constantly expanding population in which, wherever he finds himself, he will still see other men ahead of him. In an upwardly mobile society, there will always be another series of steps to be taken, another group of men to be overtaken, further victories to be won.

If a woman is forced to establish her worth only in terms of her relationships with others, at least there are many others. There are women friends, lovers, children, and of course men. If a woman has a touchstone that marks her femininity it probably lies in her sense of her "lovability" and her capacity for giving.

Depression hits many women like a sledgehammer during menopause. A woman may have half her life ahead of her in this age when life expectancy for women has reached eighty-two. Nonetheless, the fact that she cannot bear children and has passed a certain threshold of desirability in the minds of herself and unfortunately many men in her culture will be a challenge to her self-esteem. When women commit suicide, it is almost inevitably over the loss of a loved object. With men this rarely occurs. Men commit suicide at a rate of seven to eight times as frequently as women in our culture, and they do it invariably because of perceived social humiliation that is almost exclusively tied to business failures. Men become depressed because of loss of status and power in the world of men. It is not the loss of the money, or the material advantages that money could buy, which produces the despair that leads to self-destruction. It is the "shame," the "humiliation," the sense of personal "failure," all defined by a value system that we have created, for good and evil, for ourselves. A man despairs when he has ceased being a man among men.

In many interpersonal relationships, conflict arises because of the logical assumptions of one that both genders must find similar things threatening and must share similar solutions to those threats. A woman who knows that only nurturing, understanding, love, and affection will support her sense of self-worth is inevitably bewildered—and may tragically interpret it as a personal failing—when she supplies the man with whom she shares her life with such comfort and nurture during his despair, and he still continues to feel himself a failure, unnourished and unsatisfied.

She does not understand the symbolic nature of power in his world. Status, and the approval of masses of other people (mostly men), are necessary for a man to feel that he has succeeded or is worthwhile. The very nurture she offers—what would reassure her in her moments of despair—may arouse a sense of dependency in him, since it is primarily linked to a mother, which may further threaten his sense of manhood. It is not that he is rejecting her, or her love. It is not necessarily that he loves her less than success. It is that *love* is not the instrument by which worth is measured for a man.

The problem that is presented to the woman here is a complicated one. Since she wants to restore him to self-pride, somehow or other she must give the man the support he is craving when he is depressed, without making him feel dependent. This means restoring him to his culture's distorted sense of manhood. But the paradox is that her very caring and nurturing converts him into that dreaded antithesis of a real man, a Mama's boy.

A man's ego, therefore, is always tied to general and generic approval more than to specific approval. Unfortunately, it is almost always linked to a virtually unachievable sense of manhood. To be a man, one must not only learn to play the game; he must win. Winning is all.

A psychoanalyst is in a rare position. Through the pressure and pain of the psychotherapeutic process, male patients are forced to do what is generally anathema: they are forced to talk about themselves and their feelings. This introduces yet another gender difference. Men do not really talk to other men. They rarely talk to other women, and they certainly don't talk about their emotions and feelings. They are oriented toward "things" and action. Not "people" or feelings.

Women talk generally of important topics. Men disparage the talk of women by labeling it with the pejorative "gossip." By that they mean talk about people—their personal lives, their sense of failure or success, their victories and defeats, their peccadilloes, frustrations, foibles, and fancies. This "women's talk" deals with the verities and often with the philosophical questions that have dominated analytic reasoning through-

out the ages—analyzing the meaning of existence in terms of relationships, of purpose and goals.

But what do men talk about? Sports and business, inevitably. What
about business talk? Is that not truly important? Generally not. It really
is a form of shop talk. The fact that the shop happens to be the board-
room of a money management firm does not make it any more "significant" than if it were truly a shop. Men, whether surgeons, lawyers,
accountants, or engineers, will only reluctantly be dragged into general
conversations.

In the analytic situation, a man is forced to really talk, and in so
doing he exposes feelings to his therapist that he has rarely articulated
even to himself. There *is* a significant distinction between the therapy
of men and women. Over a lifetime of practice as a psychoanalyst I am
impressed by the narrowness and intensity of the subjects that dominate
men's lives. Their measure of success is a brutal and demanding vision
of manhood. Thirty years of practice has only reemphasized this common denominator: across class and culture, men still struggle to be
respected as "real men."

Psychiatric practice in New York is not quite as homogeneous as it
might seem. In the course of internship, residency, and practice, I have
dealt intensively with men of varying economic status—black, white,
Hispanic, and Oriental, Jews, Christians, and Muslims, primarily from
American backgrounds, but also English, New Zealand, Australian,
Mexican, Israeli, German, Italian, and French cultures, among others.
All confirmed the pressures of being taken seriously—"as a man."
Nonetheless, it was reassuring to find anthropologists affirming that the
constancy of the male role and the consistency of the definition of
manhood cut across cultures. From almost every culture surveyed,
whether a small Greek village or a western American town; from a Truk
lagoon to the Australian Bush; from the Dodoth people of East Africa
to the New Guinea Highlanders; whether one is examining primitive
or modern cultures, Eastern or Western, from Southeast Asia, the
mountains of Africa, or the small towns of the Pyrenees, an image of

manhood emerges that is strikingly consistent. (Often this consistency is to the chagrin of the researchers, whose natural bias is toward cultural determinants of behavior.)

John Williams and Deborah Best obtained data from fourteen countries, seeking cultural influences on masculine/feminine definitions. Their findings were sparse indeed; so much so that it caused them to "reverse" their bias for environmental shaping of gender differences. They further noted that cultures immensely dissimilar in other ways seem all to conform in their definitions of manhood and manliness.[5]

What then defines the "real man"? In almost every culture examined, he must fulfill three distinct roles—three responsibilities of manhood. First, he must be sexually a man. Sexual manhood certainly distinguishes him from boyhood. With puberty come not just the trappings of secondary sexual characteristics—the change of voice, pubic hair, muscular development, the coarsening of features of the soft child into the angularity of the adult—but also that essential sexual characteristic on which our race survives—the capability of fathering children.

In most primitive cultures, in most preindustrial cultures certainly, the first measure of a man is his capacity to produce children. Often there will be a bias for male children, but this is not necessarily a constant. To be a man without children is shameful in most cultures. He may blame his wife, and indeed it may be biologically her fault. Nonetheless, it will be seen as his disgrace. A real man must produce many children, and for this he may be entitled to many wives. The capacity to have multiple wives will vary according to wealth and rank in the social order, but it is the nature of polygamy to increase family size. (Both the pashas of Araby and the poor Mormon workers of Utah saw polygamy as a chance to increase tribal size. One man could impregnate hundreds of women in a year, if he so desired and if he was lucky, producing thousands of children over a lifetime.)

In our society, the procreative aspects of sexuality are no longer as cherished, and with disastrous results. A modern man must find some substitute for children in establishing his sexual credentials. Often philandery is the pathetic alternative. While sexual constancy is as rare as a black pearl, I would not consider most men who have occasional extramarital affairs to be "philanderers." Most men do not have the drive or the neurotic need for genuine philandering. They are more likely to be mere sexual opportunists. Doors are opened and men walk through them. Philanderers will open the doors, and Don Juans will bulldoze their way through walls. These men see extramarital sex as an escapade, an adventure. A fling on the side makes them feel virile and attractive. Adding forbidden fruit to the daily bill of fare provides both a sense of danger and naughtiness which certain men enjoy. Men who *need* extramarital affairs, who compulsively pursue them, are men on a mission. They suffer from a faltering sense of manhood that demands reassurance from multiple sources. The obsessive womanizer is a man unsure of his sexual credentials. A high percentage of philanderers are borderline impotent.

The second major role assigned to man beyond that of procreator is the protector. Man must be a warrior. He must be powerful and he must demonstrate his power, whether he lives in a hunting or a non-hunting society. Mastery is always at a physical level. Even in non-hunting societies, facing down or killing a threatening animal may be part of the initiation rituals of manhood. An essential ingredient of being the protector is the demonstration of courage, and courage is always visualized at its most primitive and physical level. In order to establish a man's courage, there must be tests of courage. If the society is developed to a point where one no longer requires physical courage to survive, artificial means of demonstrating physical courage must be established. The warrior was dependent on his body, his biceps, his limbs, his stoicism, and his conquest of fear. To be honored as a man, one must prove one's capacity in this most fundamental area.

Yet we live in a society in which physical courage counts for little in the real world, and power is rarely manifested in muscular size. A diminutive fat old man who is rich will order around a powerful young physical specimen if he happens to be his chauffeur or his "houseboy."

The trappings of power have changed, but the internal perceptions have not. The remnants of the primitive society, with its emphasis on physical courage, are but a second challenge to modern man.

The third component of manhood is that of provider. Generally, preindustrial societies were hunting and farming societies. The man, because of his physical size, speed, and agility, was the hunter. He was charged with feeding his family. If he was a tribal elder, he was responsible for making sure that food was available for the whole tribe. Notice that he must not only show that he can feed himself—to be a real man is not to be simply a procurer, but a *provider*. He must be beneficent. This means he must be generous with the goods that his power has procured. The real man is not an accumulator but a benefactor and a caretaker.

This last trait conflicts with the now fashionable generalization that ascribes a morality of caring to women and a morality of justice to men. The proposition that men are not caring is popularly accepted because it touches on a gender difference between the *styles* of caring. In almost every society the man must take care. That is what a man does. The prototypical example is the universal male role among animal herds. In the herd, the female goat, buffalo, or sheep values her own offspring; she cares little for the survival of any other young. A goat who has lost her kid after she has established bonding will kick to death any other kid that comes to suckle at her painful teats. Never mind that her kid is dead and that she is in pain. That milk is intended for one and one exclusively.

This tendency to overvalue one's own has a survival mechanism of enormous magnitude. If each goat is concerned only about the "general welfare," she is unlikely to protect her individual offspring adequately. Chaos would result. It is not surprising, therefore, that in cultures like our own, there is no particular consonance (indeed, some might argue that there is a statistical antithesis) between those individuals who weep for "humankind" in general and those who are concerned with the pain of specific human beings.

The male animal, in contrast, is concerned with the welfare of the herd collectively. This may be perceived as a selfish means to protect his sexual objects from either attack by a predator or invasion of a competitor. The motivation is irrelevant—his behavior results in promoting the common good. The male clearly is charged with protecting the herd at large. He could not even recognize his own children.

Once we come to the human animal, being a provider is obviously not merely a biological imperative. A man earns self-pride and self-respect from fulfilling his obligations to the vulnerable: women, children, and in some cultures, the elderly. He offers his body and sometimes his life to protect and feed his dependents. He must range far and wide, demonstrate courage, mastery, and power, to fulfill his biological and sociological role as the caretaker and provider. This is a manifestly different kind of caring from the tender nurturing of the infant at the breast. But it is caring.

Each gender may be only fulfilling a biological need, or each may be expressing a nurturing biological nature, depending on your view. It doesn't matter which construct you endorse in terms of the underlying or fundamental motivator. The fact is that each gender traditionally takes seriously its role of caring. In tribal society, and until very recently in Western society, each gender, to fulfill its own moral sense of worth and goodness, will inevitably be measured against some criterion of how well he or she fulfills a caring role.

In all three areas of manhood—procreator, protector, and provider —modern man has been drawn to an attenuated and increasingly metaphorical relationship with the biological directives that are part of the masculine gender. They urge him to behavior that no longer has cultural validity. These drives, cast in physical terms, do not serve the fundamental needs for which they were once designed.

Rage sets in motion the machinery for a frontal physical assault: the "animal" becomes an armed instrument for physical assault. But what is there left to assault? What dangers remain for civilized people that are satisfactorily resolved by clubbing? Often, it is not the enemy we face but only his agent. More often than not, it is not even a person but a piece of paper. How does one attack a piece of paper—even as threatening a one as a pink slip or an IRS demand for review? With one's teeth?

Because threats these days are so rarely direct and physical, we are less capable of distinguishing between real and fancied threats; we are constantly arming ourselves for dangers that exist only in our imagination. As a result, men are left with a set of built-in biological mechanisms, directives, and signals in this area of anger that diminish rather than enhance their chances for survival.

Obsolescence may be operating in all of the elements of manhood that we have described. Yet we are bound to our biology. Even in our modern culture the images of the sexual man, the warrior, and the hunter continue to be preserved in disguised forms. We still raise our men to these three roles, but we change the rules of evidence. You don't have to kill a bear anymore, but you may have to be a "killer" in the marketplace. The problems still exist: a man must satisfy these universal criteria to be a man in his own eyes and the eyes of others. Somehow or other men have to find symbolic ways of satisfying these urgent instinctive and genetic drives which shape their sense of manhood.

Men, therefore, invent metaphors of manhood. These metaphors are more readily recognizable in the simpler, rural societies than in complex industrialized urban centers like London or New York. Michael Herzfeld describes the forms and rules of manhood in the Cretan mountain community of Glendi:

One who is, in the Glendiot phrase, "good at being a man" must know how to wield a knife; dance the acrobatic steps of the leader of the line; respond in elegant, assonant verse to a singer's mockery; eat meat conspicuously whenever he gets the chance; keep his word but get some profit from it at the same time; and stand up to anyone who dares to insult him. He must protect his family from sexual and verbal threats, and keep his household at the level that befits a "master of the house." He must dispense hospitality at every possible opportunity, deprecating the poverty of his table whilst plying his guests with meat and wine. He must be ready with clever humor. And in all these agonistic domains, his every action must proclaim itself a further proof of his manhood. An action that fails to point up its own excellence is like the proverbial tree falling in an empty forest.[6]

In a Mediterranean village, the lines connecting the rituals of manhood to their counterparts in preindustrial cultures are still traceable. In the schoolrooms of the Anglo-Saxon world, the same criteria of manhood exist, but the connections to their roots are less evident, the evolution of customs of manhood more obscure, the lines of development from the biological to the cultural more convoluted. Yet they are there, and can be identified.

To fully identify and understand the criteria of manhood in our society, we must examine the various cultural institutions that are made use of to convert a "Mama's boy" into a "real man."

4 ▸ MAKING A "REAL MAN"

Manhood is universally perceived as something that must be learned and earned. Anthropologist David Gilmore sums it up well:

> There is a constantly recurring notion that real manhood is different from simple anatomic maleness, that it is not a natural condition that comes about spontaneously through biological maturation but rather is a precarious or artificial state that boys must win against powerful odds. This recurrent notion that manhood is problematic, a critical threshold that boys must pass through testing, is found at all levels of sociocultural development regardless of what other alternative roles are recognized. It is found among the simplest hunters and fishermen, among peasants and sophisticated urbanized people; it is found on all continents and environments. It is found among both warrior people and those who have never killed in anger.[1]

The job is not easy. Nature has to be helped along. One must be taught—beyond that, indoctrinated and initiated into manhood. We must teach the boy, in the inspired words of the Glendiot people, to be "good at being a man."

A more convoluted course of training and development is necessary to "make" a man than is necessary to secure feminine identity. While

46

it is guided by strong genetic directives, masculine identity will not emerge directly and naturally, as feminine identity is likely to do, since it is a two-step procedure, first requiring a *detachment* from the mother. Masculine identity is something that must be achieved and built in the formative years of boyhood.

Yet regardless of how hard we try, our society seems incapable of making "a real man"—at least to the satisfaction of the man himself. What is missing—what is desperately needed—are some symbolic markers like the "rites of passage" that are a universal experience in growing up male in all primitive societies. That marvelous anthropological term was coined, and described, by Arnold van Gennep. Across diverse cultures, he observed three distinct sets, or phases, of these rites: separation (from the mother and the feminine); transition; and incorporation (into the community of men).[2]

The rituals differ from one culture to another: in the length of time for the transition; the male mysteries that must be shared; the feats that must be performed—in one it is the killing of a large antelope, in another the slaying of a lion, and in still another the stealing of cattle from a neighboring tribe's herd (and the sharing of them with the community). The differing scenarios, however, are but variations on a common theme.

A child is taken from his maternal home. This is done either forcefully or symbolically. In some societies the mothers offer theatrical and symbolic resistance. Then the child is closeted with adult males for varying periods of isolation, purification, and initiation. In diverse societies, with similar horrifying ceremonies, a boy is forced to endure ritualistic but very real pain: whippings and lacerations, circumcision without anesthetic, slitting of the dorsal or ventral surface of the penis to expose the urethra within. Many of the specific ceremonies focus on the male organ so that no confusion exists that this is a ritual of becoming a man. The ceremonies are linked to the *right* to be a man sexually and the *responsibility* of a man to procreate and bear children. Occasionally the boy may be thrown into the wilderness with his wounds still bleeding,

with no food and no weapons, forced to meet nature naked, unarmed
—and unafraid.

The brutality is appalling to a Western observer and the stoicism—
at least as it is traditionally described—seems unbelievable. But these
are the prices of manhood, and once endured the boy no longer exists;
a man emerges from these ordeals, with the respect and privileges of
that role publicly acknowledged by all.

It is a transformation sometimes marked by ritual death: the boy will
be thrown into a river or a pit, if not literally then metaphorically, and
a new person, a man, will emerge with the marks of manhood upon
him. Often given a new name, he will then return to the village. In
some cultures, he will pretend not to recognize other members of the
community and will not be identified even by his mother and sisters as
the person who has left. The newly reborn youth will now be a man in
the fullest sense and with the entire panoply of rights of manhood,
including in many societies the privilege of sexuality with older women.

Very little of this remains in Western culture, thank goodness, but
we do pay a price. In a recent study of male identity in the United
States, the researcher described to his American subject how a Busama
youth in the highlands of New Guinea proves his manhood.

Throughout their journey the elders belaboured them with fire brands, sticks
tipped with obsidian, and nettles. They arrived covered with blood and were
received by a pair of guardians. They were beaten, starved, deprived of
sleep, partially suffocated, and almost roasted. Water was forbidden, and if
thirsty they had to chew sugar-cane. Only the coarsest of foods were allowed,
and even these were left raw. All the time the guardians gave them instructions about kinship responsibilities and duties to their seniors. The guardians
now taught their charges how to incise the penis in order to eliminate the
contamination resulting from association with the other sex. Subsequently,
this operation had to be performed regularly. A series of great feasts then
took place, and the initiands emerged richly decorated.[3]

After hearing this, the subject, Howard R. responded:

I wish I had it that easy. Run through the fire, step on the coals—then it's over and done with. You're a man. Everyone knows you're a man and that's the end of it. For me it keeps on going on and on. The uncertainty of it— at any moment you could be out on the streets. It's all tied up with money. I've got to keep on fighting for money and respect. The fire never stops; I keep running through it every day.[4]

We cling desperately to whatever vestiges of ritual do remain, and we seek proof of our manhood in myriads of symbolic tests we devise for ourselves. Nothing is explicit, or publicly defined; and we suffer for it. If only we had the wisdom that was expressed in *The Wizard of Oz*. When the Wizard is exposed as a fraud ("Ignore that man behind the curtain"), he justifies his hocus pocus as a necessary adjunct to modern society. He provides the order and reassurance that religion or magic had traditionally supplied. He provides us with ritual indications that abrogate any responsibility for having to earn something that may no longer exist, given the driving competitiveness of our society. The Tin Man *has* heart but is given a ticking clock. The Cowardly Lion is given a medal to publicly announce his valor, which may be all one needs these days when bravery accomplishes little. The Scarecrow, who has already demonstrated his wisdom, receives a diploma—the symbolic representation of, and often the alternative to, an educated man. He needs the diploma to reassure himself and to gain respect from the public at large, which inevitably responds more to the packaging than the essence of virtue. The Wizard is, if not a Freudian, at least a philosophical Idealist. There is no real world, only the world of illusion. If one can satisfy that world of illusion, one survives.

We have no recognized talisman of manhood, but some vestiges of religious and educational rites of passage still exist in sophisticated Western cultures: first communion, confirmation, diplomas and titles.

The Jewish boy is still bar-mitzvahed at age thirteen, indicating that according to the tenets of the Jewish religion he is now privileged to enter into the community of men. He is permitted to conduct the services and read the law. Ten "men" are all that is necessary to conduct a Jewish worship service. A community of ten bar mitzvah boys at age thirteen (in a clubhouse, absent a rabbi or cantor) is as realized a congregation of God as is a three thousand-member congregation with a full panoply of chorus and conducting rabbis. Unlike the Busama, however, this ritual does not mark a true transition. The jokes that revolve around the "today I am a man" theme belie the significance of a sacrament that at one time had to be deadly serious. No thirteen-year-old Jewish boy is a man in his own eyes, the eyes of his community, or the eyes of his parents.

The traditional methods for proving manhood are no longer effective—power and physical courage accomplish little these days except, perhaps, in the life of the adolescent. Since ritual and ceremonial rites of passage have been attenuated or abandoned, and manhood is never completely defined, one must prove one's manhood almost daily through elliptical and symbolic cultural rituals.

The ancient rites and rituals have been replaced by a fluid, open-ended, and ambivalent set of experiences that will be measured against internal standards that are often unarticulated, and worse, misunderstood. Without the formal statements of the society, the labeling and acknowledgments, each man must form his own self-evaluations and then seek reassurance from the attitudes of those around him. He will be constantly alert to judgment, looking for signs of respect and "disrespect," the current popular term among black urban teenagers.

Tragically, too, his perceptions may be incorrect and so compound his problems. A paranoid, competitive attitude carried through life will inevitably be a self-fulfilling prophecy in which the "disrespected" boy or man will perceive challenges and humiliations whether they are there or not. The outcome is predictable. At its best it will produce a sullen person and at its worst a dangerous one.

In America at one time, there existed a ritual of emerging manhood that included an actual involvement with the hunt, albeit a symbolic one. A boy's first gun in this culture was the equivalent of a boy's first car in an urban setting, or his first adult sexual experience in both. The fanaticism about guns and the power of the gun lobby in Congress is only in part related to the number of votes they can mobilize. The gun lobby appeals directly to the unconscious insecurities of a Congress that is still predominantly male.

The ritual of the hunt is beautifully realized in William Faulkner's extraordinary short story "The Bear," written in the late 1920s. The boy in Faulkner's story goes through a series of initiations, based on the hunt, which are as formalized as, though not as explicit and certainly less brutal than, those of the Samburu youth living in northern Kenya:[5]

> Until he was ten, each November he would watch the wagon containing the dogs and the bedding and food and guns and his father and Tennie's Jim, the Negro, and Sam Fathers, the Indian, son of a slave woman and a Chickasaw chief, depart on the road to town, to Jefferson, where Major de Spain and the others would join them. To the boy, at seven and eight and nine, they were not going into the Big Bottom to hunt bear and deer, but to keep yearly rendezvous with the bear which they did not even intend to kill. Two weeks later they would return, with no trophy, no head and skin.[6] (p. 282)

The purpose of the hunt was not to obtain game or trophies, but to join with the company of men in a communion with nature. To come to terms with one's own mortality and one's own humanity by approaching the primal, the existential, the immortal. The hunt is a search for truth and purpose. This is clearly explicated at the end of the story:

> Truth is one thing. It covers all things which touch the heart—honor and pride and pity and justice and courage and love. Do you see now? (p. 294)

The boy has been raised with images of the legendary bear and memories of his father leaving for the hunt; of the many goodbyes and the many returns with awesome stories that annually enhanced and re-created the myth.

At ten, finally, he joins the hunt. In his first hunt, he makes his kills but he knows that is not the purpose of the hunt. He must see the old bear. He will have to look at him. This is the ritual. At last he is told by Sam that in order to see the bear he must relinquish his gun, the very symbol of power and civilization. He must return to an earlier time, prove his courage by facing the bear unarmed. He must go into the wilderness alone. And he leaves the gun.

> Of his own will in relinquishment he had accepted not a gambit, not a choice, but a condition in which not only the bear's heretofore inviolable anonymity but all the old rules and balances of hunter and hunted had been abrogated. He would not even be afraid, not even in the moment when the fear would take him completely—blood, skin, bowels, bones, memory from the long time before it became his memory—all save that thin, clear, quench-less, immortal lucidity which alone differed him from this bear and from all the other bear and deer he would ever kill in the humility and pride of his skill and endurance. . . . (pp. 288–89)

This paragraph clearly demonstrates that the purpose of the hunt— and symbolically of all hunting for all children—is to reach manhood through a test of courage in which there are no trophies, and whose only purpose is the conversion of the self from boy to man. Faulkner thus takes the boy from prepubescence through puberty into manhood.

The boy does not come face to face with the bear until he is fourteen. Before puberty he would have killed his buck, marked his face with hot blood, and even killed the bear; not so in his maturity. He finally faces the bear, unarmed and alone except for the companionship of a small mongrel dog, a symbol of pure courage, unadulterated by ratio- nality or civilizing influences, the raw courage to which all men aspire.

In a sequence of overpowering beauty, Faulkner describes the boy's confrontation with the bear, and here one senses the author's conviction that only in coming to grips with nature, his place in it, his fear and his courage, can a boy emerge into manhood:

> Not white nor black nor red, but men, hunters with the will and hardihood to endure and the humility and skill to survive, and the dogs and the bear and deer juxtaposed and reliefed against it, ordered and compelled by and within the wilderness in the ancient and unremitting contest by the ancient and unmitigable rules which voided all regrets and brooked no quarter. . . . (p. 293)

The men sit as a community around a fireplace passing the bottle, and the boy is now with them and of them. This, too, is a ritual of acceptance into manhood. To Faulkner, this drinking of the liquor, which "not women, not boys and children, but only hunters drank," represented "some condensation of the wild immortal spirit."

The deterioration of the meaning of the hunt, and the degradation of rituals of manhood, are evoked in two other wilderness stories that also involve hunting: James Dickey's *Deliverance,* and Norman Mailer's *Why Are We in Vietnam?* The decades that separate Faulkner from Dickey and Mailer have seen profound changes in American culture and in the industrialized Western world. While all three authors are quintessentially American, they are men of different times and different subcultures. Still, just as the transcultural studies showed the similarity of Truk Islanders in the South Pacific to the Andalusian peasants in southern Spain, these authors illustrated how peripheral cultural differences are when placed in juxtaposition to the universal central struggle to achieve manhood.

What a difference those fifty years that separate Faulkner from the other two authors make! The hunters and the hunts described by Dickey and Mailer are kindred stories, seemingly unrelated to the experience described by Faulkner. Their similarity is particularly noteworthy when one remembers that Mailer is the quintessential urban Jewish wise guy and Dickey bears the heritage of the southern poet.

On the surface, Dickey in *Deliverance* seems closer to Faulkner than to Mailer. It is a hunt, but this time for adult men. They enter the wilderness not to confront nature at its most primitive—not to learn "the humility and pride" that the boy must ultimately learn in Faulkner, but to reestablish manhood by playing at the hunt on their own terms. As the story develops, though, they are confronted with the primitive in their own kind. It is not animals they meet but the animal still residing within man, and ultimately the animal within themselves.

The story is essentially one of homosexual rape and assault on manhood, and the recovery and reassertion of manhood through a return to an earlier time of brutal vengeance. The wilderness that ultimately brings deliverance is the wildness inherent at the very heart of the concept of masculinity in our society. Here the gun *will* be used and must be used. This is a story of the big stick, of phallic power, of individual combat, vengeance, and redemption through ritual slaughter.

The story is post-Freudian, not just in the implicit way that Faulkner's may also seem to be, but explicitly. Its language is everywhere phallic, and its metaphors are framed in terms of consciously drawn sexual symbols which will be examined more fully in later chapters.

What can one make of Mailer's primal scream of a novel, *Why Are We in Vietnam?* In contrast with the other two writers, Mailer moves from the spiritual to the psychological to the political; but as in all of his work, politics and sex are barely distinguishable.

Outraged by the injustice of an indecent war in which young men are endangered to satisfy the macho anxieties of their fathers, Mailer tells this story as a parable. Specifically, it is an attack on Lyndon Johnson and the politics of his age. It is not just chance that in Mailer's book it is a Texan who takes his son into danger in the wilderness.

What occurs in Mailer is the exact opposite of the fusion of father and son in manhood that we witnessed in Faulkner. For, in Mailer's hunt, the bear *is* killed, and the result of that kill is shame and disgust, not pride. It is an event that marks the ultimate separation of the son from his father and his father's values.

Starkly and irrevocably, the son is betrayed by his father, Rusty. When the father's cowardice is exposed, he attempts to recover his own manhood by usurping that of his son. As in the Vietnam War, the young men will be sacrificed to support the fading potency of their fathers. In the end, the son even refuses to recognize kinship with his father.

The teenage narrator teases us, the readers, with whom he directly converses, by assuming the role of a black teenage disc jockey (hence D.J.). It is a Texas boy's painful attempt to dissociate himself from the image of manhood presented to him by his father. Mailer contrasts the concept of masculinity tainted by power, money, and civilization represented in Rusty by juxtaposing an unspoiled "true" man in the persona of the guide, Luke Fellinka.

In Mailer's story the trappings are all sexual, but the substance is all power. The gun is no longer the symbol of the phallus. Rather, the phallus is the symbol of the gun. Power is all—and sexual power is everything. D.J. describes an imaginary psychiatrist:

> Listening to Dallas matrons complain about the sexual habits of their husbands, all ex-hotrodders, hunters, cattlemen, oil riggers, corporation gears and insurance finks, zap! . . . Well, every one of those bastards has the sexual peculiarities of red-blooded men, which is to say that one of them can't come unless he's squinting down a gunsight, and the other won't produce unless his wife sticks a pistol up his ass—that man is of course a cop.[7]

Mailer has been called a modern Hemingway, but there are significant distinctions. While both men are obsessed with masculinity, they are products of different times. There is no nobility, no nineteenth-century romanticism left in Mailer, although he is surely the last of our romantics. A late twentieth-century cynicism pervades all; a post-Vietnam consciousness. Everything now is paranoia. Everything now is an extended shriek of pain. Gone is the model of speaking softly while carrying the big stick—that image perpetuated in every bar scene in every Western across decades, epitomized by the lonely man of few words and great quiet courage, from Tom Mix to Gary Cooper, John Wayne to Clint Eastwood. No longer is the gun sheathed and invisibly resting in the folds of the gunman's clothing. Like everything else in our time, the implicit has become explicit, the private public, and the symbol of modern man is represented by the "fuck you" shouted more in fear than defiance—preferably from the confines of an 8,000-pound automobile whizzing to safety.

For a city boy, there are no hunts, symbolic or otherwise. But the directives to hunt and destroy, confront and attack, persist in our genetic makeup. The intransigence of a little boy's primordial fascination with struggle, competition, and power is epitomized in his games and instruments of war. The psychology of the sixties playing on the Vietnam generation bred a group of parents determined both to minimize gender differences and to prohibit toys that glorified militarism. The power of androgens and genes confounded these optimistic parents. I have now observed both the "insensitivity" of pre-feminist parents and the "consciousness raising" of the post-feminist generation, and can discern no significant difference between their male progeny, all of whom still delight in weapons.

My first grandchild was a boy. Not only his mother but his father —particularly his father—was determined that he would not be permitted to play with mock weapons. His favorite playground happened to be his grandparents' yard, filled with rocks, hills, and woody places—perfect for forts, barricades, bunkers, and retreats. This yard was swiftly littered with hidden caches of sticks shaped like guns; clearly recognizable "arrows," "daggers," and "swords" piled neatly in cleverly constructed redoubts; and everywhere the neatly stacked, frighteningly realistic caches of hand grenades that pine trees so generously supply with their abundant cones.

Faced with the inevitable, even these resolute parents capitulated, and the water pistols, cap-guns, and other paraphernalia of aggressive combat began to appear on birthdays and holidays. Further evidence of the incessant preoccupation with shoot-up activities of little boys is of course seen in the vast commercial success of Nintendo and other video games which bring combat more realistically to life on the little screen. The protector and provider persist in the boy, and must find outlets in power games and power symbols.

In my midwestern childhood, more suburban than urban, the automobile was the symbol of power. But it was late in arriving, well past puberty, and later than the rural boy's introduction to the gun. The right to operate a motor vehicle is one of the few formal rites of passage left in our culture, being regulated by law, demanding a test of competence, and limited to those over a certain age. One could not drive in the state of Ohio until sixteen—that is, one could not *legally* drive. All of us had learned to drive at least a year earlier and were often indulged, accompanied by our fathers. We envied the farm boys who at thirteen and fourteen were driving powerful vehicles, tractors and pickups.

Before the car, of course, came the bicycle, and in our adolescent stages to manhood, it may have been more important than the car. It granted us power and freedom such as we had never felt before. The bicycle gave us the energy, the kinetic drive, and the motion that seemed so much a part of the masculine genetic endowment. Movement and speed in every aspect are part of the male sense of biological self; speed, strength, and courage are the fundamental attributes of the warrior and the hunter. Boys love speed, whether on a roller coaster, skiing, roller-blading, skateboarding, racing on the basketball court, or even purposeless and hysterical running through empty streets and empty lots.

The bike also gave us a sense of enhanced mastery and potency by fusing us to machines which by definition embody leverage and expand biological power. The machine, like a baseball bat, or a rifle, extends the self. It is an empowering instrument.

Finally, the bicycle was a distancing instrument, essential in our perpetual struggle to free ourselves from maternal supervision and maternal identification. "Back in a half hour," yelled out by the son meant he would return in an hour or more. The distances one could go and the things one could do in that hour were enormously enhanced by a bicycle. I remember the extraordinary power I felt when, on my twelfth birthday, I received the ultimate two-wheeler—a big red Schwinn. Along with my Schwinn I also got "long pants."

When I was a boy, there was a strict code of dressing imposed by the social standards of our community, beyond those enforced by schools. Young boys before school age routinely wore shorts. In the winter, to protect their legs, they wore high socks. The change of length of a boy's trousers became a mark of his maturity. One he entered school he was usually introduced to the world of "knickers," loose trousers tied slightly below the knee and bloused over sufficiently to allow freedom to move and run. These were worn over high socks, or in the cold winter months high-top boots, which laced up to a height that cleared the calf. One can see this style of dress in period movies of the thirties and the great still photographs of the Depression. A shirt, sweater, and jacket in wintertime completed the outfit.

The prepubescent boy waited with longing and envy for his first long pants. It was a mandatory change of costume before entering junior high school (grades six through nine). If a boy were tall and matured early, he might prevail upon indulgent parents to give him his first long pants before then. This made him the envy of his fellow classmates. Occasionally, however, there was the poor soul, who—whether for economic reasons, or because he was small and had not yet outgrown his knickers, or simply because of parental indifference—was seen with knickers in junior high school. Usually he was teased mercilessly. He was a "baby," a "sissy," a "wimp."

These standards of age-appropriate dress have since been eradicated. All boys now wear long pants almost from infancy on, and shorts, when worn, are accommodations to weather. Boys' clothing increasingly looks like men's clothing of an informal nature.

Beyond clothing, there were still other publicly accepted behavior or ceremonials that were reserved for certain ages. One of the most malignant was of course cigarettes. I list this as a ritual because it was age-oriented. During my coming of age the health hazards of cigarettes were less apparent than they are now. Still, it was considered inappropriate for a child to smoke. (Indeed, in my childhood, it was considered inappropriate for a woman to smoke in public places.) There was almost an intuitive sense that smoking was harmful, and few parents were pleased to see their children smoking. But by the time young boys were in high school, most of them were smoking. The tougher or less rigidly supervised boys were smoking at thirteen or fourteen. Young boys were perpetually stealing cigarettes from their parents and smoking in covert secret places.

The relationship of smoking to manhood and masculinity is evidenced in the methods of marketing cigarettes. In those days there were only three legitimate brands, Lucky Strikes, Chesterfields, and Camels. To break open the cigarette market with a new brand was considered almost an impossible task for advertising.

When it became increasingly apparent that cigarettes were toxic, filter-tip cigarettes were introduced as a deceptive device to encourage wary consumers to continue smoking while assuming falsely that they were protected by a fluff of cotton. Since filter-tips were only smoked by those concerned about safety, however, they had a sissy quality and young boys—the prime market—were reluctant to adopt them. Brand loyalty in those days was extraordinary. It was imperative to snare a customer when he was young to keep him committed to a lifetime of smoking.

The Philip Morris Company, a large but secondary manufacturer, had marketed a brand in their own name that never succeeded against the big three. Then they invented the Marlboro Man—a calculation that was to be repeated later on with the Virginia Slims campaign to attract women—and outsmarted the competition. Marlboros quickly cashed in on a rising anxiety over lung cancer. Generations of young boys, reassured by the fact that tough wranglers smoke filter-tips, switched brands. The advertiser who knew that cigarette smoking was not just an addiction but a mark of manhood won the allegiance of innumerable gullible boys.

There are still some other rites of passage remaining. If the automobile is a symbol of phallic power and sexuality, then surely the first experience of intercourse is more directly so. This differs enormously with socioeconomic groups. In the hurly-burly of the cities, a boy's first intercourse may be as early as the prepubescent years. In the middle class, the first intercourse was traditionally observed later and as part of a sequence of sexual activities often discussed freely and openly with one's peer group. The first pubic hair, the first wet dream, the first ejaculation through masturbation—all markers bragged about when they occurred, or for that matter before they occurred.

Masturbatory activity, while almost inevitably producing shame and therefore done in private, could occasionally be incorporated into games. The "circle jerk" was a common form of destigmatizing masturbation, though more common in puberty or just before. In the postpubescent years, with true sexual involvement, such intimacies with other men become too threatening as the possible homosexual implications of shared sexual experience grow more obvious.

"Scoring" was always important. Autobiographical and semi-autobiographical fiction, movies, and television have charted the preoccupation with the stages toward intercourse—from kissing to feeling, to feeling naked flesh, to seeing and sharing nudity, to mutual masturbation, to intercourse. All these stages have profound significance to the growing boy, beyond the sexual pleasure involved. They are markers on the road to manhood.

Sex with the domestics was common in Victorian times and was almost an assumed pattern for certain upper-middle-class boys, and while no such coterie of young domestics appears to have existed in twentieth-century America, the amount of sex that was "arranged" was significant. Most of my middle-class patients describe initial sexual experiences that were arranged either by a parent (rarely in America) or a surrogate—an older brother, a young uncle, a friend of the family. Or, first sex was part of a group activity, involving a prostitute or a girl from another neighborhood or class. One went outside the boundaries of the "tribe." For the city boys of New York, it meant going to a Harlem brothel for the initiating sexual experience. For the boys of midwestern cities, it was often going to a blue-collar neighborhood or bar and picking up either a prostitute or a working-class girl.

Prior to the sexual revolution, we saw "totemic taboos" as firmly in place here as in the tribal structures of Africa, where sex was forbidden with members of the same clan or totem. One had girlfriends from the same social class and neighborhood ("the totem") with whom one had sexual activities, but not sexual intercourse. Sex was with the "others"—at least publicly acknowledged sex.

The separation between affection and status—the girl one marries and the girl one screws—was firmly established. The sexual revolution did not liberate men to feel free to have sex. They had that liberation all along. The sexual revolution in this sense only served women. What the sexual revolution accomplished for men was to make it somewhat easier to combine the social role of girlfriend with sexual partner. This could be done even before the sexual revolution; but before the sixties, sexual activity with a girlfriend was usually deferred to a later age.

The initiation into sex was a ritual of interest to the father even while not engineered by him. Young men rarely discussed sex explicitly with their parents of either sex. Nonetheless, somehow or other they tangentially communicated to their fathers the knowledge that they had become "men." They were aware that the fathers wanted to know and were relieved to hear about it. When a boy went off to college, it was reasonably common for some fathers to ascertain whether their sons were still "virgins," and if so to make some suggestions to prepare them for their independent adult lives.

Now, with the sexual revolution, sexual activity is more open and starts earlier. It is less ritualistic, less fuss is made over progressing from one stage to the next and on to intercourse, and frequently sexual intercourse is achieved before either party is emotionally ready for it.

Of course we still have other markers of manhood: the first shave; the first mustache or beard; the first unescorted trip away from home; the first time drunk; and so on. These are still important, but often they are not publicly announced except to the small public of one's gang, where bragging rights are sustained. The true rite, the public ritual, whereby the community acknowledges manhood at a given time through a given ceremony and with a formal announcement, has disappeared forever. Nonetheless, the boy is still stuck with the same biological directives for power, assertion, competition, benevolence, and all those other aspects of masculinity we know to be fed through biology and amply supported by mothers and fathers of most cultures. This biological diversity is still supported via gender stereotyping which, while mitigated by the new feminism, remains essentially intact and firmly in place.

A man must make himself a man. Wanting the public acknowledgment, he must, as poor Howard R. said, "keep running through it every day." He must demonstrate in some way that he is still a procreator, a protector, and a provider. He must demonstrate, somehow, that he has the courage and wherewithal, the power and significance, to maintain his own status and his own self-respect as a man. He must establish his independence—the primary marker of manhood.

Look Homeward, Angel may well be the paradigmatic American tale of a boy's attempt to find his manhood by freeing himself from his parents. Eugene Gant's attempts to escape his purse-lipped, demeaning mother were a message in hyperbole to an entire generation of American boys. The almost purple prose was particularly well received by self-dramatizing adolescents. After five hundred pages Thomas Wolfe liberates his hero, Eugene, in the following scene:

> "Unnatural!" Eliza whispered. "Unnatural son! You will be punished if there's a just God in Heaven."

"Oh, there is! I'm sure there is!" cried Eugene. "Because I have been punished. By God, I shall spend the rest of my life getting my heart back, healing and forgetting every scar you put upon me when I was a child. The first move I ever made, after the cradle, was to crawl for the door, and every move I have made since has been an effort to escape. And now at last I am free from you all, although you may hold me for a few years more. If I am not free, I am at least locked up in my own prison, but I shall get me some beauty, I shall get me some order out of this jungle of my life: I shall find my way out of it yet, though it take me twenty years more—alone."

"Alone?" said Eliza, with the old suspicion. "Where are you going?"

"Ah," he said, "you were not looking, were you? I've gone."[8]

Lacking ceremonial liberations, each boy in our culture is required to find the door to manhood on his own. Whether freeing himself from hated parents or adored ones, he still has to escape from childhood and from the mother with whom he so lovingly first identified. With or without ritual, he must crawl toward that stereotype of masculinity by shedding the feminine parts of himself. Unfortunately, the feminine parts so shed may be fused with crucial capacities for love and tenderness, which in the process will also be abandoned.

Modern man now carries his stick with anxiety. No longer sure it is big enough, he will find ways to measure himself through symbolic acts. He must establish himself in competition with other frightened and insecure men, who surround him with their (bigger?) sticks.

PART II

FEELING
MANLY

PROTECTOR, PROVIDER,
PROCREATOR

5 ‣ CARRYING A BIG STICK

In a previous, more modest generation, the following anecdote was passed off as a true event. A little girl with no exposure to male nudity on seeing a little boy take out his penis to urinate against a tree said: "My, that's a handy thing to have along on a picnic." This might be interpreted by some psychoanalysts as "penis envy," an ambiguous and highly politicized term. Little girls, on first recognizing the presence of the male genitalia—and noting the absence of the same in their anatomy—often express feelings of deprivation, inadequacy, and anxiety. Enough women patients over the years have confirmed their sense of incompleteness, with the accompanying anxiety, to accept that there is something that can be labeled "penis envy." That it is a universal developmental phase through which all women must pass is problematic. That it is the central focus—the principal dynamic—about which all feminine consciousness rests is of course absurd.

What has been missing in all such discussion is the awareness of penis envy in men. Castration anxiety was presumed to dominate male sensibilities in prepubescence. According to classical Freudian theory, the little girl is not spared castration anxiety either. All anxiety, whether experienced by boys or girls, was classified as castration anxiety. If one reads Freud metaphorically, the argument is less mystifying. Think of the male genital as a symbol of power; what castration anxiety then represents is disempowerment, weakness, and helplessness.

"Castration" technically means the removal of the testes, but Freud always visualized castration anxiety in terms of the fear of loss of the penis. The "moral superiority of men" to women (Freud's original premise, not mine) was dependent on the assumption that castration anxiety made the man more vulnerable to terror of loss, and therefore more "controllable." If you are a man, castration is a very real threat. The possession of the penis made man a moral agent. The early view of "male superiority" is well summarized by Robert Stoller, a distinguished psychiatrist and pioneer in modern psychosexual research.

Freud accepted as a given the belief that the superior sex is male. He felt this was a fact established throughout mammalia by males' physically superior strength; life or death struggles select males as superior because they are stronger. This fact, with the penis as the most compelling symbolic representation, was then reflected in mythology, folk tales, institutions of society, artistic productions, religious worship, dreams—everywhere. . . .

It is a corollary of the thesis of male superiority that the prime feature of maleness, the penis, is a superior organ physically and symbolically; and Freud could point to phallic worship, in its myriad forms, for proof for those who do not listen to the dreams of men and women. In the concept of castration anxiety he found reason to believe that men consider the penis the prime organ of the race, and in penis envy he found the proof that women also agree on the primacy of the penis. Because it is visible, can change so in size, is shaped like a weapon, can penetrate, frightens women, and is such an intense source of sensation from infancy on, it also demonstrates its superiority. Then, when it is contrasted with the female genitals, the case is again made. The female phallus, the clitoris, is much smaller, not visible, cannot penetrate, has not seized mankind's imagination, is never symbolized or exalted, and—Freud thought—is not a competent source of pleasure. Its significance is further weakened since it must share its fate with another organ, the vagina, which Freud felt was universally considered an inferior organ—it is hidden, dark, mysterious, uncertain, unclean, and an undependable source of pleasure.[1]

Freud in this instance was wrong, notwithstanding a couple of generations of psychoanalysts—male and female—who bought this party line. The difficulty is that the world of men out there in this late twentieth century still shares the biases, attitudes, and anxieties that influenced Freud in the late nineteenth century. If Freud was led astray, it was because his culture seemed to indicate the truth of these observations. Freud did not create male chauvinism, he was its victim, as were most Victorian men and women. With the changes wrought by the Industrial Revolution, two world wars, the biological and the feminist revolutions, it is somewhat incredible that these biases still remain intact in so large a part of the population.

One must not rule out all of Freud's insights on manhood because of this one ill-devised theory. He remains the most profound authority on human behavior to date. Where Freud is absolutely correct, where his guidance proves invaluable, is in his awareness of the power of the symbol and the metaphor embodied in the phallus. He saw this emerging most strongly in dreams. All instruments of power were simply representations of the only true source of power, the phallus. How could we believe otherwise? Freud had decided all energy was sexual energy, all motivation sexual motivation; therefore, all fear was sexual fear and all aggression was sexual aggression.

It was Freud's great discovery that when a person dreams of a gun (or a large stick or a baseball bat), the symbol might really represent a penis; many things that are visualized as instruments of power are really phallic symbols. What Freud failed to recognize was that the phallus itself might be a symbol, representing a big stick or a rifle. Freud's great insight was that everything may be symbolic, not that everything is sexual. And just as power may be a form of sexual satisfaction, sexual satisfaction may be an act of power. Today, we differ in our readiness to accept the universality of symbols. To some of us at least, at times a cigar may be only a cigar.

I vividly recall my first dream in analysis. I had enrolled in the Columbia Psychoanalytic Institute—a radical, suspect, breakaway group from the orthodoxy that dominated psychoanalysis in America during the 1950s. Knowing that I was part of a splinter group, I decided to have my training analysis with a "classical analyst" from the New York Psychoanalytic Institute, then the temple of orthodoxy and respectability.

In those days I was unaware that despite the rhetoric and invective, whatever separated the psychoanalytic schools in theory bore little relationship to what happened in practice. As in every other area of life, what a person said was not necessarily what he did.

My dream was simple, unromantic, and terribly disappointing. I would have elected to start my grand adventure with finer stuff. My dream was simply that I noticed a tear in my tie. That was it; the whole story. My analyst, sternly Freudian (in those opening days and months of analysis, at least), said nothing. I knew that it was my job to free-associate. All right, I thought, let's go!

The tie immediately directed my thoughts to my father. My father was a man I adored. Quiet, strong, hardworking, devoted, a person of absolute decency and integrity. And I, the eldest of his three sons, had always felt a special relationship and affinity to him. One of his foibles was his love of ties. He had literally hundreds of them, even though he was not a wealthy man. Most of them were of extravagant design and color, the only extravagance I knew in this conservative man. He allowed himself the freedom, joy, and self-indulgence denied him in his mundane and constricting job by wearing these flamboyant ties.

The dream, which when first recounted had seemed so trivial, when put in the context of my everyday existence began to take on new meaning. As I began to "associate," the meaning of the dream became apparent as in an epiphany. This small dream focused the entire drama of my life. With my wife, a fifteen-month-old child, and a newborn baby, I had come to New York to pursue my psychoanalytic education. We had left behind, in Ohio, all our family, all our friends: a community we had known and understood, where we felt accepted and at ease. We came from sentimental families who celebrated holidays together. Now we were completely alone in a city that was rude, vulgar, somewhat frightening, and while challenging and exciting, ultimately confusing and disorienting. In this setting, in this mood, we faced our first major holiday—it must have been Thanksgiving—isolated, cut off, unattached.

We were forced, finally, to recognize the price of independence. All our ties with the past had been cut. There was a poignant sense of separation, focused on the image of my father, the powerful figure whom I had chosen to leave. This, then, was my final rite of passage, my graduation, my initiation, my wandering in the wilderness. I thought I was ready and eager for it, and in most ways I was. At twenty-seven, married to an independent and loving woman, the father of two daughters, a physician, I was beginning a new career—and my own personal analysis—both of which I hoped would expand my possibilities and my sense of self. Life was all promise and excitement, despite the economic hardships that faced us.

In the tradition of men everywhere, I rarely looked back. It was my wife who thought to call home, and prodded me to do the same. This persisted throughout the lives of our parents. "Call your folks" was her weekly reminder, well aware that a call originating from me had more powerful impact than any she placed.

During my father's lifetime I rarely thought of him or, for that matter, of my mother. Only since their deaths do I think of them with great regularity, and particularly with my increasing age. Yet during this first holiday season away from home, my emotions were centered on an area that my conscious thoughts avoided. It is the power of the dream to drive thoughts into consciousness and expose true feelings. It seemed strange on Thanksgiving to be alone with no family, to have a small dinner by ourselves. I was in the grip of nostalgia. The dream made it perfectly clear that while I seemed to be reveling in my independence, a part of me mourned the loss of my family ties. I had identified a parallel emotion emerging from my unconscious that I had not recognized: I was lonely and felt adrift.

From the point of view of my home school, Columbia, I had traced my dream to a basic "dependency conflict." This was consonant with the psychodynamics of the Columbia Psychoanalytic School. Sandor Rado, the most brilliant of psychoanalytic teachers, had been brought to New York from Berlin to head up the first psychoanalytic school in the United States. He had left the New York Psychoanalytic School to start the Columbia Psychoanalytic Center. Rado had broken with orthodox psychoanalysis over its insistence that only sexual conflict could produce neurosis. In classical analysis, maturity and health were equated with the resolution of the Oedipal complex; with Rado, it was the resolution of one's dependency. By the standards of my teachers I had traced the dream to its root conflict.

My analyst, on the other hand, was an *echt* Freudian. In treating me, he had a dual agenda. His job was to analyze me, but in the process he was determined to "educate" me; he would not have me lost to an alien school without some exposure to the true faith. When I completed my analysis of the dream to my satisfaction and was prepared to go on to other matters, he asked why I had stopped. I thought that I had already extracted a mountainous interpretation out of that psychic molehill; nonetheless, I dutifully returned to the dream.

Then I remembered a ritual characteristic of Jewish funerals. A black ribbon, worn by a mourner, is cut with scissors. The ceremonial cutting is a symbolic substitution for the rending of one's clothes in grief. I, myself, on observing this had concluded that, in addition, it must symbolically represent the need for the survivors to cut their ties to the past, to sense the limits of mourning, and rise—as David rose from the ashes of his despair on hearing of the death of his son—and continue the obligations to life and the living. I offered this new gem, which my analyst acknowledged; yet when I wanted to turn to other events he still seemed dissatisfied and disturbed.

He asked me why a tie and what I thought of the shape of a tie. It was then I realized that by the definitions with which he worked, I had yet to analyze the most "profound" element of the dream. I became aware that to enter into the Oedipal conflict by standards of traditional analysis the tie must be a phallic symbol, and, in my separation, I must be experiencing castration anxiety. I was not aware of being anxious. I was aware of being lonely and nostalgic. But emotions were not given credence in traditional analysis. Therefore, all emotion—rage, disappointment, hurt, guilt, shame—was seen as modifications or forms of anxiety.

The dream was ultimately interpreted as my striving to return to the mother (home), competing with the father, attempting to usurp him by establishing my independent role as a father, fearing the punitive backlash—and suffering from a sense of impotence that derives from castration anxiety.

Is this the "correct" interpretation? I have no idea. Is it essentially different from the interpretation that would have been made by my reformist teachers? Probably not. Once the ritual languages are discounted, the stories are the same. Cast into a language and metaphor acceptable to my analyst, the interpretation was now completed. It was not difficult to accommodate myself to his language, and once we were speaking the same language we got along swimmingly.

Both interpretations abided by the quintessential Freudian principle that we live in a symbolic world; that things are not what they seem, or if they are, they are also more; that everything is metaphor, and that in the world of men the phallic metaphor is an overwhelming one.

The penis is more than just the primary instrument of sexual gratification. It is a symbol of power and potency to every man in our society, and to too many women. The two boys in their little game seeing who can pee further faster are tragi-comic prototypes for the games men will play for the rest of their lives.

The average size of the penis—like height or any other biological measurement—falls within the traditional bell-shaped curve, with very few people being either inordinately large or small. Yet generations of boys are stretching to measure that extra fraction of an inch to prove . . . what?

Certainly in the performance of the sexual act for either of its purposes, fun or reproduction, size doesn't make a bit of difference except at the extremes, which might create separate problems. The vagina is an accommodating organ. It tends to wrap itself around whatever is presented in a congenial fit.

Yet, not just for men but for many women also, the size of a man's penis somehow seems to carry symbolic weight in the measurement of the man. Can anyone imagine a symbolic equivalent for women? Some might mention that large breasts provide a competitive edge, but on analysis that varies with cultures, what is considered pleasantly large in one culture being unseemly and obese in another. One need only compare the typical Rubens nude with the flat-chested nudes of the Art Deco period in the late twenties to see how culture determines the value placed on breast size. No culture to my knowledge has ever glorified and romanticized a teeny-weeny-peeny.

Even when large breasts are admired, they are generally revered as sexual adornments. When breasts have symbolic meaning beyond the sexual, it is not in the area of the power struggle, but rather in terms of their most fundamental function as organs of nurture, and therefore maternal love. Breasts say nothing of power, except indirectly: the "power" to attract a man, and thereby gain a powerful protector. Penis size is something else again. Beyond its cachet in the sexual arena, the penis is a transcendent symbol of male competition, power, and dominance.

In the prehistoric world of the cavemen, an emphasis on body size was justifiable. Big men with big muscles were more dependable defenders of family and property. When the only weapon might be the jawbone of an ass, the muscular power of a Samson was a necessity. But this has long since ceased to be the case except in the more primitive societies or the more primitive areas of industrial society. A small man carrying a small gun, or for that matter a big checkbook, is in most situations more than a match for an Arnold Schwarzenegger type. Yet a bias for size and strength exists. How else to explain the phenomenon of the real Arnold Schwarzenegger.

We now live in a world where we have machinery doing the heavy work of our lives. With the creation of agricultural machinery, robots, and assembly lines in developed societies, the economic exploitation that reduced men to beasts of burden or to living human machinery is about over.

The positions of power in our society require little muscle. To be a Supreme Court justice, a senator, a chief executive officer, to be a physician, lawyer, money manager, editor, politician requires no physical strength. A compact real estate tycoon might be ordering around hundreds of men half his age and twice his size. And they call him "Sir." Power is exercised in the forms that have leverage in the modern world—money and position.

Generally speaking, in everyday life physical power no longer serves survival: the ability to run fast or far, to jump high, to throw javelins and hammers, to wrestle or box an adversary into submission, all of these have real value only in the symbolic world of sports. True, an awe and reverence for the man of strength lies hidden in the unconscious of most men. Boxing matches draw millions of spectators, and even the fake, gladiatorial combats of the wrestling world attract giant audiences. Big is still beautiful in the male world of ideals, if not in reality. Big muscles, physical strength, endurance, height—the tall man *is* somehow still seen as more of a man. Men who are inordinately small suffer severely into adult life, and the so-called "small-man syndrome" has a modicum of reliability within its generalizations. Except for certain sports like football and basketball, what is the advantage of a powerful, muscular frame and a height of 6 foot 6? Yet the vast majority of men would build a powerful musculature if it weren't so exhausting, tedious, and time-consuming.

The infatuation with size endures beyond rational explanation. At the end of World War II, with the Westernization of Japan, dramatic nutritional changes occurred in that country. To the delight of the Japanese, the introduction of a higher-protein, higher-fat diet resulted in a steady gradual increase in the average height of the population. To the world at large, this proved that nutritional deficiencies—probably the lack of essential amino acids—had limited Japanese growth to less than their genetic potential. The bias for size is such that it assumed the larger size was preferable. Yet, were there a bias for smallness, an entirely different approach could have been taken. One could have argued that the corrupting Western diet had caused abnormal growth, hypertension, arteriosclerotic heart disease, stroke, cancer of the breast, and cancer of the uterus. All of these diseases *were* markedly increased, along with height, in the Japanese population. All are products of a high-fat, high-protein diet.

During the 1970s the Hastings Center, an institute devoted to research in bioethics, began discussing the ethics of genetic engineering. With tongue in cheek I suggested that our first task might be to engineer a new population of *Homo sapiens* that would ideally be between 3 feet and 3 feet 6 in height. I argued that the smaller-size human being would diminish the resources of the globe at a 50 percent lower rate. Tiny people need smaller things, consume less raw materials. We could eat less food and therefore distribute it more equitably. Cars could be smaller, using less rubber, steel, etc. Automatically the parking spaces in New York would be doubled! We would contaminate our globe with throwaway products at half the current rate. We would be buying time to cure ecological disaster. We could even begin to breed down our pets, so that Great Danes became the size of miniature poodles.

In every way it seemed an admirable solution to all the pressing problems of the time. I loved the idea that roads would automatically be doubled in size, two-lane highways becoming four-lane and bridges monster superbridges. Nonetheless, my idea was rejected out of hand. I did not offer it as a serious blueprint; but, on the other hand, some of the blueprints that were taken seriously seemed counterproductive and positively dangerous. Even had I been serious, it would not have been an easy sell. The concept that big is beautiful is too ingrained in our unconscious. Instead of lowering the basket in basketball so that it becomes a game we can all realistically identify with, we "breed" seven-foot-tall basketball players to present us with a super-world young boys observe with awe and envy.

The primary vestigial remnant of brute force—beyond sports—resides in the universal attitude to the size of the penis. Penis size is a statement of a relative position in the male hierarchy, and the "big prick" suggests control and power—and beyond that, a meanness and dangerousness that is so often insinuated into the image of masculinity. It is the most persistent and dangerous vestige of the earlier equation of size with power. This idea is perhaps most dramatically defended in the somewhat paranoid writings of the French sociologist Emmanuel Reynaud:

> The principle is simple: as the penis is supposed to be a sort of biceps, the more it is used, the larger it will become: in the same way the bigger it is, the better it can subdue women, thus the more successful the man is likely to be. We have come full circle—a big penis guarantees success and success guarantees a big penis.[2]

Reynaud is speaking of power, even though he talks in terms of subduing women. The purpose is not sexual pleasure but domination:

> Man does not generally envisage relationships other than as power relations. He chases, approaches or seduces a woman to conquer her; the language he uses is revealing and sounds more like that of a sailor, hunter or warrior than of a lover. A woman is not a person to be discovered, but a body to

be undressed; he does not really "know" her until he has penetrated her vagina.[3]

In this world the woman is merely a trophy, a public statement of victory over some other man, since all of modern man's pursuits are in the service of establishing power:

Relations between men center around the struggle for power; whether individually or in a group, they are permanent rivals in the appropriation of women, wealth, and glory. Friendship, so often proclaimed as a typically masculine sentiment, is more a pact of non-aggression, a brief respite from the fight. . . .[4]

One doesn't have to buy the hyperbolic generalizations of Reynaud to recognize the presence, if not the preeminence, of the dynamics he is describing. In our culture the need to prove masculinity is narrowed into a few symbolic areas: money; sports; and particularly, and unfortunately, women.

One of the confusing aspects of penis size is the inconsistent role it plays in self-evaluation. Most people *overvalue* their own assets. Is there anyone who does not feel he is above average in his good taste or common sense? Who does not have a "superior" sense of humor? Self-evaluation will always be skewed, usually in the direction of one's own superiority. Penis size seems to be a startling exception.

When I first started practicing in New York, I became aware that the vast majority of my male patients assumed they had a penis smaller than average. At first, I thought it could be a statistical fluke. One of my friends jokingly suggested that maybe it was a comment on me— on the kind of men who present themselves to me for treatment.

Nonetheless, I puzzled over it, often coming up with some bizarre conclusions, like my "theory of parallax." The average heterosexual male doesn't have much opportunity to examine the phalluses of other men. When he observes the penis of another, it is with a surreptitious glance that must be fleeting and quick, lest the observation be seen as either an invitation, or worse, an assault. In New York, just looking directly at someone in the subway can be seen as invading his space. God knows what looking at his exposed genitals could mean. At any rate, from a distance one gets a direct view, whereas when one looks down at one's own penis, the foreshortening of perspective may make it look smaller—the parallax effect.

Well, such were the fanciful flights of young imagination. What I had actually stumbled upon was yet another manifestation of the essential insecurity of men in our culture: the difficulty anyone has in accepting himself as powerful, successful, or a man among men.

It has been repeatedly noted that mastery, power, and achievement dominate the world of men. What may have been neglected in all of this is the tendency of men to interpret failures in all these areas as an attack on manliness. In the unconscious of most men, everything is reduced to a symbolic ritual to prove one's manhood that must be repeated daily in multiple metaphoric struggles.

Being a "person" means being a man. And being a man is still measured by the traditional standards of power and courage. Impotence in any area of activity is visualized as a reflection on sexual potency, the foundation of manhood. Eventually, sexuality itself becomes desexualized, stripped of its pleasure functions, in the service of gender identity. Sex is too often perceived as a conquest and a victory. By perceiving sex as yet another index of status and power, we destroy the joyful and tender aspects of that most intimate and central of human experiences.

For the most part, phallic power and competition will not be exercised by dueling or physically struggling with another powerful man. Sure, we may do hand wrestling, and certainly sports have become an institutionalized means by which we can directly test our competitive powers. But even in sports we are likely to convert active into passive, direct into symbolic. We become spectators and affirm our own superiority by identification with our team. We have eschewed the field of physical competition for that of symbolic competition. But at the core of the male psyche, all power struggles are still visualized in terms of the physical. On those rare occasions when we are confronted physically, we can be reduced to irrationality, rage, and terror. The U.S. newspapers are filled with altercations over parking places and slights at bars which produce the murderous rage necessary actually to acquire a shotgun and kill another human being. Even those of us who do not kill *feel* like killing.

Most of us, still, will not get into physical encounters. We act out our power plays subtly in the course of our daily pursuits of money and status. True gladiatorial conflict is more likely to take place today in a private office or over the phone, where the opponent is not even present. Or we experience our victories in our fantasies. In fantasy, the thought may be expressed directly: there is no attempt at disguise, no imaginative dislocation or symbolic substitution. It is man the hero: the robot cop, Clint Eastwood, Rambo, John Wayne, the vigilante. All here is power, muscles and sinew, the big gun and the big prick.

Sometimes, to better conform to the facts of our lives, the hero will seem like us—mild, well mannered, civilized, bearing taunts and turning away. He is the strong, silent man who endures—as most of us must endure—until a line is crossed and then he demonstrates his terrifying power—as we hope we would if justified.

A handicapped man played by Spencer Tracy in *Bad Day at Black Rock* epitomizes this kind of ready identification. Older, crippled during World War II, he bears humiliation and taunts from the lesser villains who see his endurance and stoicism as weakness. The major villain, however, "knows" that only a strong man will endure so much; only a confident and brave man can afford to accept such provocation and not feel humiliated. The elephant does not trumpet at the stings of the gnat. Quietly, we wait for the line to be crossed when our hero—the heroic man with only one arm—will demolish his petty tormentors in hand-to-hand combat.

There are at least two other major areas of our everyday life where we see the direct linkage to the physical power of the warrior and hunter: in the predominantly male world of guns and automobiles. What is the fascination with weaponry? Well, obviously, the gun is the great equalizer. The small man with the gun is more powerful than the big man without. The gun is a vestigial link to the warrior. It is an instrument of combat. So, you might say, is money, but the financial victory is delayed, more subtle and circuitous. One does not usually have the dramatic and romantic gratification of instant subjugation of the enemy. The gun is there, in child play and in adult male fantasy, but also in adult male games.

What excuse is there for still permitting automatic weapons to exist in the hands of the general public? There is little justification even for simple hand guns. The patently hypocritical cant about sportsmanship is sheer nonsense. If every gun owner were required to spend an hour a day on the rifle range or even in the woods, we would not have to worry about gun control. We would have imposed our own form of it. The presence of the gun is in the service of fantasy. The fantasy that we might all become the avenging figure of *Death Wish* supports the American gun lobby.

There are hunters with genuine love of the country, of the simple life, the companionship and slow pace of the hunt. Yet, women love companionship and nature, and for the most part they do not hunt. The blood lust that underlies hunting and shooting can be seen in the corruption of private game preserves where animals are supported strictly for slaughtering; in shooting compounds on private lands that are stocked with pheasant and other game birds to be released by servants on command. The clay pigeon will not do. There is something about the actual bloodletting that appeals; everything else is secondary.

The fisherman is generally different. He, too, finds a primitive identification with an earlier self. He is testing himself against nature, and often to the limits, using lighter and lighter lines, slimmer and slimmer rods to give every advantage to the game fish. He delights in the catch—which is often released. In hunting and shooting, there is no way to release the dead creature. And if there were, would the hunter do it? A decent percentage I know would not, even though the game is usually left to rot in the fields. The hunt maintains our links with an earlier past, but also reflects the failings of our current culture. There is little communion with nature and less nobility than when men hunted with primitive weapons in a true wilderness.

What about automobiles? What is there about the automobile that makes it the ultimate phallic symbol of our male culture? First of all, it is a machine. It used to be called that, and a machine by definition is a device to apply force and power efficiently—to enhance human musculature through human ingenuity. When man was incapable of lifting a giant boulder he invented the lever, automatically increasing the efficiency of his own muscle mass. He invented the hoist and pulley to raise giant timbers. He invented gears and wheels. And he put those gears and wheels together to provide him with the ultimate machine of our culture—the automobile. In this one symbol we have combined power, status, speed, armor, and sex. I do not think it is too far-fetched to suggest that this, too, is yet another phallic metaphor—a represen- tation of the "complicated machinery" of the male genitals, which, enlarged and expanded, is viewed as an instrument for overcoming women and outdoing other men.

The car became not only a sexual symbol but a sexual vehicle. It gave one status with the girls. But more important—in the crowded world of the middle class, in the prudish world before the sexual revolution—the car was a private place, a locus for sexual activity, even if sexual activities were only "making out," or more accurately, to use the antiquated terms of those innocent days, "necking" and "petting." In the days when sexuality was covert, families intact, and supervision de rigueur, the car was the only place one could make out in relative privacy.

Most of us could not afford cars. It didn't matter. One relatively affluent person would have the $50 or $75 for a junker, fix it up, and in triple dates (four in the back, two in the front) would go out, enjoying the innocent sexuality that served passion in those days.

Now, however, the car has become primarily a phallic symbol. The fast car, drag racing, the games of "chicken," enable the car—with all its latent power—to be converted into an alternative for the actual wrestling matches of non-technological cultures.[5]

The car games of the adolescent are immediately recognizable as extensions of the pissing contest of the six-year-old, but with more power, because they involve real risk. Speeding cars in a drag race can get out of control. They introduce a note of derring-do, courage, and potential danger reminiscent of knights' tournaments in the Age of Chivalry.

Here, too, there is generally an audience. It is a public event. There is a victor and the vanquished. There is a sense of empowerment or impotence. The game changes subtly and dangerously when it is made into a game of "chicken." Here, two young maniacs in speeding cars approach each other from opposite directions, waiting to see who will turn aside first. Victor and vanquished are instantly recognized—the one acknowledged as leader, the other forced to admit his inferior strength. He is not just beaten, he is revealed and exposed.

The adult male buys cars that are capable of speeds of 150 miles an hour, in a country where anything over 55 miles per hour is generally illegal and in cities where anything over 25 miles an hour is impossible. These sports cars are revved up on the moving parking lots known as the Long Island Expressway and the Los Angeles Freeways, rarely getting up to 30 miles per hour and never going at their maximum speed.

How is one to explain the adult infatuation with the "sports" car, whether it is the blue-collar version, the Pontiac TransAm; the bourgeois Corvette; or the affluent Lamborghini and Maserati? The cars are not more comfortable or more serviceable. In the Lamborghini class, a man is lucky to find a windshield wiper that works or a defroster that clears the windows. Surely no one needs the much-vaunted acceleration from zero to 60 that these cars provide. Where in God's name can one practice such acceleration except all by oneself on a distant stretch of road? And where's the fun in that? The purpose after all is to leave the other guy standing at the light.

There is no real need for the creation of such powerful automobiles except for the psychological purpose they serve. Sitting behind the wheel of these extravagant cars helps disguise our own sense of inadequacy. The behavior of a man enclosed within this protective structure changes dramatically. Overt epithets and rude gestures are passed back and forth with an impunity that could not be risked in the bodily proximity of a subway train or a movie line. Cars can be vehicles for intimidating or even killing, which embody not just the power for hurting but the power of escape.

A car is a distancing machine that protects a man from retaliation. It is visualized almost the same way the tank is in war. Protected by steel armor, capable of flight if things turn against him, the average man can be reduced to a competitive, aggressive idiot. Life-threatening behavior is a commonplace event on our highways. If someone cuts you off, endangering your life while traveling at 60 miles an hour, the logical action would be to keep your distance from him. But a man rarely responds that way. He interprets this aggression as humiliation, as a personal assault, and further, as a challenge to manhood that must be met. If his life was endangered, he will get even by racing ahead and cutting the other fellow off, thus endangering his life a second time.

Such behavior has not been empirically studied, but I think evidence would suggest that men are worse than women in this area. Women seem to prefer another kind of aggressive behavior in automobiles. I have observed that women more often than men will hug the passing lane and refuse to move for a flashing light or a tap on the horn. At first I assumed that this behavior was induced by anxiety about being in the middle lanes of a fast-moving highway, where cars might pass on both sides. Recently I have been questioning men and women about driving attitudes, and now I am not quite so sure. A number of women, independently of one another, have offered the same explanation. Yes, they said, they hug the passing lane because they feel more comfortable in it; but they also refused to budge on hearing the horn because "I was traveling at the legal speed limit. No one has to go any faster than that. If they want to break the law, let them just go around me." No man I queried offered this explanation. There is something self-righteous about this behavior; but in addition it is characteristically passive aggressive rather than directly aggressive.

The loving attention a man pays to his car is akin to that a Marine expends on his rifle—or that the narcissist spends in building his own beautiful body. In an earlier day, psychoanalysts would glibly describe the man rubbing, polishing, and sweating over a wax job on his new car as a "masturbatory equivalent," and while we are reluctant these days to make such glib and direct analogies, there was a seminal truth to these global interpretations. It is the self that is being massaged, built up. It is the artificial extension of the self that sticks out, is noticed and admired. Truly, in the words of the younger generation of today, "awesome." The expensive car bespeaks a man of means; it is a form of male jewelry. Surely then the automobile is the phallic symbol supreme—a metaphor firmly identified in our culture with masculine power.

Everything can be corrupted and transmuted into a measure of manhood, a symbol of power. One would hope at least that sexuality itself would be spared, that here manhood would be fused not with power but with affection and love. But even this primary function may be corrupted by concerns of power. Sexual pleasure itself is often sacrificed to a man's need to reassure himself about his position and potency.

The discussion of sexuality will be elaborated in a later chapter. At this point I merely want to indicate that the concept of penis-as-weapon will intrude into the most primary functions for which the phallus was intended: love and procreation. The power struggle exercised by men in a world of men will also play out in men's relations with women.

Power inevitably means different things to men and women; power plays different roles in their lives. To the man, power defines his self. Ego strength is built on a sense of physical strength. The penis is the symbol—the scepter—of male power and authority. The phallus is the performing instrument. But in procreation, it is a secondary instrument, being only the conduit for delivery of the semen. A man without a penis can father children; a man without testes cannot. The fundamental male sexual organs are the testes. These have been endowed with their own mystique. They are the symbols of that primary male virtue—courage.

To be a man as distinct from a boy one needs the instrument of the man, the big stick. But to be a man among men, to "deliver the goods," to father children, one has to have balls. In the Spanish culture, with its emphasis on machismo, the focus of masculinity is on the testicles. Big balls rather than a big penis are more likely to be cited as a sign of manhood by an Hispanic. Power alone is not enough; courage too is needed. Power may be an accident of nature. Courage is an act of will, a true measure of man.

6 ▸ COURAGE AND COJONES

Power and strength are universally coveted by all men. But these attributes are not necessarily respected. They are just as likely to produce fear as admiration, perhaps because such might is too close to the animal, or to the machine.

Mythic figures of power often were depicted as foolish. There is a buffoonish quality about Samson, who allows himself to be deluded by Delilah and is forced into humiliating servitude. Only after a protracted period of impotence and weakness does Samson learn to respect his own power, to honor it; and then we respect him. Hercules, while certainly a heroic figure, was not by accident pictured as a clod by Robert Graves.[1] His brute force seemed uncontrollable and irrational. He was devoid of both the bodily form and the ideals of manly behavior revered by the Greeks. Power alone is not enough. Power can be ugly. A bully is not revered nor a psychopath admired. To be seen as a virtue, physical power must be in the service of a larger image of masculinity.

Courage is the one incontrovertible virtue associated with masculinity. In the history of Western culture and from the data evident in current tribal cultures, courage has always been the substance of masculinity. The Stoics had only four cardinal virtues: practical wisdom, justice, courage, and self-control. No one of these was possible without the other. Plato enunciated these identical virtues, substituting only temperance for self-control. Balance and self-control were introduced to help draw a distinction between the rash and reckless fool and the true hero. One must control both the impulse to carry out a meaningless and foolhardy action and the impulse to run from the dangerous and threatening. Aristotle, therefore, more carefully defined courage for us as the means between an excess, which is foolhardiness, and a deficiency, which is cowardice.

While in modern times we recognize all forms of courage (we think of moral courage—the courage to face adversity or illness, the courage to do an unpopular action), the image of courage that comes down from Greek culture and is central to the male ego is almost always physical courage. To this day, it is visualized this way in the male unconscious. Even though tests of physical courage rarely are required in adult life, to be a man one must feel he has the mettle, the stuff to face physical danger with resolution. Courage is synonymous with bravery and valor. In the measure of manhood, courage will be the yardstick.

Courage is often in opposition to power. It is not courageous for the powerful to attack the weak. Courage demands the ability and willingness to put oneself at risk. Obviously, then, courage demands an understanding of risk and a capacity for choice.

Courage cannot, therefore, be the absence of fear. Without fear, it is hard to visualize a courageous act, as it is difficult to praise virtue if there is no temptation. If an action comes easily, or is an automatic and reflexive response of an organism, we may view it as "courageous" (or "altruistic"), but it is difficult to view it as virtuous. We do not ascribe morality to animals, which are instinctively patterned to do only "good." It is the human animal who is the moral creature because we have choice. We have the freedom to do either good or bad. Beyond that, only we have the knowledge of good and bad—which is what the ancient Jews unquestionably meant when they said we not only are made in the image of God but we have the knowledge of God. We also have the knowledge of our own vulnerability and our own mortality. We know what death is, and we assume that it is once and for all. If we value the sweetness of life, we must inevitably feel fear when it is placed in jeopardy. How we behave in such situations will tell us a great deal about our own moral character.

All creatures with sentience, and even some without, respond to danger with the fight or flight mechanism. They either destroy the danger or run from it. Only human beings have other alternatives; only human beings may consciously and willingly embrace the danger for "higher values" than survival.

The human being, therefore, is constantly redesigning himself in a way that no other animal does. If courage is an ideal of manhood, it is not one that comes easily. If it is prized, then it must be defined, nurtured, and reinforced.

In a section of *Mankind in the Making* entitled "Men Are Made, Not Born," David Gilmore summarizes various masculinity rituals that are strikingly similar. Widely diverse societies show an awareness of the need to instruct and condition boys to conform to a universal ideal of manhood—which always includes courage.

Gilmore concludes that "maleness in New Guinea is a complicated venture, a long, restless journey that not all men can complete." He sees adult masculinity as

an artificially induced status . . . achievable only through testing and careful instruction. Real men do not simply emerge naturally over time like butterflies from boyish cocoons; they must be assiduously coaxed from their juvenescent shells, shaped and nurtured, counseled and prodded into manhood. . . . Unlike femininity, which comes naturally through biological maturation, the fulfillment of masculinity does not "occur naturally" among the Awa. . . . In general, throughout the Highlands, men are thought to be incapable of living up to masculine-role expectations without the intervention of cultural artifices. Male gender is "created" rather than "natural." . . .

Roger Keesing summarizes: "Growth and strength, bravery and manliness are achieved through sequences of isolation and ordeal, instruction and revelation." In New Guinea, "A boy is made into a man."[2]

This was precisely what Gilbert Herdt had said in *Rituals of Manhood*. These rituals of manhood involve exposure to danger and pain of the most awful sort. Boys must not only accept the infliction of pain but must do so stoically. Since courage is seen as a manly trait, the pain is traditionally inflicted on the central identifying organ of the gender, the phallus. Circumcision rites exist across cultures. Gilmore tells us that

The first test for the boys entering manhood is the traumatic circumcision procedure, a trial of bravery and stoicism. The operation is intensely painful, and no anesthetics are used; nor is anything done to lessen the anticipatory terror of the initiate, suggesting that the purpose is specifically one of testing. Each youth, placed on view before his male relatives and perspective in-laws, must remain motionless and silent during the cutting, which may last four minutes or more. Even an involuntary twitch would be interpreted as a sign of fear . . . if the boy makes the slightest movement or sound, there is a collective gasp of shock and dismay; he is forever shamed as a coward and will be excluded from joining his age-set in his march towards adult status. . . . Besides being cruelly ostracized himself he brings ruin upon his entire lineage forever. In the Samburu proverb, all of his people must publicly "eat their respect" because one of their boys has run.[3]

Several distinct and important purposes are served by the rituals of scarification, whipping, and torturing. They are not arbitrary. These are life-training initiations. They expose a young boy to the kind of pain he may have to endure in the hunt. The pain of brambles, of lacerations and wounds, the deprivation of food. Stoicism is part of the hunter's life. They remind the boy of similar, if mitigated, anxieties and pains he must endure to fulfill his role as a man. He must be courageous and brave; must place the hunt—on which the food of his wife, children, and tribe will depend—above his natural fears.

The rituals are explicit. The price to be paid is clear. It is a test that once passed allows for ready acceptance into the club. The youth may rest his mind in peace; he is indeed a man. He will be treated so by his colleagues in the village and also by the women, who now see him as a man, with all of the sexual privileges that the tribe reserves for manhood.

With the industrialization and urbanization of our society, physical power and actual physical courage became less a part of the survival needs of our culture. We did not have to plow fields with the sinews and muscles of our own bodies. We did not have to cross wild frontiers, risking death, in pursuit of free land. We did not have to enter the wilderness, hunt for food to stave off starvation during periods of crop failure. Granted, there are jobs where one knowingly puts one's life at risk. For the most part those are "glory" jobs: test pilots, policemen, firemen, the jobs children aspire to. These professions compose that small segment of the population who are still permitted to enter the ranks of the heroic.

In our society, there is little opportunity to demonstrate courage on the physical level, but when such events do occur, the public at large responds with awe and admiration. Despite this, men perceive themselves as constantly facing symbolic tests of courage. Most of these symbolic conflicts will demand courage in the moral or sociological sense: can I face down my boss; can I defy accepted wisdom and take an unpopular but correct stance on a public issue? The effect of the decision will, however, be perceived as reflecting on the man's *physical* courage. Either I still have it, or I don't. "It" being guts, fortitude, balls.

During that transition period when the industrial cities co-existed with the rural landscape, boys were still taught to be brave and courageous, to face the wilderness in pursuit of those virtues that would serve the community.

Since one does not normally have to risk one's physical self in order to survive in our culture, the training for such courage disappears. Yet, some vestigial awe of physical prowess and physical courage persists. Never mind that it has no utility. We value many things that serve no utility beyond an ideal or principle. Forget that occasions to prove physical courage are rare to nonexistent. Each individual man, within himself, inevitably anticipates the ultimate test of manhood as arising either in the bedroom or on some field of battle.

Since physical courage is an essential part of a man's masculine identity, he will often seek out, even invent, tests of courage. Most of these tests are ad hoc and uninstitutionalized, but some are formal, with specific rules of the game that define success. A prime example is the field of sports; but before even such organized and disciplined activities, there are the unofficial games of childhood. The "I dare you" and the "I bet you can't" games of the prepubescent are a testing and baiting ritual that will lead these boys—it is almost always boys—to significantly more dangerous activities in adolescence: climbing a tree or clinging to the back of a moving bus, jumping from one roof top to another, or the current deadly games that involve riding on the tops of moving elevators. These games of chicken and derring-do, which seem idiotic to an adult, must be fulfilling some primary needs of the emerging male.

War, of course, is not a game, but it can be viewed again as an extreme event that brings us back to an earlier time when fear had to be conquered and the self sacrificed to a group; where rights gave way to duty and obligation. In conditions of war we return to a more primitive lifestyle, where combat is physical and the stakes are survival, not just status. It may be, as some feminists have said, that men love war, and that war is an institution that is encouraged to permit a return to the fundamental manhood game. Perhaps. Yet some of us believe there are just and necessary wars.

All wars are popular in their opening phases. They create a sense of purpose in a society that often seems purposeless and a sense of community in a culture that has progressively eroded the nature of community. During the Gulf War, the sense of elation was palpable. Admittedly it was a peculiar war, since it had a beginning and an end and no middle. It is the middle that usually erodes our euphoria about war.

The Gulf War was a tonic, an antidote. Americans were washed clean of their frustrations. It was a phallic thrill for both men and women; a giant surge of power to replace a limp and flaccid self-respect that was the residue of the Vietnam War and the hostage crises. In addition, the war molded Americans into a community, and the hunger for community is great in America in these closing days of the twentieth century. It returned us to heroism and ritual on the most primitive level of life-and-death combat. The pride of courage could be at least vicariously experienced by those of us who sat comfortably huddled around our television sets. We could watch men and women of valor, courage, and honor.

Wars are an ideal locale for literary analysis of fear and cowardice. Stephen Crane's *The Red Badge of Courage* is subtitled: "An Episode of the American Civil War." This book, tracing a boy's passage into manhood, is a study of the nature of courage. When "the youth," as he is described throughout the book, first hears that he is to enter battle, it is with a sense of excitement and romance. "He had, of course, dreamed of battles all his life—of vague and bloody conflicts that had thrilled him with their sweep and fire. In visions he had seen himself in many struggles."[4] (p. 7)

He didn't much trust that the war at home would live up to his expectation. It had to be a "play affair." He longed for the sort of battles the ancient Greeks had fought, which he had read about. Men were better then, less timid.

His mother was less sanguine about the war than her son. She knew his limitations, and she wanted him home and alive. He in turn was disappointed by her unromantic attitude to his enlistment. He had wanted her to say something to him about "returning with his shield or on it" (p. 8), the traditional admonishment of the Spartan mother to her son leaving for war.

When reality is part of a barely visible future, we all can anticipate fantasies of courage and valor. Like a typical adolescent, the boy has no sense of his own mortality. He assumes he will live forever. When he visualizes his body returning inert on a shield, that is not the essential self. "He" will still be there—somewhere—enjoying the encomia and wallowing in the tears of love shed for him. He will actually, like Tom Sawyer, enjoy attending his own funeral.

Shortly after, everything changes. As battle approaches, the youth feels his first anxiety. Then he becomes terrified, not of the impending battle, for he has no real knowledge of what a battle will be, but of his anxiety and unpredictable performance. "He felt that in this crisis his laws of life were useless. Whatever he had learned of himself was here of no avail. He was an unknown quantity. He saw that he would again be obliged to experiment as he had in early youth . . . he resolved to remain close upon his guard lest those qualities of which he knew nothing should everlastingly disgrace him." (p. 11) This is the same performance anxiety experienced constantly by men today.

The youth has difficulty controlling his anxiety and turns to other soldiers, older, more experienced, often taunting them. He is not a very attractive person, this young Henry. Full of himself, callow and insensitive, he is contrasted with other men, barely a few years older, who have an essential dignity that emerges out of their early testing period. He begins to panic.

The youth perceived that the time had come. He was about to be measured. For a moment he felt in the face of his great trial like a babe, and the flesh over his heart seemed very thin. He seeks time to look about him calculatingly.

But he instantly saw that it would be impossible for him to escape from the regiment. It inclosed him. And there were iron laws of tradition and law on four sides. He was in a moving box. (p. 21)

Now we are in the world of the adolescent. What drives him is social approval. He is less interested in virtue than in possible shame, humiliation, and disgrace. He must look good in the eyes of the peers who surround him and will judge him. He *is* in a moving box, as are all teenagers. As are all men in our society.

Crane picks as his hero a boy purposely defined as more cowardly than others, whining and complaining, in order to explicate the nature of courage. The youth *is* a coward. He begins to feel that he has not enlisted "of his free will." He had been "dragged by the merciless government," and now look what is happening. They are "taking him out to be slaughtered."

Yet, in the first flush of battle, he finds an automatic behavior emerging that has been experienced by almost every soldier in combat, the special courage that comes of being part of a group:

He suddenly lost concern for himself, and forgot to look at a menacing fate. He became not a man but a member. He felt that something of which he was a part—a regiment, an army, a cause, or a country—was in a crisis. He was welded into a common personality which was dominated by a single desire. For moments he could not flee no more than a little finger can commit a revolution from a hand. (p. 30)

Crane quickly defines that essential ingredient, identification with the group—so lacking in our time—which permits one to draw on a sense of reserve strength that exists unawares in a communitarian individual. The power of the group to sway behavior is enormous. It usurps the sense of autonomy of self. Whether the group is an army of liberation or a lynch mob, we are capable of submerging our "self" into a group identity.

Later the boy begins to feel frightened, and does what we all do when, humiliated by our fear, we begin to lose self-respect. He converts fear into rage:

> Following this came a red rage. He developed the acute exasperation of a pestered animal, a well-meaning cow worried by dogs. He had a mad feeling against his rifle, which could only be used against one life at a time. He wished to rush forward and strangle with his fingers. He craved a power that would enable him to make a world-sweeping gesture and brush all back. His impotency appeared to him, and made his rage into that of a driven beast. (p. 31)

The youth comes through his first battle feeling like a hero and prematurely embracing his proven heroism. His short-lived glory and self-satisfaction are shattered, however, when he finds that this is but the first skirmish, that there will be yet another and another. When the battle renews, he runs, giving way to panic. His response is pure rationalization and projection, the stuff of a typical psychoanalytic hour. The youth convinces himself that all is lost anyhow and only a fool would stay. He deserts his company and flees, protected by the knowledge that they will all soon be dead and he has made the only wise decision.

Then to his consternation he finds that the line has held. Now his worst fears will be realized: he will be exposed for the coward he is. Overwhelmed by self-pity and the dread of exposure, he wanders in his own wilderness, beyond the lines. Now he watches the wounded soldiers with envy. "He conceived persons with torn bodies to be peculiarly happy. He wished that he, too, had a wound, a red badge of courage." (p. 46).

The bulk of this book is preoccupied with the humiliation of this adolescent boy. He is terrified that at any moment he will be exposed as the non-man he feels himself to be. The youth shares with every human being the feeling that somehow or other our unconscious thoughts and feelings must be apparent and visible, that there is no hiding within the self. A psychoanalyst is constantly reminding his patients, often to little avail, that no one can read their thoughts, that an individual is responsible for his conduct, not his wishes and feelings. Yet a patient inevitably reacts as though the internal self is somehow publicly exposed. And to a certain extent the patient is right. Our self-image will inevitably inform the perception of us held by others.

Toward the end of Crane's novel, to Henry's surprise as well as that of the reader, he does become a heroic figure.

> He had fought like a pagan to defend his religion. . . . By this struggle he had overcome obstacles which he had admitted to be mountains. They had fallen like paper peaks and he was now what he called a hero. And he had not been aware of the process. He had slept and, awakening, found himself a knight. (p. 90)

Henry, almost despite himself, is finally on his way to becoming a man, having experienced "a temporary but sublime absence of selfishness." (p. 96)

> He felt a quiet manhood, nonassertive but of sturdy and strong blood. He knew that he would no more quail before his guides wherever they should point. He had been to touch the great death, and found that, after all, it was but the great death. He was a man. (p. 121)

War is a terrible way to have to prove one's manhood, and most of us are spared that true trial by battle. Further, Henry is a man of a different time from our own. Identification with the group, social responsibility, and fear of shame and humiliation are the ultimate forces that drive Henry to overcome his natural fear. Courage, then, is seen by Crane in a psychological sense as the subjugation of one fear—the fear of death—by what is perceived as a greater fear, the fear of social humiliation in a time and period when social acceptance is all. We do not live in such an age. Crane's novel and Faulkner's short story are separated in time by fifty years, yet they seem of a time and a place in terms of values. And both seem alien to the present.

Norman Mailer is a man of our time. In what I have to assume is a direct reference to Faulkner, Mailer in his novel *Why Are We in Vietnam?* returns to the ritual of the hunt in order, I suspect, to show how far we have deteriorated from Faulkner's time. Here the adolescent hero D.J. and his boyhood friend Tex have completed the formal aspects of their rites of passage, but with entirely different consequences, emphasizing the degradation of our values and our civilization during the Vietnam period.

D.J. bags his bear, only to have his arrogant, macho, and ultimately cowardly father take credit for the kill. He is disgusted, humiliated, and sets out with his friend to cleanse his system of a sick despair:

> Tex feels like he's never going to hunt again which is not unhorrendous for him since he's a natural hunter, but then with one lightning leap from the button on his genius belt to the base of his brain-pan he gets the purification ceremony straight in his head, and announces to D.J. that they gonna wrap their weapons and lash them in a tree, and then they going to walk through the forest and up to the peak with their Randall bowies, and their binocs, and packs, but nothing to protect themselves with except the knife. They each know even as he says it that this is how you get the fear, shit, disgust and mixed shit tapeworm out of fucked-up guts and overcharged nerves. . . .
>
> About the time they cache all belongings, they own clean fear now, cause they going to live off the land. And they as light as if they lost gravity. D.J. could take a ten-foot spring. If it wasn't cold ass this morning, he'd be ready to go naked. Oh, that country looks big and mean ahead.[5]

Here the ritual is the same: Abandon the accoutrements of culture and technology and cleanse your soul. Not this time to join with the community of men, as in Faulkner, but to separate yourself from the community of corrupt men. To find affirmation not in manhood but in the defiance of youth.

Mailer represents the ultimate expression of the libertarian times in which we live. Society, culture, human beings are all contaminants. There exists only the macho individual as exemplified by Hemingway and Mailer, his self-appointed heir.

This is the moral universe of the late twentieth century in America. One does one's own thing, lets it all hang out, preserves one's own life. All morality is cast in terms of the individual, self-preservation and self-expression. We make myths out of the isolated mountainman, the vigilante, the loner.

Short of wars, what can men do to display their courage? They can invent games to play with one another, as boys do before puberty and into adolescence. Occasionally, mature men resort to such games, but the results may be disastrous, for with men the stakes are higher. There is no tomorrow, and the judgments could turn out to be humiliating, even unbearable. James Dickey in his novel *Deliverance* has his hero, Ed, set out on such a "game."

Ed is impressed by his friend, Lewis, a hard-as-a-rock, back-to-nature fitness freak, whom he observes with part incredulity and part awe. Lewis pressures Ed and two other friends to join him on a river trip in the wilderness of Georgia to fight the white water and commune with nature. Lewis is a romantic and a borderline fanatic, whose purposes go beyond fun and games.

"I just believe," he said, "that the whole thing is going to be reduced to the human body, once and for all. I want to be ready."

"What *whole thing?*"

"The human race thing. I think the machines are going to fail, the political systems are going to fail, and a few men are going to take to the hills and start over."

I looked at him, he lived in the suburbs, like the rest of us. He had money, a good-looking wife and three children. I could not really believe that he came in from placating his tenants every evening and gave himself solemnly to the business of survival, in so far as it involved his body. What kind of fantasy led to this? [6] (pp. 40–41)

Ed finds out sooner rather than later when he himself becomes victim of the same romantic fantasy.

Why in God's earth am I here? I thought. But when I turned back to the car to see what Lewis was doing I caught a glimpse of myself in the rear window. I was light green. A tall forest man, an explorer, a gorilla hunter. I liked the idea and the image, I must say. Even if this was just a game, a charade, I had let myself in for it, and I was here in the woods where such people as I had got myself up as were supposed to be. Something or other was being made good. I touched the knife held at my side, and remembered that all men were once boys, and that boys are always looking for ways to become men. Some of the ways are easy, too; all you have to do is be satisfied that it has happened. (p. 62)

As the story develops, Ed will face sheer terror and the need to kill or be killed. Throughout this novel, Dickey uses the knife and the bow and arrow, penetrating instruments of death, as the phallic symbols of male power.

When Ed, the civilized urban male, is about to kill another man, this is how he responds:

Everything was right; it could not have been better. My anchor was good and firm, and the broad head seemed almost rock steady. I was full of the transfiguring power of full draw, the draw hysteria that is the ruination of some archers and the making of others, who can conquer and make it work for them. (p. 163)

Given the absence of any physical tests, doubt about our courage will persist. It is a doubt that brooks no trivialization. Women who teasingly make fun of a man's need to assert physical courage usually find that this is the point at which a masculine sense of humor seems to depart. To question a man's courage is to question his balls, his very identity as a man.

Kriegel, in his book *On Men and Manhood,* expressed it well:

> For we have discovered that the real issues facing men today are not really sexual at all. The real issues still have to do with courage, with the willingness to risk one's substance as a man, with the ability to capture that self one claims. . . . In our time, even parody in the service of manhood seems braver than what we possess.[7]

What men actually experience today is less a need to demonstrate courage than a fear of showing cowardice. This omnipresent fear of cowardice is a rare phenomenon among women. Women do not feel they have to be brave or courageous. This does not mean that they lack courage or bravery, nor that they lack respect for these virtues. They simply do not measure themselves exclusively by this standard. As a result, they do not fear the exposure or failure.

One can speculate about the essential differences between men and women. We know that aggression in almost all animals is strongly influenced by the presence of male hormones. On a physical level, women are less aggressive than men. This does not mean women are less assertive than men, nor does it deny the presence of aggressive women. Aggression, violence, and power do not and could not serve survival for a woman. The essential difference in body size and strength puts women at risk in a contest with men. A genetic endowment for direct confrontation and attack would be maladaptive—suicidal—in a physically smaller creature destined to lose in direct combat. If she is to survive, surely a better adaptive mode would be necessary. Intelligence, rationality, accommodation, wiliness, ingratiation are all more suitable for the smaller of the species than the larger.

A second reason why women may not have the fear of cowardice is that in the traditional woman's life she will inevitably experience pain.

In the Book of Genesis, it is "the judgment of God" that the price women would pay for choosing freedom, autonomy, and knowledge over dependency is that God will "greatly multiply thy sorrow and thy conception; in sorrow thou shalt bring forth children. . . ." (3:16)

Women traditionally anticipate pain. In giving birth, they have a biological rite of passage that demands courage and the embracing of pain for a nobler purpose. Until such time as we pass into a culture of artificial deliveries, women will still expect to endure this painful trial. This, combined with the fact that courage is not a hallmark of their essential self, frees them from the fear of cowardice; allows them to admit vulnerability; and allows them, I would guess, a greater compassion for the vulnerability of others.

This compassion for the vulnerability of others can cause great difficulty in their dealing with men. A woman may assume that a man will be comforted by having the person who loves him recognize his vulnerability. She can then indicate that, coward or no, her love for him endures; physical courage is not important to her. Nothing could be more disastrous. Men generally do not respond well to conversations whose substance is: "Don't feel you have to pose. I know you're afraid and it's all right with me. I understand." It is *they*, the men, who will not understand. And to protect their pride they must deny their fear. Since the inevitable result of fear denied is rage, it will often be the woman who is assaulted.

A typical example was described to me in the course of therapy by a young man in his early thirties. Out on a date, standing in line with his girlfriend at one of the large movie theaters in downtown Manhattan, he was waiting patiently, chatting with the people around him. The line extended around the block. Three tough-looking, aggressive late teenagers, viewing the long line, walked up to the front and said to the young man, "Why are you standing in our place? Move your ass." His temper began to rise; his girlfriend, frightened, said, "Let them in." He hesitated for a moment, but recognizing that a few more people in front of him would hardly make a difference, he prudently controlled the animal instinct that was both inappropriate and dangerous. His girlfriend pulled him around so his back was to the teenagers and engaged him in conversation. The teenagers, however, seeing a sport that might be more fun than the movie, began to taunt him.

In the traditional sociology of the New York crowd, people backed off and turned away, leaving a small area of apathy between them and the encounter. In fact, the encounter never took place. This was not the movies, only a line for the movies. In the cinema itself, Charles Bronson would pull out a giant gun and blast holes in the intruders, instantly becoming a folk hero. A series of movies—*Deathwish I, II,* etc.—based on the unconscious fantasies of intimidated males in the inner cities have become runaway hits.

But our man left the movie line and dropped his girlfriend off at her apartment. And the humiliation of this frustrated man then turned to anger, which was deflected from the self and directed to his girlfriend. Where else could he safely express his horrible humiliation? He had been confronted as a man; his "woman" had been insulted; he had failed as a protector; he had run from the scene of battle. All rational, intelligent, sane ways to stay alive in the inner city.

In analysis, the rationality of his behavior was no comfort. His only actual mistake had been to go to a major downtown movie house. He should have stayed on the Upper East Side or in suburban areas where encounters that inevitably become losing encounters are minimal. Nonetheless, he felt humiliated, exposed, and impotent. He knew that if he had spent the night with his girlfriend, he could not have made love. Sexuality was the last thing on his mind, at least tenderness and heterosexuality. His dream that night was a thinly veiled symbol of homosexual rape.

Rage and fear are "emergency emotions" established biologically, in those barbaric eons before civilization, to protect us from danger when the meaning and nature of "danger" was unequivocal. A threat to our survival was present. The danger was real and physical—a beast, an enemy horde, a rebellious kinsman.

In modern life, danger arrives obliquely. Since it is defined in terms of the balance of power between us and the threat, anything that diminishes us enhances the danger. No new element of danger need be introduced into a man's life to make him less secure. Simply raise doubts about his strength, reliability, or stature, diminish his self-respect or self-confidence, and the identical environment will seem more hazardous. It is the assault on self-esteem and self-confidence that particularly enhances our sense of vulnerability and impotence.

Men are most likely to feel threatened when they sense disapproval, deprivation, exploitation or manipulation, frustration, betrayal, or humiliation. These are the lions and tigers that stalk our civilized environment, and men have sharpened their senses so that they detect their signs everywhere.

Fear and anger were intended to serve as responses to threats to our survival. To our *survival*—not to our pride, status, position, manhood, or dignity. Yet somehow men have established a crucial linkage between affronts to their status and their very sense of survival. Men respond to an affront with biological defenses appropriate for physical assaults. Manliness, designed to facilitate the survival of our species, has run amok in a culture that seems to have changed the rules about survival. Today, physical courage is life-threatening rather than life-saving, but it is still a pillar that supports masculine pride and self-respect. There is now a potentially explosive dissonance between nature and culture. We have to redefine manhood to accommodate this anachronistic aspect of male identity. Perhaps we can redefine courage in new terms, but I am not sanguine. Physical courage is deeply rooted in the constitution of manhood—supported by both physiology and genes.

Man the protector is out of synch with his culture. How well does biology continue to serve us in that other crucial area, man the procreator? We naturally assume that in an area as central to survival as sex, a consonance between biological and social man must continue. The facts are somewhat less reassuring.

7 ▸ MALE SEXUALITY: NO PRIVATE PARTS

All sorts of strange creatures large and small, animal and vegetable, reproduce "sexually." Sex does not necessarily mean inserting a penis into a vagina. It simply means that an "offspring," which could be a tree as well as the monkey who occupies it, is a product of two different parents—male and female—each of which contributes half the genetic endowment of the new creature. This ensures that for the most part no two offspring of the same parents will be identical, identical twins being the prototypic exception.

We all recognize the fact that male and female plants may be widely separated and dependent on amiable others—the birds and the bees— to consummate the sexual act. But this is true in animals, too. In many marine animals, the male and female have no physical access to each other during sex except in their mutual presence at the breeding site. The eggs are laid, the female departs, the male appears and sprays the sperm over the eggs. Not romantic, but very efficient.

This simplified introduction to sexual reproduction is intended to dispel the anthropocentric view that "sex is sex" and that man is at his most animal in his sexuality: the stuff that binds us to the tigers and the elephants. While most of us are unprepared to see the apple tree as a participant in any sexual activity, what the dog does in the street seems very similar to what we do in the privacy of our homes; we will equate these two activities. This is a dangerous and false projection. There is a world of difference between these two forms of copulation.

For one thing, we do not do it in the streets. There are few cultures that will tolerate that. The unique role of privacy in human sexuality is a part of the *biology* of human sexuality, which distinguishes the sexual behavior of human beings from even their closest primate relatives. Many have been bewildered by this. What kind of adaptation is this for human beings? Here is an animal, *Homo sapiens,* which is as dependent on copulation for its survival as the pigeon or the rat, yet it approaches sexuality with modesty and shame, even guilt and trepidation. This seems perverse, downright non-functional. Why should not human sex be as unencumbered by psychological trappings as it seems to be in most other animals? For that matter, why should sex be so different from the other drives that sustain life—thirst and hunger?

This was the paradox, the contradiction, that Freud confronted. Freud was fully aware that human sexuality differed significantly from animal sexuality. He was particularly interested in the role of sexual guilt and shame, and developed two separate theories of their origin, one drawn from his clinical observations of human development and the other from anthropological and sociological speculation.

In his "libido theory," Freud postulated that normal human development was genetically fixed and biologically driven. The primary energy, the force that drives all human activity, is the sexual instinct.[1] According to this theory, the human child is a hedonic animal, driven by pleasure needs that are always specifically and uniformly sexual. At first this sexual drive is focused on his own body parts. If left to his (or her) own devices, he will enjoy masturbation, exhibitionism, voyeurism, and the like without shame or guilt. By age four or five, the child integrates his sexual drive and begins to seek an object other than himself. It is at this point that he directs his sexual interests to the parent of the opposite sex. The attraction of the little boy to his mother and the little girl to her father is understood by Freud to be instinctually determined. This sexual interest initiates an incest dread, which Freud also assumed to be both universal and biological. The incest dread produces guilt, shame, and fear of retaliation from the parent of the same sex.

To avoid this perilous condition, the child will suppress all sexual desire and enter into a latency period, where sex is permissible only when sublimated into seemingly non-sexual activities. Sex remains hidden in the unconscious until the power of puberty drives it back into consciousness and, with luck, toward a non-incestuous object.

This incest dread always dictates a precarious balance in sex between desire and shame, which will then require that sex be secretive and private, as distinguished from such other survival-serving drives as hunger and thirst. The privacy that shapes the sexual behavior of the parents will also protect the child from his compelling incestuous appetites.

Freud covered the territory of sexual guilt and shame from what would now be labeled a "sociobiological" point of view in his book *Totem and Taboo*.[2] Here, Freud speculated that in its primitive beginnings, the human social structure resembled that of the hordes of primates. A dominant male copulated with a female group, which consisted of his "wives" and his daughters. At puberty, male offspring were banned from the primal horde to keep them away from the father's sexual consorts. Eventually the banned brothers joined together, forming a secondary group. With maturation, this group became powerful enough to raid the primary horde, kill (and eat) the father, and appropriate the mating females. In time, Freud stated, these memories (through mechanisms now discredited by modern biology) became imprinted on the unconscious of the new horde leaders, resulting in religious taboos. These taboos forbade eating certain foods associated with tribal totems, forbade the killing of the father or leader, and protected against incest by regulating marriage within the various totemic units. (This is a brutal oversimplification of a fascinating speculative work.)

Freud's conclusions in *Totem and Taboo* remain identical to those expressed in the libido theory. Incest dread and incest taboos are universal parts of the human conscience, a response to genetically determined incestuous appetites. Shame, guilt, privacy, and the other rituals of human sexuality are part of an apparatus essential for the survival of a species with contradictory demands. Sexual drive in the human being is an essential for species survival just as it is in lower animals. But *individual* survival demands some suppression and repression of sexuality, given the eccentric factors of human birth and development. These unique features include: a continual sexual drive; a prolonged dependency period—demanding a tight-knit family; a great potential for individual diversity; and freedom from instinctually fixed behaviors. All these distinguishing traits demand the special environment of privacy.

We pay a price for our sensibilities. Our sexuality is less fixed and more fragile than that of the lower animals. Before considering the profound vulnerability of our sexual behavior to sociological and psychological influences, we must look at the specific biological characteristics of human sexuality.

The assumption that in our sexuality we come closest to our animal forebears is false. Human sexuality is not the same rutting, obsessively driven, genetically derived procedure that we recognize in other primates and in such lower animals as horses, dogs, and sheep. While their copulation looks embarrassingly like what we do, the differences are more extensive and intriguing than the similarities.

The most dramatic difference is that we do it all the time. The human being is the only continually—although not, thank goodness, continuously—sexed animal. We have no mating season and no distinct estrus. Most animals, male and female, live out their existence with specific, defined periods reserved for their reproductive functions. Certainly this is the model that prevails in the insect community. As we climb the ladder of complexity in animals, we find that some *male* animals, particularly among mammals, are liberated from a periodic and isolated time of sexual arousal. But since it still takes two to copulate as well as to tango, a mating season can be defined simply by controlling one half of the copulating pair—having a relatively brief period of receptivity on the part of the female.

In the female animal, sexual desire and sexual receptivity are always linked to the potential for reproduction. As a result, a mating season is defined according to the occurrence of ovulation and a fertile period in the female. In some but not all animals, female estrus will also influence and control the sexual appetites of the male, who will require the pheromones (the specific sexual olfactory stimulants secreted by the females only during estrus) to trigger the brain centers initiating his sexual appetite.

Estrus, then, establishes two conditions central to animal sexuality. First, sex in animals, though it may be pleasurable, never serves pleasure alone, but is closely linked to reproduction. Second, all sexual activity is limited to a severely constricted period of time, a mating season. The differences between human beings and animals are now only too apparent.

Of course, the primary function of human sexuality is also to ensure the survival of the species. The intense pleasure of the sexual experience for the individual is the driving force that will guarantee the performance of this species-serving function. But the activity of human sexuality is now so divorced from its reproductive function that, for most people at most times, the *reproductive* aspect is an annoying and limiting imposition on the now transcendent *pleasure* purposes of sexual intercourse.

The advantages of estrus are obvious. During the period of mating, but more particularly during the period of tending the young, the animals are at risk from predators. Young suckling animals are particularly vulnerable, and the species depends on their survival. Having all of the young born at the same time when the herd is together and the males present for maximum protection is crucial. There is a further advantage to having estrus limited to a relatively short period of the year. The herd is vulnerable during periods of mating and childbearing. If the herd can be kept together during these specific periods, which coincide with times when food is abundant (and extensive grazing is not required), the length and extent of vulnerability is narrowed.

The most dramatic condition distinguishing human sexuality from animal sexuality is the biological liberation of female sexuality from the limiting conditions of an estrus. This separation of fecundity and appetite resulted in the emergence of a continual sexual appetite which alone was quite capable of transforming human sexuality into something entirely different from the models of other animals. But, as in all things human, the essential biology is only the raw material that will be shaped and transmuted by the psychological and sociological forces forming our perceptions and behaviors.

It is not difficult for most of us to imagine the advantages of a human sexual function that can operate twenty-four hours a day, seven days a week, all year long. But what adaptive end could this characteristic of human sexuality have served? And what does it say about the human condition?

The distinguished biologist E.O. Wilson has seen this continuing capacity for sexual activity—and the human elaborations that create diverse forms of human sexual activities—as assuring the bonding that precedes marriage. The everyday and heightened hunger for sex links the mating couple in desire through the years:

> Human beings are unique among the primates in the intensity and variety of their sexual activity. Among other higher animals they are exceeded in sexual athleticism only by lions. The external genitalia of both men and women are exceptionally large and advertised by tufts of pubic hair. The breasts of women are enlarged beyond the size required to house the mammary glands, while the nipples are erotically sensitive and encircled by conspicuously colored areolas. In both sexes the ear lobes are fleshy and sensitive to touch.[3]

Wilson tends to see sexual love and the satisfactions of family life—like almost everything else—as based on "enabling mechanisms," fixed genetically through programmed behavior mediated by physiology. In most animals, sexual activity is a semi-automatic phenomenon, stimulated on a basic chemical level. With human beings, nothing is automatic. Nothing is immune from the power of the human mind. Imagination can transform pleasure into pain and pain into pleasure. As a result, sexuality and the role it plays in a man's life extends well beyond biological fathering. Wilson, almost reluctantly, introduces the concept of human imagination as an influence on the sexual drive:

Human beings are connoisseurs of sexual pleasure. They indulge themselves by casual inspection of potential partners, by fantasy, poetry and song and in every delightful nuance of flirtation leading to foreplay and coition. This has little or nothing to do with reproduction. It has everything to do with bonding. If insemination were the sole biological function of sex, it could be achieved far more economically in a few seconds of mounting and insertion. Indeed, the least social of mammals mate with scarcely more ceremony. . . . It is consistent with this trend that most of the pleasures of human sex constitute primary reinforcers to facilitate bonding. Love and sex do indeed go together.[4]

Wilson assumes the importance of human bonding without explaining why it is so essential to our species. The extraordinary dependence of the human infant demands the full occupation and cooperation of at least two parents—or did so in the hundreds of thousands of years that antedated the development of a culture that could provide child-care services. The human child is born utterly helpless, and remains thus for such a ridiculously long time that a full-time caretaker is required. The infant would encumber the wide-ranging hunting activities necessary to feed and support the incipient family unless an arrangement were made for a division of labor, with one of the family pair dedicated to the care and feeding of the child while the other seeks the wherewithal of survival. In the early history of our species, when we were essentially a hunting-and-gathering society, a dedicated pair, at least, were required to support the needs of the helpless creature.

Male animals in most primate groups have no special interest in their own progeny, if indeed they even recognize or acknowledge them as such. The protective devotion to the specific child is the purview of the female. The male is responsible for the collective safety of the horde. In non-herding animals such as the tiger, the mother must defend her young against male tigers—including the father—who represent one of the major threats to the offspring. This is not so in *Homo sapiens*. The overvaluation of one's child is gender-neutral in human beings. It may be argued that, given the traditional patterns of caretaking, it assumes a greater intensity in the mother; but the human father knows and zealously guards the interests of his own children.

The bonding of the male to the female assures that he will support her needs above those of the general community. Beyond bonding, desire and love will drive him to return to the waiting mother and child. In turn, the bonding of the female supports her fidelity to the male during his absences. Unlike most other monogamous creatures, who cling together only during the mating period, humans have a mating period that is forever and continuous, even surviving the long absences necessitated by the food-gathering activities of the wide-ranging male. The female of this species experiences sexual appetite whether or not she is ovulating, and whether or not her mate is physically present. It is the emotional elaborations of sexuality that bind the couple together in commitment and love and fidelity, and secures the stability of the family unit.

This need of the dependent child for a family setting, combined with the continual nature of sexual appetite, may help to explain further the paradox presented earlier: why so essential an activity as sex should require privacy and be endowed with a mantle of shame. One hypothesis is that the covering of the genitals so common across cultures is an attempt to inhibit or constrict sexual arousal in order to facilitate such other essential activities of life as building shelter, getting food, and rearing children. Modesty is also a public statement about the non-public aspects of the genitalia and their sexual activities. For human beings, sexuality is never a casual public affair.

Despite his awareness of many subtle and unique factors of human sexuality, Freud in his libido theory inexplicably postulated an automatic and animalistic mechanism of sexual energy. Sexual pleasure was cast in purely physiological terms. But pleasure cannot simply be the physiological product of released sexual tension, as Freud presumed. Sex must be placed somewhere within a broader, more sophisticated concept of attachment and love. These institutions of commitment will indicate a great deal about our society's values; about the people we relate to and the world we live in.

But isn't there a macho drive for sex in men that transforms everything? Wrapped into the rituals and romance of human courtship and love, isn't there something operating, in men particularly, that is equivalent to the pure sexual instinct that drives the lower animal? Isn't this the touted "big difference" between men and women: women need attachments, whereas men simply need "to get it off"?

If there is an animal drive in men, the term "lust" is likely to be used to describe it. Some serious scholars of love assume it exists. Pure lust is the desire for casual and anonymous sexual feeling—an erection that occurs without intention of romantic pursuit; without any particular evaluation of the object. A penis looking for a convenient hole in which to insert itself. Certainly, both men and women have experienced a surge of sexual excitement on seeing an attractive member of the opposite sex who may or may not be an appropriate object—a lustful feeling. The anonymity of the feeling is what social theorist Roberto Unger felt characterized lust, which he defined as "Sexual satisfaction untransformed by love or generally uninspired by the imagination."[5]

C. S. Lewis defined lust by saying that "Sexual desire without eros (love) wants *it*, the thing in *itself*, whereas love wants the lover. . . . We use a most unfortunate idiom when we say of a lustful man prowling the streets that he 'wants a woman.' Strictly speaking, a woman is just what he does not want. He wants a pleasure for which a woman happens to be the necessary piece of apparatus."[6] With the sexual liberation of the past three decades we have seen an attempt to detach sex from love and commitment, to demysticize or deromanticize sex—to make it "a natural thing." But it is, as Freud completely intuited, a fact that it is "natural" for sex to involve anxiety, a certain amount of guilt, and some shame. It is natural for sex, like most profound actions between people, to be a metaphoric and complex activity.

Despite the power of the sexual drive, it is rare to find human beings for whom sex is pure, unadulterated instinct. The most passionate lovers might like to think so, but they do not behave like rutting bears or bitches in heat. All human sexuality, like all human behavior, is shaped by emotion and imagination, by fantasy as well as reality. Only in animals and in the animalistic behavior of such aberrant people as rapists does one see pure sexual drive, unadulterated by other contradictory sensibilities. With the rapist, sex may be totally separated from affection or knowledge of the other person. But even here sex is often a secondary factor in the attack. Rage and fear of women may motivate the rapist more than lust.

Some subcultures in our society have attempted to separate sexuality from the sexual partner completely. This isolated and sad sexuality exists, among other places, with those male homosexuals who are attracted to the anonymous sex of public toilets and public baths. These men have an obsessively driven need for a sexual—or, more exactly, a phallic—experience stripped of all human association. The pseudonymous William Aaron describes his experiences in this world. The desire for anonymous sex leads to activity whereby one may be anally penetrated repetitively or perform fellatio on twenty to fifty "partners" a night.[7] The degradations of anonymous sex are further amplified in Larry Kramer's novel *Faggots*.[8]

Even in this kind of sexuality, the anonymity does not make for freedom from fantasy. Indeed, fantasy is an essential ingredient of the excitement. But another human presence intrudes on such fantasy. Here it is the isolated phallus that has meaning and is desired. Sexual pleasure is totally incidental to some secret scenario of power and humiliation, dominance and submission, anxiety and reassurance. The driven behavior is only barely sexual. That the sexual act is not gratifying is evidenced by its insatiability and the compulsive need to repeat it constantly.

Sexuality, divorced not just from affection but from human contact (the heterosexual equivalent has been described by Erica Jong as "the zipless fuck"), turns out to be sexual in form only. It usually represents a compulsive use of sex to fulfill other, quite different, unconscious needs. The real motivating force behind this activity in men is part of the complex domain of male competition, dominance, submission, and dependency cravings in our culture. Such aberrations are also distinctly human, though not characteristic of human sexuality.

For animals, sex is sex, not a symbolic substitute for anything else. Of course, power struggles occur in the competition for a mate, but procreation is the ultimate goal. Power and dominance are used in the service of sex, never the other way round. And sex is fixed and instinctually driven. The rat, seeing and smelling a receptive female, is not concerned with the aesthetics, personality factors, or status of the particular female rat available. A male dog is attracted to a bitch in heat because of an olfactory stimulus, a pheromone, that operates like a chemical switch, turning on a mechanism so impelling that the male animal is driven toward the consummation of the sexual act, often at the risk of its own life. A dog will get into fights with dogs twice his size and more powerful and terrible than he is when under the automatic spell of the sexual instinct. He is not thinking; he is drawn as though attached by a wire on a pulley. He does not care whether the female dog is well formed, misshapen, well bred, or mongrel, black or white, one tenth his size or five times as large, old or young, his daughter, his sister, his mother, or simply the dog next door.

None of this is conceivable as a model for human lust, let alone love. It *does* matter to us whether the object of our desire is our mother or the girl next door. The sexual act, even when it is not a part of romantic love, is always modified by the imaginative aspects of the human psyche. The sexual object must be perceived as "attractive." She must be of a certain age, style, manner, or personality to elicit desire.

And what of the consummation of the act in animals, once the contact is made? It certainly doesn't seem to be much fun! Despite the fact that the courtship and competition may be elaborate and thrilling, the consummation seems unbelievably stereotyped and passionless. Considering the exhausting and often dangerous maneuvers the male goes through to gain permission to mate, the activity itself seems an anticlimax. The same stereotyped behavior exists all the way up the animal line from simple to complicated species: copulation remains the same dull (to the observer, at least) and predictable entity, whether one is watching guppies or "our cousins" the chimpanzees.

Perhaps we misjudge the subjective experience of the animals. The male animal must derive intense gratification of some sort with ejaculation. Otherwise, why risk life and limb for the privilege? But the female animal is not thought by most ethologists to achieve anything approaching the orgasm of women. To the casual observer, the mating of animals seems humdrum and tedious compared with the experience—or expectations—of human intercourse. The female usually appears fixed and staring. No moans of delight, no shivers of ecstasy. The male rhythmically pumps away until the charge wears down like the actions of a cheap wind-up toy. Sex among animals, whatever it is, seems genetically wired, physiological, and non-memorable. Forget about romance; where is the passion? Apparently only in the chase, not in the consummation.

Pure lust, or pure sexuality—as animals do it—operating as a release of tension in the same way that urination releases the tension of the distended bladder, is an unlikely phenomenon in human beings. Even at their most distorted and perverse—perhaps more so in such cases— sexual appetite and behavior are laden with obligations to the past and hopes for the future. Sex is rarely expressed or enjoyed independent of other emotional relationships with the sexual partner. We will not generally have sex with people who repel us.

Human sexual excitement is always an amalgam of endocrine and imagination. The response is more religious than reflexive. It always has and always will have an unanalyzable, mystical aspect. When a man approaches a woman for sex, he is rarely looking for sexual release alone. He is surely looking for that, but he may also be looking for affection, approval, romance, status, reassurance about his manhood, a sense of power, an affirmation of his masculine abilities, perhaps a feeling of domination of the woman or at least liberation from anxieties of such, and so on. He may not even be aware that he is looking for one or many of these things, but he can be quickly made aware.

The male capacity to perform this direct and seemingly simple function of copulation on which the survival of the species is dependent is vulnerable to erosion because of the "romance" that has been introduced into the physiology of sex. He adds imaginative feelings and meanings to mating that convert "screwing" into "making love." The same human imagination can allow him to draw false conclusions; to add two plus two and get five, i.e., to draw conclusions that are incorrect about "the meaning of having sex with a woman." All of these leave the man— given the peculiar fragility of his sexual organ—open to possible failure.

In human beings, sexuality has become so highly symbolized for both genders that one has to strip layers of metaphors to find the "simple" procreative biological drive at its root. For men, sexual behavior is the ultimate expression of their manhood; beyond manhood—their personhood. Courage, strength, and power should have nothing to do with sexual performance. Try telling that to the average man who manages to vest his sexuality with all of the above, and more.

It is this fusion of aspects of power with sex that forms the foundation of the cult of machismo. The prototype exists in the Mediterranean. David Gilmore has summarized the work of Julian Pitt-Rivers, who pioneered in this area.

The Andalusians of Spain's deep south are dedicated to proving their manliness publicly. Even more than other Iberians, they are fervent followers of what the Spanish critic, Enrique Tierno Galvan, has called a quasi religious Hispanic "faith in manhood." If you measure up in this regard, you are "very much a man" (muy hombre), "very virile" (muy macho), or "lots of man" (mucho hombre). If not, you are flojo, a weak and pathetic imposter. The polysemous term flojo literally means empty, lazy, or flaccid; it is used also to describe a dead battery, a flat tire, or some other hopeless tool that does not work. It connotes flabby inadequacy, uselessness or inefficiency.[9]

The phallic significance of this general term of uselessness is only too painfully evident.

To Spanish men, as to many Mediterranean men, it is not only important to be successful with women, it is important to publicly announce this. In the American tradition there is still a place for the opposite image of manhood, speaking softly and carrying a big stick. The shy, gentle heroes who will not talk of their sexual or heroic exploits represent a powerful alternative tradition, perhaps going back to the silent and isolated men of our frontier: the mountainman, the trapper, the cowboy. It might be labeled the "Natty Bumpo syndrome," for James Fenimore Cooper's strong, silent scout. Of course we have our other tradition, our swaggering swashbucklers, our Don Juans. The Mediterraneans, however, seem primarily occupied with the macho man. Sexuality is not enough. Assertive sexuality is essential. Gilmore points out that "Sexual shyness is more than a casual flaw in an Andulusian youth; it is a serious, even tragic inadequacy. The entire village bemoans shyness as a personal calamity and a collective disgrace."[10]

This tradition exists throughout the Mediterranean area up into the Balkans: for Sicilians, Andalusians, Turks, et al. Gilmore states that

A real man in these countries is forceful in courtship as well as a fearless man of action. Both sex and economic enterprise are competitive and risky, because they place a man against his fellows in the quest of the most prized resource of all—woman. Defeat and humiliation are always possible.

In Sicily, for instance, a masculine honor is always bound up with aggression and potency. A real man in Sicily is "a man with big testicles" . . . his potency is firmly established. Among the Sarakatsani of Greece, also, an adult male must be "well-endowed with testicles," quick to arousal, insatiable in the act.

Such beliefs also hold true for much of Spain, especially the south, where a real man is said to have much cojones, or balls. Such big-balled men, naturally, tower over and dominate their less well-endowed and more phlegmatic fellows.[11]

Gilmore takes issue with some other students of Mediterranean and Hispanic cultures in still seeing—despite all the bravura—the primary role of the man as being the reproductive one. He maintains that "Even in those parts of southern Europe where the Don Juan model of sexual assertiveness is highly valued, a man's assigned task is not just to make endless conquests but to spread his seed." Clearly, the ultimate test is producing children, says Gilmore, pointing to countries where only a wife's pregnancy could document her husband's masculinity. "Most important, therefore, the Mediterranean emphasis on manliness means results; it means procreating offspring (preferably boys). . . . It is legitimate reproductive success, more simply than erotic acrobatics."[12]

The male capacity to perform this direct and seemingly simplest of functions is more vulnerable than the woman's, purely on biological grounds. The cultural weight of all the symbolic attachments of machismo further burdens the already finicky machinery of male sexuality. Sexual failure is devastating to a man.

Men *are* different from women. They are tyrannized by their anatomy. They are different both morphologically and psychologically. While most of the latter differences (and some of the former) are susceptible to cultural modifications, all these differences are genetically sponsored.

Some are crucial in understanding the special agonies of male impotence.

The average man knows, often all too well, what his genitalia look like. He sees them daily. He also knows what other men's genitalia look like and how he "measures up." The average woman, until very recent times, had no idea what her genitalia looked like; many still don't. Many women are unaware that the vagina, the labia majora and minora, the vaginal wall and its excretory gland, are as complicated and "interesting" a set of genital organs as the man's.

In my early days of practice I was appalled at how many young women could not even make a simple drawing of the clitoris and surrounding areas. Young men had none of these problems. They not only knew exactly what their penis looked like, they usually could give me its circumference and length (undoubtedly exaggerated) upon erection and when flaccid. To a girl, what she has may appear to be simply an empty space where the penis could have been.

For better and for worse the male genitalia are therefore public organs. Like the tail on a dog, it is an external appendage not easily ignored. The worst is that it is a "tattle-tail." A man has no private parts. Not only is it there to be seen, but embarrassingly, it is an instrument of public record to announce his innermost thoughts, his most private cravings, and his most covert fantasies. Remember Mae West in *She Done Him Wrong* turning to Cary Grant with her delightfully caricatured sexual come-on: "Is that a gun in your pocket, big boy, or are you simply excited about seeing me?"

Every man recalls periods in his boyhood, and unfortunately also in his maturity, of embarrassing erections. The terror of the young boy in puberty fearful of having an erection while dancing with a young girl has led to some of the more bizarre prophylactic measures of concealment.

A little boy tends to discover his penis earlier than a little girl does her clitoris, perhaps again because of the anatomy. Male babies can be observed masturbating to points of erection with a regularity not visible in infant girls. In addition, a male infant will have his genitals handled by his mother and nurses regularly in a way that a little girl will not; bathing and cleanliness require manipulation of the uncircumcised penis particularly. But mothers are careful not to penetrate the infant girl's vagina. The area is treated gingerly and delicately, to preserve all the signs of virginity that were so highly valued in earlier times. Eventually both sexes can discover masturbation and do so, although the compulsive masturbation of male adolescents is rarely described by young girls.

Further, parents can attempt to discourage masturbation in both genders with threats and veiled admonitions. This is more difficult to enforce with a little boy. He is, after all, encouraged to handle his genitalia. We don't want him peeing all over the bathroom floor or dripping down his pants legs. He is instructed to direct the flow of urine into the toilet, which requires handling the penis. In addition, simply getting in and out of the clothes requires touching, tucking, and maneuvering, all of which may be in the covert service of masturbatory pleasure.

Another essential difference between the genders is that a woman may go into adult life without ever experiencing an orgasm. A normal man cannot. Again, the basic difference in physiology is crucial. A man's orgasm, unlike a woman's, serves a secondary and crucial function of releasing the tension of retained semen and sperm. After puberty, the boy is constantly manufacturing semen and sperm. This is dammed up and eventually will create pressure that is both painful and sexually stimulating. To release the accumulated fluid, a spontaneous nocturnal emission accompanied by an orgasm will be physiologically induced. Since it is often accompanied by an erotic dream, this is euphemistically called a "wet dream." The wet dream is frequently a transition phenomenon directing the late-blooming boy to masturbation. He has the spontaneous ejaculation and then begins to learn that with a little manipulation and friction, he can induce ejaculation. Producing a stimulating fantasy—no big production for an adolescent—is ample substitute for the dream. I have never met a man who has not experienced an orgasm, nor have I met a man who is confused when I ask him how frequently he has experienced orgasm. A man knows what an orgasm is. A woman, on the other hand, is often confused and unsure whether she has experienced orgasms. It is possible for a culture—determinedly and viciously—to psychologically destroy all sexual pleasure in a woman. It is not possible to do this in a man. Physiology protects his orgastic pleasure.

Beyond that, no culture could survive if the male population were permanently crippled. A woman can perform whether interested or not; she can even perform under duress. She can certainly perform as a loving service to a mate. A man, unlike a woman, cannot "oblige" his partner. A man who is not sexually aroused cannot procreate. A woman—perhaps with the help of a little lubricant—can for reasons of affection, duty, consideration, desire for a child, be a loving sexual partner and a potential mother. A man cannot by the peculiar nature of his genitalia do what it is not exciting to do. If he has no desire, or is frightened for any number of reasons, he will fail. Just as his sexual appetite is advertised, that same "tattle-tail" will publicly announce his impotence. The male genitalia do not allow for dissembling, accommodation, or affectionate service in another's interest.

Impotence is a blow to the male ego of the most devastating nature. It is the one psychological symptom most likely to drive the most macho and conservative man with his contempt for things psychological into the arms of a psychotherapist.

Male impotence is more than a failure to achieve pleasure; nor is it just about procreation. Impotence cuts to the heart of that very manhood to which his pride and self-respect are bound. Impotence is almost always the intrusion of fear into the sexual act. The roots of this fear may be multiple and are usually unknown to the individual. Occasionally underneath the fear is a primary rage at women, at a specific woman, or at the idea of sexuality in general. Often both fear and rage are present, and it is difficult to know which is primary and which derivative. We know we will become angry at whatever frightens us; and we also know that our own rage can be frightening. In therapy, we focus on these emotions that impound the sexual drive.

Impotence takes a number of forms. The simplest, and the one most recognizable by the man or his partner, is the inability to get or sustain an erection. Two other very closely related forms also exist. One is premature ejaculation and the other is retarded ejaculation.

Premature ejaculation is often misunderstood. Many patients complain of "premature ejaculation" which on examination turns out to be nothing of the sort. They mean they ejaculate "too early," which may mean before their partner has achieved orgasm. If the partner has problems with orgasm or requires other stimulation besides penetration, and either or both partners are ignorant of this, a man can pump away for hours and still choose to call it "premature ejaculation." When we psychiatrists use the term, we consider not just the time factor (although that is one significant aspect) but also the nature of the ejaculation. Active copulatory movements will produce an ejaculation within a relatively short time. Thirty, forty, fifty strokes will do the job, and that is perfectly normal. Men may choose to slow themselves down to prolong the sexual excitement; in order to gratify both their partner and themselves; or to make "lovemaking" out of sexuality.

Premature ejaculation means ejaculation at the moment of penetration, or almost immediately thereafter. The man will have an erection and, just as he attempts to penetrate, he will ejaculate. This ejaculation has a different quality from the normal ejaculation after full sexual activity. Some men describe it as ejaculation without orgasm, or with an attenuated orgasm. The semen often drips out rather than spurting in a projectile, pulsating manner.

A less common form of impotence is often not recognized as impotence at all, but viewed as its opposite, virility. In this condition, a man is capable of maintaining an erection almost indefinitely, but has great difficulty in ejaculating during the act of intercourse. This is called "retarded ejaculation." Some men—and some women—take joy or pride in this, interpreting it as a sign of hypervirility. What it really represents is an "anesthetic" penis: the man assuages his anxiety or anger by refusing to discharge the semen or abandon his erection. The term "refusing" is used metaphorically and psychoanalytically here. This is not a cognitive or conscious act over which the individual has any control. Otherwise it would not be a symptom.

Central to all three forms of impotence—inability to maintain or achieve an erection; premature ejaculation; and retarded ejaculation—is the intrusion of powerful, dominating primary emotions. In treatment, we assume that confronting the man's irrational anxiety will allow the sexual drive to emerge. So we start by looking for the fear.

When I ask a man who is sexually impotent (particularly in the case of inability to maintain erection) what is frightening him, he will acknowledge fear, but give a totally useless answer: "I'm afraid that I won't have an erection and that I will be embarrassed and humiliated." Patiently a therapist must work with the patient to avoid this pattern of circular reasoning. He must be brought to recognize this as secondary performance anxiety. He has to understand that he does not have an erection in the first place because he is afraid of something involving the sexual act. First comes the fear; then the impotence; then the fear of impotence.

At this point the patient does not consciously know the answer. He must start the process of examining his attitudes about sexuality, about men, women, the nature of their roles, and so on—all that encompasses the dynamic exploration that is part of any "talking cure." But dynamic therapy and self-awareness are not the only forms of psychotherapy. Impotence, particularly if not too profound, responds readily to behavioral therapy, to simple conditioning. Perhaps the most popular treatment today, the basis of most "sex therapy," is a conditioning program to alleviate the performance anxiety which—whatever may have initiated it—soon becomes the dominant factor. The assumption is that by overcoming the performance anxiety, a routine and ritual sexuality can occur that will bypass the unconscious anxiety mechanisms. Even if there is an unconscious dynamic present, solid regular performance will create a corrective emotional experience to alleviate the fear. This is precisely the mechanism that is used in any phobic situation, whether fear of sex or fear of flying.

The prototype of this treatment is the basic technique designed by Masters and Johnson.[13] They tell the man and his wife (or surrogate) that they must begin to explore each other for purposes of pleasure and tenderness, but they are *absolutely forbidden* to have intercourse. Regardless of how much they may want it, it is not allowed. Indeed, ejaculation is forbidden in the first stages, unless it occurs accidentally. Freed of the "need to perform," given authoritative permission not to have an erection, with even intercourse "forbidden," physical stimulation will do its job. Gradually the couple are allowed to move closer and closer to intercourse. Within ten days to two weeks, intercourse will often be achieved.

The number of individuals who respond to this kind of sex therapy with success is considerable. This disturbs many dynamic therapists, for there remains the concern that the unresolved underlying conflicts will then be displaced into other areas. There is no evidence to date that behavioral treatment of impotence is in any way a dangerous or inadequate treatment. It is a cliché of analysis that when sex is good it is 10 percent of a successful marriage and when sex is bad it is 90 percent of a failed one. Getting sex on track will allow the other 90 percent of the successful marriage to take hold.

Each sex therapist has his or her own special elaborations. One very successful New York sex therapist creates scenarios with her woman "accomplice" (the patient's spouse or girlfriend) when treating an impotent man. If a man wakes up with an erection in the middle of the night—knowing it is probably pressure of the bladder creating what has been traditionally called a *Wassertur* (water tower)—he is instructed to wake the woman, who immediately is to exclaim how beautiful the erection is—big, powerful, scary, awesome, humungous, or whatever the language of that twosome may be. It is important to link the erection to concepts of potency, masculinity, power, and awe. The woman is instructed in the artifices of this game.

The sex therapist who has perfected this technique happens to be a woman. It is questionable whether a male therapist could get away with such manipulation given the political climate of our times. This role could be seen as demeaning to the woman. On the other hand, the woman in question is generally one who loves the man and wants to restore the relationship. This sex therapist is operating on her awareness that what has occurred is a breakdown in the man's system of pride and his masculine identity, not just of the sexual apparatus.

A sophisticated woman does not have to be told that she gets nowhere by making comments about the male organ as a "cute little thing," but she may still need to be forewarned. While the penis is often discussed by couples in the third person, it must not be taken lightly. It is to be revered. It is a big stick. It is to be seen as powerful and treated as awesome. Women who choose to play the game know that most men will respond positively to mock fear, to such statements as: "Oh my God, you're killing me . . . it's too much . . . I can't get it all in . . . it's too big . . . you're driving me crazy!" It is a peculiar language for love, but often necessary for that pathetically fragile creature, the male animal, particularly in a society that has never allowed him to feel fully a man in any other way. If a woman says she finds him "adorable, even though small," it is not acceptable. "Adorable" is not what he wants to be and "small" terrifies him, since in all probability he is one of the majority of men who is not sure that he measures up either physically or psychologically in potency to the "average" man, whoever that may be.

Some knowledge of the more basic fears that can intrude on sexuality are worth noting. What should be scary about doing one of the most natural things in the world: inserting your penis into a woman's vagina in order to bring the two of you pleasure and draw you together in a primal experience?

Traditionally, psychoanalysts have seen all impotence as the product of failing to resolve the Oedipal complex. What is meant by this? It simply means that the first heterosexual love in a boy's life is his mother. These feelings produce an incest dread which Freud specifically felt to be a biological and genetic phenomenon of the human race. The boy struggles with this and attempts to repress all of his sexuality, but under the burden and the immense pressures of puberty the sexual drive is so powerful that it cannot be contained. The child's job then is to transfer his sexual feelings from his mother to a heterosexual object other than her. Fortunately, most of us seem to do this without too much difficulty. Some do not. The reasons for not doing it involve a series of complex scenarios as variable as the impotent patients presented. But whatever the reason, a certain number of individuals are considered "fixated" (arrested, developmentally stuck) at the Oedipal level. Since for these young men all sex is sex with the mother, it produces true terror.

Some of these men will handle this problem by the development of what Freud referred to as a "Madonna-prostitute complex." We tend to use this term now in precisely the opposite way from which Freud used it. Freud saw the mother as the whore (for having sex with the father). Nowadays we see the whore as the alternative to the mother. The mother—good, loving creature that she is—will be viewed as a-sexual. These men will tend to form friendships with and marry women of their "class" and culture. But they will only be able to enjoy sex with "debased" women who are whores. One can see such behavior simply as the resolution of this terrible conflict of desiring sex and yet not wanting to have sex with one's mother.

In either case, what emerges is a clearly evident constellation of events that the psychiatrist meets frequently: A man who divides women into "good girls" and "bad girls," who marries or is attracted socially to the good girl but is impotent with her, and who can only have satisfactory sex with the "whores," i.e., anyone who for any reason is déclassée.

The elaborations on this theme are elegant and manifold. There are men who *can* have sex with their wives, but it is perfunctory and unsatisfying. True passion is reserved for affairs. By definition any woman in the affair is a whore. (Affairs, however, are more complicated, serving multiple needs, and must not always be seen as satisfying only this particular fixation.)

A man can often have sex with his wife if she speaks dirty words to him and acts in a totally unmaternal and unfeminine way. In one common variant, it may be necessary for a sadomasochistic game to be played out. This game may involve humiliation of the man or simple subservience. Metaphorically speaking, it confirms the incestual need, while pretending to deny it. No, she is not the mother because she is sexy, uses dirty words, dresses like a whore, paints her nipples with rouge, whatever. But yes, she is the mother, in that once again he has returned to early childhood, where the mother is the beloved tyrant who is capable both of giving and of depriving all pleasure. This sexual game avoids certain nurturing aspects reminiscent of the mother, while replicating the early childhood drama of power.

The intricacies and elaborations of the Oedipal complex can fill volumes. For many generations of psychiatrists, the basis of *all* neuroses —not just sexual problems, but all neurotic problems—was a failure to resolve the Oedipal complex. In the grand tradition of the Talmudists, who were forced to spend centuries devoted to the five books of Moses, early psychoanalysts devoted their lifetimes to the small body of Freudian work. Therefore the number of variations on the Oedipal theme exceeds the number of angels who could dance on the head of a pin.

In the Oedipal triangle, there are two other major components besides the boy's sexual fixation on his mother. In addition to the desire for the mother, there is a keen awareness of the much more powerful father. The mother belongs to *him*. In order to get the mother—who at this point represents any or all women—the boy is brought into competition with the powerful father. Anxiety, therefore, derives not just from some biological and genetically fixed incest dread, but from the very real developmental, everyday awareness that to take a woman means to take her from another man, usually symbolized by the father and therefore a more powerful man. One other major variable that emerges from all of this is that sex becomes a competitive phenomenon, which pits one man against another more powerful man.

This terror of the avenging father leads directly to the castration anxiety that has been thought to underlie all impotence. If you use your big stick to gain a woman, a man with a bigger stick will come along, castrate you, take away your instrument, and further might subject you to a feminine role by making you the homosexual object of his choice. A sense of one's own inadequacy, for whatever reason, in the competitive world of men can lead to an abandonment of women, thus avoiding the competition.

Again, almost every imaginable variation and metaphorical disguise occurs. Some men can only be excited by "unavailable" women, or women who belong to other men. The secret usurpation is a source of joy, and a disguised and emblematic acting out of Oedipal needs. Much of this discussion can be read in Freud's papers, peculiarly titled "Contributions to the Psychology of Love."[14]

Premature ejaculation involves yet another dynamic. Here, rather than a persistent desire for the mother, fear of the dominant, or phallic, mother is the primary factor. In this pattern, a boy raised by a domineering mother will often see her as the main source of power. Sometimes, a boy's fear will focus on her genitalia as the area of danger rather than the whole woman, who can still be nurturing.

The term "vagina dentata"—a vagina with teeth—was an early psychoanalytic construction. The vagina was seen as a dangerous place. Castration anxiety can be converted into this vagina dentata fantasy: the little boy observes the absence of a penis on, perhaps, a little sister; he assumes that she had one to begin with, but it was ripped away by the powerful mother because of some transgression. He then assumes the same may happen to him. The original elaboration of this theory can be read in Freud's fascinating and brilliant study of "Little Hans."[15]

Another source of fear of the vagina rests with the male child's confusion about the female organs. Since the female genitalia are less easy to examine than those of men, many boys—and sadly some young girls—have a cloacal image of the vagina. They conflate the anus, vagina, and urethra into one large cloacus, which serves all purposes. They then see the vagina as a dirty hole. The irony is that a whole generation of men were more terrified to stick their tongue in a woman's vagina than they were to stick their tongue in a woman's mouth, though the mouth is often the dirtier orifice.

From whatever source, a boy may begin to perceive the vagina as a dangerous area—to be avoided. This underlies the phenomenon of premature ejaculation. The frightened man, like the thief in the night, must get in and out quickly before being discovered. Safer still, he will not enter at all.

Anything that makes occupation of the vagina seem dangerous can lead to premature ejaculation. Another example: the vagina may be the private vault and reservoir of the powerful man, which one enters at great risk. Think of all the myths, fairy tales, and legends about entering the giant's private cave and stealing his jewels. Premature ejaculation is a specialized way of handling fear of the woman who is still regarded as a prize possession. The boy will handle this sexual problem through such "compromise formation." He gets in and out quickly.

The third major category of impotence is represented by the Don Juans, who are reputed to be able to screw for hours without exhaustion or depletion. These men are misunderstood and overpraised. They usually suffer from retarded ejaculation. Such individuals with an "anesthetic" penis equate ejaculation with the loss of power. The prototypical example is Samson and Delilah. Only a woman is capable of making the virile male impotent. A woman is of course capable of making any man "impotent" in the sense that ejaculations will eventually drain him and limit his capacity for an erection. The totally satisfied man has physiological difficulty in gaining successive erections. If he is young and vigorous, maybe he can have two, three in a row, but beyond three ejaculations he is usually "spent."

This image of being spent is a common one in childhood. I recall only too vividly a memory of early adolescence. I was scrounging through old books in the attic, seeking some form of titillation to augment what seemed my insatiable need for materials for masturbation. Pornography, at least in our household, was not available. The soft-core pornography *Playboy* and *Penthouse* magazines were yet to come of age. Hard-core pornography did exist—I remember clearly a "Big Little" book in which the sexual exploits of Popeye and Olive Oyl were illustrated behind the mundane scenes of their life as documented in the daily funnies—but it was hard to come by and tended to be reserved for the high school crowd. We poor fellows in early pubescence, at age thirteen or fourteen, were relegated to the meager pickings of the *National Geographic* with their occasional bland images of bare-bosomed natives of Africa or Australia; or even worse, resigned to the humiliation of looking up "sexy" words—"vagina," "breast," "vulva"—in the dictionary.

One day in our attic, I discovered a treasure trove in a book entitled *Eugenics*. It was filled with biological and anatomical illustrations of the human body; with explanations of the "scientific" nature of physical and mental health, and the conditions that encourage or deplete it.

Being a master of the index, I immediately turned to masturbation. To my horror I found a section which, with great scientific certitude, explained that masturbation depleted the cerebral spinal fluid and that excessive masturbation would eventually lead to insanity and blindness. I had never met an insane person and the term had a certain romance about it from the Gothic novels I had read. It certainly didn't represent any threat. Blindness was another thing. There were at least two blind men in the neighborhood and they always struck me as pathetic figures. After that many an hour was spent wandering around the attic with my eyes blindfolded in practice for what I felt was an inevitable destiny.

One would expect this kind of "scientific knowledge" from a nineteenth-century book on mental health, but one does not expect it in the modern world. Still, the concept of draining one's strength is omnipresent. Athletes are warned not to have sex with their wives or girlfriends before "the big game." Dating, girlfriends, wives, are barred from training camps, and if rumors are correct, the Italian soccer teams live by this motto. Given the culture of Italian men, this represents a profound, if not religious, sacrifice for the glory of the game.

Retarded ejaculation conserves the sperm. Further, it then allows the man to have sex with a woman—bring her to an orgasm which in his competitive view of male-female relationships disempowers her— while at the same time demonstrating his iron discipline. The more orgasms he provokes in the woman, the greater his power. Meantime he remains cool and in "total control." It might be noted that even men who do not suffer from retarded ejaculation often find this fantasy exciting. The man in turn never releases his sperm and never loses his erection. Thus he "retains" both.

The concept of sperm as masculine "fuel" or energy, which must not be depleted without being replaced, is a central one for the Sambia people of New Guinea. The Sambians go so far as to insist that young novices perform fellatio on elderly males as a means of empowering them with enriched fuel. With retarded ejaculation, beyond retaining sperm the big stick remains intact, not reduced to the sorry and useless postcoital instrument of the typical man after intercourse. Finally, the male suffering from retarded ejaculation supports his own self-deception by the endorsement of certain women, who will also interpret this failing as a sign of increased potency, a superstud.

Whatever its source, impotence or the threat of impotence will haunt many men throughout their lives. The importance of the threat to the mainstay of the man's pride is suggested by the symbolic meaning of the language of sexual failure. "Potency" literally means power. To be impotent is to be disempowered, and to the man, for whom power is almost everything, to be impotent is to risk being a non-person. "Impotence" is a term reserved exclusively for men.

With women, we use a different word. And the distinction between these two words is a powerful metaphor for the distinction in our attitudes about male and female sexuality. A woman who is incapable of sexual pleasure is called "frigid." The implication here is that she is cold, unnurturing, unreceptive. It is seen not as a failure of strength, but as a sign of rejection and lack of love. Or worse, as an incapacity for feeling. She is "withholding" the fluids that nurture and lubricate the act of lovemaking. Why should the inability to achieve sexual plea- sure be seen as a failure of "power" in men and not in women? The answer lies in the firm union between potency and performance that exists in the man (and that does not exist in the woman). A woman can perform the procreative role independent of the capacity for any pleasure in her action. The two functions are not fused. A man must be interested, must be aroused, in order to father children, at least through the normal methods of copulation. He cannot be raped by a woman, only seduced or encouraged.

Obviously there are significant consequences resulting from this dis- tinction between the male and female genitalia. Just as the public and private nature of the two profoundly influenced our culture, our atti- tudes, and our practices, so too will this differentiation in the linkage of pleasure and performance have its influence. A woman who is "frigid" may be made to feel unloving and uncaring, but not necessarily un- powerful. It is a serious price, but a different price. To a man, sexual failure is impotence in all senses of that word. Sexual potency equals power equals manliness.

The metaphors for impotence go well beyond the sexual arena. Any- thing that reduces a man in any field can also make him *feel* sexually impotent, powerless at this seminal level. Reciprocally, any signs of sexual impotence will diminish his sense of power among other men in the competitive worlds beyond sexuality. A man's system of pride is governed by his sense of power. This in turn is fed by his ability to fulfill the fundamental role of procreator, which joins with that of pro- tector and provider in supporting the male ego. The tragedy is that the tripod of pride depends on all three legs, and that reducing any one can topple the entire structure.

The waning sexuality of adult age, coming as it often does along with waning power in the work community, becomes a double blow to many men. It is one of the reasons that the need for work, beyond middle age and well into old age, is progressively being seen as an essential for modern-day men.

8 ▸ WORK: MAN AS PROVIDER

Nothing is more important to a man's pride, self-respect, status, and manhood than work. Nothing. Sexual impotence, like sudden loss of ambulation or physical strength, may shatter his self-confidence. But that does not mean that pride is built on these. They are the subsumed attributes of manhood. Pride is built on work and achievement, and the success that accrues from that work. Yet today men often seem confused and contradictory in their attitudes about work. The modern man "dreads" Monday mornings; counts the days until his vacation; and endlessly plans for retirement. But without work he is likely to withdraw into self-contempt and humiliation. Work is a part of the function of the human animal in the way that it is for no other living creature. Yet we remain confused about whether it is an obligation or a privilege.

Even God seemed ambivalent. The punishment of Adam for daring to become a free and autonomous creature was that he would be obliged to earn his bread "by the sweat of his brow." But Adam was a worker *before* his banishment. Twice before in Genesis God refers to Adam's role as a worker—and in much more benevolent terms: ". . . for the Lord God had not caused it to rain upon the earth, and there was not a man to till the ground." (II:5) Only after Adam had been created would there be a garden at all! The Garden was to be a collaborative effort between God and Adam: "And the Lord God took the man, and put him into the garden of Eden to dress it and to keep it." (II:15)

According to the Bible, Adam was "created in God's image." God, too, was a worker and His work required energy, toil, exhaustion— and satisfaction. "And on the seventh day God ended his work which he had made; and he rested on the seventh day from all his work which he had made." (II:2)

Thus the banishment and the injunction to labor simply meant that pain would be introduced into the occupations of Adam. Work was not his punishment. Work was and is his nobility. Work distinguishes the human species from all animals and joins man in creativity with God.

The fact is that animals do not work. Those activities which are seen as work are mechanical obligations, built into the organism to serve survival needs exclusively. The idea of work as a form of creativity does not exist.

Students of labor and work recognize this exclusive capacity of the human being and have speculated about its potential meaning. It was recently underlined by Pope John Paul II in what may be considered his most elegant and compassionate encyclical to date:

> Work is one of the characteristics that distinguish man from the rest of creatures, whose activities for sustaining their lives cannot be called work. Only man is capable of work, and only man works, at the same time by work occupying his existence on earth. Thus work bears the particular mark of man and of humanity. And this mark decides interior characteristics; in a sense it constitutes its very nature.[1]

Work is thus intended as a component part of the essential pleasure mechanism of the human being. It is linked to a sense of a larger and enhanced self. When we *choose* to work at something we do not enjoy, simply to make money, it is a very poor trade-off indeed. It is tragically a necessary one for the typical working-class person, who must take any job which presents itself. He does not think about whether he is "being fulfilled" or whether his work is serving some purpose of gratification or "self-actualization." He becomes a miner because he lives in a mining town, or he works in construction because his father did so before him, or he becomes a truck driver because his uncle was a member of the union and he could get into that union. The average workingman does not think of work as pleasure; he thinks of it as a condition for pleasure. When work takes up forty to sixty hours of one's week, this is a heart-breaking accommodation.

I remember my own father laboring six days a week, twelve hours a day, in work he loathed. Having come out of the Depression and being denied the opportunity to go on to college, he became an insurance salesman and supported his family throughout the Great Depression in comfort and security, when relatives were desperate for even the $15 a week afforded by the WPA. His lesson to his sons was a constant one: No amount of money and nothing that money can buy can possibly compensate for the hours spent in drudgery, indentured to a joyless job. You sinned if you traded pleasure in work for material goods. If you had this choice and made the wrong decision, you had sold your birthright for a mess of pottage.

It goes without saying that most men do not have this privilege. It is particularly tragic, therefore, when men trade the gratifications of a rewarding job for the security, the status, or the purchasing power of a stultifying job. There are few things that money can buy that are truly worthwhile. One thing of great value it *can* buy is the freedom from horrors of poverty. Another is the freedom from having to do something unattractive to earn money. Finally, it buys the sacred privilege of time. One can hire services to liberate oneself from doing the mundane, and free one's time for true pleasures.

Work is part of the substrata of our ego, our pride system, and our sense of identity. Obviously, I am not talking about the back-breaking labor that primitive man had to endure to supply food for himself and his starving family during meager times. This labor he shares with animals. We must distinguish "labor" from "work." There is a classical distinction that goes back to Locke's second *Treatise on Government,* in which he refers to "the labor of our body and the work of our hands." Hands, of course, are those dextrous instruments that carry out many of the fine creations of the human mind. Among the traditional semantic distinctions that have emerged since Locke's time, Hannah Arendt in her book *The Human Condition* offers a brilliant analysis of work.

"Labor," according to Arendt, produces no lasting product. "Work" in the traditional definition produces a product, "the work," which is independent of its producer's literal survival and may outlast him. "Work," in this context, is independent of the toils of survival.[2]

"Work" is not necessary; it is an occupation, a form of creativity, a special privilege of the human being. Other animals must scrounge for food, flee from predators, adapt to the environment, migrate, burrow, build nests, dam rivers, cut trees; but none of this is "work." There is no product and no choice. These activities are necessary for species survival. The only meaning in animal existence is survival. As has been said, the chicken is simply a convenient machine for creating an egg that is capable of producing a chicken.

If "work" exalts and distinguishes humankind, what are we to make of the harshness and pain that inevitably accompany even true work? I believe that the pleasure exists not *despite* the agony but because of it. True pleasure is a feeling of well-being, a joyous feeling, a good feeling, a feeling of satisfaction. It is first and foremost a *feeling,* or an emotion. Despite the differing forms in which pleasure occurs, one basic ingredient is common to all. Those activities that give us pleasure will inevitably enhance, expand, enlarge, and elevate our sense of self. Pleasure makes for a bigger and richer self.

There are discrete categories of pleasure that differ in their source and quality. Simple sensory pleasure corresponds most accurately to the pleasures of an animal—the pleasures from eating, from orgastic release, or from being stroked. But even here the human being also experiences pleasure from the secondary elaborations of these simple sensory inputs. The joy in observing nature—the power of the sea, the majesty of the mountain, the delicacy of a flower—is not in the actual seeing but in the conceptual additions that transform that sight into a perception, a symbol. No animal contemplates the sunset or the chasm of the Grand Canyon with awe. The things that "delight" an animal are probably limited to the sight of prey, the smell of a mate in estrus, and possibly the parent's view of its cub. The human eye *perceives* as it sees. It integrates the simple sensation into an embroidery of past remembrances, future anticipations, related events, and symbolic meanings.

The category of pleasure which is closest to the essential nature of work is something I call "mastery." Human beings love progress. We take gratification in change and growth. Our delight in observing our mind in successful operation is in every way equivalent to our joy in sensing our working bodies in athletic activities. I am not at all convinced that a product is an essential of work. What is the product of the teacher, the social worker, or the physician? Yet all three represent honorable and rewarding fields of work. In a world that is increasingly abstract, service and mastery may be as central as a product to a concept of proper work. The very nature of the satisfaction with both these joys involves effort and pain, the feeling that "I did it."

It is said that many men these days do not achieve this sense of mastery, of accomplishment of a "job well done" from their daily work, and those who do are progressively becoming a smaller minority. They turn to sports, hobbies, or extracurricular involvements for this gratification. Although games do not fulfill the traditional definition of work in that they do not create a product, they do involve effort and mastery.

I enjoy gardening—the original work of Adam. Not the planting of seeds and the gentle and patient satisfaction of nurturing them to bloom—no, I am in for grander stuff. I like building retaining walls, moving bushes, battling against unruly growth, chopping, sawing, pruning, heaving, and sweating until nature and I, in antagonism and collaboration, have created something I consider beautiful, a garden.

It is not *despite* my bruises, my sweat, my scratches, my aching back that I enjoy the activity, but because of them. Having done this difficult thing, I have proved something about myself and my worth.

One might speculate that Paleolithic man was *not* distinguished from the animals; that he did no work for its own sake. It is conceivable that all of his time was occupied, as is that of certain animals, with securing the means of subsistence. Although we can never completely know the nature of the earliest history of human beings, every new increment of knowledge reinforces the belief that early humans managed to find work or to manufacture occupations. We humans find work because we "need" the activity and are gratified by the results. Our device to justify work is a devious one. We redefine the "necessities" of survival. No longer do we need shelter from the elements; we need a "house," and the definitions of adequacy in that term—a "decent house"—extend far beyond considerations of shelter.

The slim evidences of the Paleolithic period reveal remarkably diverse examples of the need of primitive man to accumulate "things," not for their survival but for their imagery, their suggestion of status, power, or wealth, or simply for their aesthetics. Only recently a discovery was made which revealed that human beings twenty thousand years ago— ten thousand years before they had learned to cultivate the earth and domesticate animals—were already stringing together beads of animal teeth and claws, manufacturing artifacts of adornment, accumulating symbols of wealth and power.

And there is evidence from the Paleolithic period that an early aesthetic also existed. The European cave drawings are testimony not just to man's imagination, but to his need to create, to make things that involve an aesthetic or even spiritual life—things that bear no relationship to physiological survival. These early records of our artistic endeavors are testament to the strangeness of our species. Here is an animal who—beyond subsistence and survival (often to the detriment of both)—is preoccupied with the *significance* of existence and the *meaning* of survival.

The descendants of Adam and Eve, from the primitive existence in the caves of Africa before tools and fire, before agriculture and manufacturing, may only have had time and energy to labor for survival. But they managed, in an incredibly short period of discovery, to develop technology. Through the development of this technology—through the use of their hands and their minds—they created an existence that spared their bodies. The human being became, as Benjamin Franklin called him, "the tool-making animal."

The development was really remarkable. A clam shell might be the model for a sharpened stone that would ultimately lead to the forging of metal tools. What may have started out as the chance use of the sturdily bent branch of a tree to upturn roots and edible tubers soon gave way to much more sophisticated instruments. The piece of wood, so conveniently bent to provide a lever, led to the construction of the lever and then, with the grand leap that truly defines our species, to the discovery of the *principle* of the lever. The lever is the simplest of "machines." A machine is a mechanism for taking a small force and allowing it to move a larger load. Try opening a lid with your hands, and then use an old-fashioned bottle opener, to appreciate the enhancement of power. The discovery of the principle of the lever would lead to the awareness of the pulley, the inclined plane, the screw, the wheel and axle. These five simple machines are all there are. The entire complicated machinery of modern physical life consists simply of variations and elaborations on these five themes.

Eventually human beings, through their keen, observing eyes, would also discover the relationship of the seed that falls to the plant that grows to the cultivation of grains—the seeds that nourish. They would discover agriculture. The piece of wood would then be converted into a primitive hoe, and the human being could evolve a culture where he need never go in search of food, but could actually cultivate it in his own "backyard." That extraordinary mind of early man was operating in exactly the same way as we do today when we penetrate the molecular nature of living things.

The horizons early men were probing with the discovery of agriculture and the domestication of animals were in no way less dramatic than our flights to the Moon and our Venus probes. The domestication of animals required the same time and patience, the same imagination and intelligence, the same abilities to accumulate data, synthesize them, draw conclusions, and then test the conclusions to separate the false ones from the correct. It took thousands of years for human beings to discover the relationship between copulation and procreation, in themselves as well as in lower animals. There were primitive tribes existing in the twentieth century who still did not acknowledge this relationship in either man or beast.

The first animals to be domesticated were probably seen as a form of living tool—dogs to assist in the relentless pursuit of game. The dog could be regarded as an extension of the same intelligence that developed spears, javelins, bows and arrows. But sooner or later human beings would realize that the exhausting activity of the hunt was itself no longer necessary. As one domesticated the dog to facilitate in the hunt for the food animal, one could also domesticate the food animal. Compared with domestication, hunting is unreliable and energy-inefficient. Sheep could be slaughtered, pigs roasted, and cows milked, all again at one's own convenience and in one's own backyard.

There were still further ways in which man could extend his dominion over the beast and by so doing reduce his toil. In addition to eating them, he could exploit them to perform his labor. The bent twig which had become a tool for digging could then become a plow to be drawn by oxen, who were gelded specifically for such uses.

All of this paved the way for a life that could be theoretically free from toil and sweat. Yet it was not to be, and the "why not?" becomes a critical question in illuminating the nature of the modern human being. Suppose for a moment that, after all these discoveries, men and women had stayed in the cave, had not, so to speak, been upwardly mobile, but had maintained their early, primitive standards of living. Suppose all the conditions of existence had been the same: we stayed in the cave, did not build cities—or even huts—did not advance our culture, aspired to no more than the lion or the ape, worked only for food, air, water, and protection from the elements. With our discovery of technology and agriculture, we human beings might well have existed—despite God's injunction—without pain or exertion. But that is not the history of the human species. The questing beast that is *Homo sapiens* insisted on upping the ante at each turn, as he persists in doing to this very day. The cave would give way to a thatched or mud hut, which in turn would give way to a primitive stone or wooden lean-to, which in turn would give way to a palace, which in turn was a direct antecedent to the cathedrals of Salisbury and Chartres.

The history of human culture seems to be a perverse one, the human being constantly expanding his definitions of what is "necessary" for life—life clearly meaning not mere survival but the good life—and in so doing fulfilling the prophecy that he must earn his bread by the sweat of his brow. The young men and women graduating from Ivy League law schools today who are seduced by a major Wall Street law firm's offer of $85,000 a year will earn their money. They will be sweated out by seventy to eighty weekly hours of work of extraordinary tedium, which will generate a despair so vast that the majority of them will quickly develop a loathing for their profession and a cynicism about the law. Only a small percentage will persist in the field with pleasure and gratification. Yet they will stay in their professions. And the question is why? For some, it may be a simple matter of entrapment. By the time they are aware of their dissatisfactions, they are committed to a way of life and a standard of living to which they are indentured. There is also a real degree of pleasure in being good at something, even if that something is not rewarding. Finally, they achieve pride in the byproducts of work rather than in the work itself. They value positions, perquisites, and power. They take comfort in the prestige of the profession. They take pleasure in the packing rather than the package. They come to need the wrappings and ribbons of success, but the substance and sustenance are not there.

Hannah Arendt contemplated this intensive expansion of our "needs" and came to the conclusion that it was an integral part of a requisite *need for work*. There is a limitation on how much we can consume. But we *must* continue to consume things if we are to continue producing them, particularly when there is an inexhaustible labor force. One danger of having the toil taken out of work was that for many men the opportunity for *any* employment would disappear. "How can we rev up consumption when we seem already to have an unlimited accumulation of wealth and goods?" Arendt asks. The solution

> consists in treating all use objects as though they were consumer goods so that a chair or a table is now consumed as rapidly as a dress, and a dress used up almost as quickly as food. . . . The Industrial Revolution has replaced all workmanship with labor, and the result has been that the things of the modern world have become labor products whose natural fate is to be consumed, instead of work products which are there to be used.[3]

This quotation explains literally as well as figuratively what we mean when we say that we now live in a consumer society. In the battle between what Arendt has labeled *Homo faber* (man the worker) and *animal laborans* (man as laborer), the laboring animal has won. We live in a throwaway world. Everything is to be consumed, nothing saved. But in the process of doing this, we have paid an enormous price. We have changed our normal work into labor. No one starts and finishes anything any more. We do little pieces, small, precise actions to produce things of no real value. We live in a world of paper towels and paper napkins, of built-in obsolescence. In the process, we have managed to destroy our pride in products and our joy in work. What has also resulted is the trivialization of work.

We have now degraded work in many of our industrial factories to the extent that our own product, the robot, works more efficiently than we do. The robotization of the assembly line may start a new age of liberating humankind from the pieces of work that are no longer creating whole things out of unwhole things. We have not yet gone that far. Instead, we are exporting this kind of labor to less developed countries and to less privileged people. We are closing our steel mills, reducing our assembly lines, and importing more and more of our products from the sweatshops of countries that are one or two generations behind us, either in their development or their aspirations. Still, ironically, most of us seek work and need work.

We are readjusting our economy to more technological ends, which demands a work force with a greater education and more technical skills. There is nothing new in this; surely something like it happened in the many generations that were necessary to bring us out of the caves and into the sunlight, although probably without the current speed of change, the modern condensation of time. All through history craftsmen and artisans existed who performed work that had meaning. There was a time when farmers worked rather than simply labored. Although they produced consumables, these were for others, not themselves, and they were building farms that would outlast themselves. They may have worked desperately hard, for example in the nineteenth century, a period that did not honor the sweat of their labor—a period of such vast class distinctions as to repel and disgust our modern imagination.

Yet the small farmer worked in a way that had its own nobility. It is good to plant seed, nurture it, see it grow, harvest it, to separate the chaff from the wheat, to produce a product of value and worth. Beginning with one season of planting and ending with another of harvest, it is good to take that wheat and mill it, grind it into flour, mix it with yeast and water, and bake it into bread. It is good to create food, to start with raw materials and end with a useful product. It was good for the artisan working in his shop to create a chair, a bench, a table, or, more elegantly, a violin or a cello, which would be used with pleasure and passed on after the death of its user to still another user, thus gaining a kind of immortality across cultures.

I do not mean to romanticize labor in primitive cultures. None of us would have wanted to be a serf in feudal times. There were always laborers, and most of humanity during this period only labored. But the emergence of a better, more egalitarian society should have produced a greater conversion of toil into work—not the opposite. There is something very sad in the way we lay waste our powers getting and spending for all of these artifices and gadgets whose only purpose is to satisfy status needs and in the process convert all work, that genuine source of pride, into common labor.

The conditions of unrewarding work are egalitarian. They exist for the privileged as well as the disenfranchised, for men as well as for women. Now that we have a labor force of both women and men, it will be a double tragedy if we are not able to reconstitute some of the aspects of work that support pride.

The answer to unrewarding labor is not "non-work." We know that although leisure time alleviates the strain of toil, it is not a substitute for the empowering aspects of work. It is true that, once we are freed of the constraints of earning money, many forms of volunteer work should be available. But the evidence emerging from experience with the population of the retired has not been encouraging. Retirement is simply a different form of agony for many men.

For *men*, even unrewarding work is better than no work at all. Work is necessary to supply the needs of survival. With luck it will provide him with some pleasure of mastery. But for *men*, unlike women, it fulfills a third essential purpose. It defines his manhood. Even when work has been stripped of all joy, even when alternative sources of income are available (a working wife), the idle man sees himself as an incomplete man. His ego, his essential self, demands that he be a breadwinner. The growing schism between the conditions of the real world and a man's self-image demands attention. We must liberate male pride from the role of worker, by supplying alternative structures that allow him to see himself as a "provider" and benefactor independent of his role as a wage-earner. Primitive societies often viewed the non-working elderly men with reverence and awe. They were models, teachers, sages. These were the repositories of knowledge and the transmitters of learned skills in an age before the written word made these roles obsolete. Some new and prideful use must be found for the man who, because of age or social conditions, can no longer work. Men need work, they shrivel and despair with the forced indolence and the symbolic meanings of both retirement and unemployment.

In the days when social legislation was first being considered to ease the misery of old age, the concept of a government-guaranteed retirement was created. When the principle of social security evolved in Germany at the turn of the century, it was decided to set the optimal retirement age at the median age at which people would normally be forced to retire because of disability. When German Social Security laws were first passed, that median age, at which half the population was disabled or unable to work, was sixty-five. The institution of retirement at sixty-five was then established—not arbitrarily, but with statistical validity.

In the 1930s, when America under the New Deal began to structure its Social Security system, the same sixty-five-year cutoff point seemed appropriate. No one at that time could have anticipated the dramatic progress in medicine after World War II, when medicine truly became a life-saving profession instead of merely a caring and comforting occupation. This medical progress caused a profound dislocation and conflict between the verities of age and the principle of retirement, making the social welfare programs of the New Deal counterproductive.

We are not only living longer; we are living healthier and "younger" for longer periods of time. If today we were planning a retirement based on the mean age of disability, we would set the age at *eighty-two!* This suggests two problems. First, the enormous burden of an aging population will rest on a young population, who must labor to support the Social Security system. Second, the so-called "free ride" of the now vital and not disabled elderly will extract its toll from them, too.

We know from early studies of retirement that some unexpected results occurred. Men, relieved of the burdens of modern labor, did not flourish. Depression and despair were more likely the lot of the

indolent human being, unless he could invent for himself a new occupation. Some found it in games. Those with sufficient income could
retire to the "work" of golfing, one of the most exasperating and demanding of tasks.

Women, on the other hand, tended to do much better in the post-
retirement period. For most of them, their "work" continued essentially
unchanged. They were not given the freedom of retirement, since they
were never paid for their labors or, for that matter, honored for them.
Women simply continued doing what they had always done—cooking,
cleaning, tending, if not their children their grandchildren now, or
perhaps an ailing spouse or parent.

At the same time, it is important to notice that such work was never
fragmented into meaningless parts. Women did actually both labor and
work. Given a choice of being an assembly-line worker (or beyond the
assembly-line worker, a pediatrician who spends his entire day examining well babies, with an occasional child in need of a standard remedy
of antibiotics) or a mother, I would much rather be a mother.
Provided—and what a proviso that is—that it paid the same, that it
commanded the same respect and honor, that it endowed one with the
same power.

In the early days of the feminist revolution, women assumed that
there was something noble about men's work and wanted their share
of the marketplace. But the intellectuals who led the feminist revolution
were thinking of the jobs that *they* could achieve—as senators, judges,
editors of magazines, surgeons. The average man, however, was working in the mills and the mines, or sorting envelopes in the post office.
This is the marketplace that most women are now entering. The irony
remains that with their final freedom, women are free to enter an area
that has been depleted of joy for most men.

But work—even when reduced to meaningless labor—is still a source
of self-respect for men. Most men still manage to derive some pride of
mastery in their work. They can find ways of making the performances
of even routine jobs important. I recall overhearing a delivery man

whose truck had been improperly loaded complaining—with thinly veiled pride—how the system had "collapsed" during his vacation. "Jesus Christ! Don't they know I've got to get the whites out before the ryes!" Yes, there is some pride left in work; but it is often a thin veneer that remains to protect the essential self.

Most of the pride that is left lies not so much in the work itself as in being a provider—in fulfilling one's manly responsibilities of caring for the wife and kids. In the tribal life from which we all have but recently emerged, the role of the man was clear. He had to be a warrior of courage and bravery, and he had to be a provider. Strength and courage must be combined with beneficence, generosity, and service.

The role of the warrior has little direct translation into the conditions of modern life. The role of the provider, on the other hand, is fully and well understood. Men work to support their basic survival and to support their needs and desires. Those needs and desires are part of an ego mechanism of status, competition, and establishment of self-worth. While no longer requiring a formal hunt, the workingman is still expected to "bring home the bacon" for his family. Although he increasingly shares this responsibility with women, the role of breadwinner is most central to a man's sense of pride. The loss of a job will always be interpreted by men as a failure of the essential self. When a man "fails" at work, he is failing in his fundamental role as a provider. His fear of this type of failure is equivalent to the terror the more primitive earlier man felt in seeing his food supply disappear. But he faces more than destitution—he faces humiliation. Although most work has been reduced to mere labor—a hunt without glory—its loss produces more than terror and anxiety. The loss of a job is not merely a financial blow but a blow to self-respect and pride—pride in being a worker, if not in the work itself.

In late twentieth-century America we do not, for the most part, allow people to starve: unemployment insurance, welfare aids, and various benevolent government institutions guarantee that the unemployed laborer and his family will generally not go hungry. Some, of course, still fall between the cracks. Yet, during the recession of the early 1990s, television screens were filled with poignant pictures of anguished unemployed mine and mill workers suddenly finding themselves unneeded and useless in industries that were under assault from more cost-efficient societies. The sense of despair, but even more, the sense of humiliation in the eyes of those blue-collar workers will not easily be forgotten by those of us who publicly viewed their shame.

What these workers had lost and mourned was certainly not the *pleasure* of work. Their jobs were miserable—they were the coal miners in the hills of Kentucky and steel workers in the mills of Gary, Indiana. These men did not enjoy their back-breaking toil and labor. Unemployment actually relieved these men of heavy burdens, but in their perceptions it deprived them of their manhood. It did not matter that there was bread in the house independent of a man's work; it was his *job* to supply food for his family. His pride, his identity, his masculinity, his ego were involved in *his* bringing home the food.

The role of the provider and the meaning of work have been neglected in modern psychological and sociological considerations of gender difference. There is still a difference in its significance for men and for women. Providing is a man's form of "mothering," of caring for the young. Working is man's form of nurturing.

The man's job in both his role as protector and provider is to "take care," in a particular masculine way; to provide for the safety of the helpless and dependent. The distinction between the caretaking of men and women is clear. The caretaking of the mother to the newborn infant is hands on: loving, warm, nurturing, caressing, *involved*. The "caring" of the father is one step removed: detached, distant, territorial, rather than direct and immediate. The male as warrior provided the safe environment for the care of the helpless infant; the male hunter provided the nurture.

With the decline of the warrior role in our society, the burden of manhood rested even more heavily on man the provider. Most men take their work very seriously indeed. Work is the way most of us make money, and money has an essential role to play in the average person's life. It pays the bills. It is the necessary commodity to sustain survival in a civilized society.

But money does more than pay the bills—it encompasses more than simply obtaining food and shelter. Money is the universal medium of exchange by which something we do or something we possess is transferred into something we want. And we want a great deal more than the necessities of survival. Money is involved in power, social position, status, and the establishment of ourselves and our worth in relationship to those about us. Dollars are power. Money buys everything from sex to public office. Money is the true instrument of power, and the bank account, as it swells, is the ultimate phallic representative.

The job confers special social status and power on the most successful. We have carried the trappings and the use of that special power to an extreme that would be ridiculous in a hunting society. We find ourselves working more for support of status needs than survival. And we pay an enormous price for this in premature deaths of men from hypertension, heart disease, and other stress-related phenomena. We cannot assert our masculinity directly in the ways that are most biologically satisfying—we can't "wrestle" for power; we have no rites that clearly label us "successful." The internal standards of success are almost impossible to reach in an upwardly mobile society where each step only brings into sight another step ahead. We drive ourselves to more and more accretions of useless and unusable things, whose primary purpose is a desperate attempt to establish our identity as powerful male providers, not only in the eyes of the world but in our own gut.

A man who loses his job—whatever it is—is faced with both the anxiety of being cut off from the supplies of survival, and the guilt of failure in one of his primary responsibilities. When a man loses his job, or even fails to advance in a job, this may be interpreted as a sign of his impotence. It erodes his self-respect and self-confidence, and can lead to depression and suicide. (In fact, the leading cause of suicide in men persists in being failure in the work place.)

Men love their children. They love their mates. But they endure their loss. Their self-respect is less threatened by the loss of loved ones than by their loss of status in the marketplace. The same is not true for women. Most important for those who would comfort men bedeviled by failure is this knowledge of how central work is to a man's identity. One might presume that love and understanding would compensate, as it often will for a woman. But a man in our society is rarely reassured or supported by such comforts. It is failure in work that destroys his sense of manhood, and there is rarely anything beyond work that can restore it.

A man can view himself as a failure in his lights while he seems so obviously a success by the norms of the world around him. We all live in a world of our own creation; reality exists only as perceived through the deceptive and distorting filter of our own imagination. Never mind that a man has $50 million. If he has seen the crumbling of an empire of $1 billion, he may perceive himself as humiliated, destitute, and an "economic" failure, despite the fact that his $50 million could easily generate an income of $3 million a year, more than most of us dream of accruing in a lifetime.

I have treated such men, and struggled with their depressions. In the course of depression they will literally see themselves as destitute. They will cry in anticipation of the humiliating ruin of their reputations in the newspapers and they will weep at the impending hunger—yes, hunger—of their children. I can think of at least a half dozen cases of patients of mine (all men) who had what can only be called "delusions of poverty," since even accepting the worst-case scenario of the bankruptcies of their business, the failure of all their hopes and aspirations, they would be left comfortably rich, as would their wives and children. Such men under the distortion of depression nihilistically visualize their downfall in primitive terms of homelessness and starvation.

Reduction in status means loss of power, failure as a man. This sense of personal failure can be experienced as deeply and painfully at a symbolic level as at the more fundamental level of failure to supply the needs of survival. Very few of us ever experience that failure. The scenes of the Great Depression, and books and works of art of that Depression, are the stuff of true tragedy. In our society, that sense of "tragic loss" can exist at a very high material level indeed.

Meaningful work is scarce. But even meaningless work is essential for male pride. Unemployment and premature retirement deprive a man of even the unrewarding labor of a technological age. He is no longer the protector. Increasingly, he is no longer the sole provider. And procreation is no longer highly prized. So, the three pillars of his essential pride system are now shaky and vulnerable. What, then, supports masculine pride? He is forced to turn to the narcissistic reassurances of "male jewelry" and the mock triumphs of "games."

PART III
▶▶▶▶▶▶▶▶▶▶▶

SUPPORTING THE MALE EGO

9 ▸ MALE JEWELRY

In pursuit of a sense of superiority, men create categories and castes. Men look for statements to announce their credentials. The English have it easy. They are constantly conferring titles. A "Sir" before the name is a tonic for the ego. Public announcement is the ultimate purpose of jewelry. It is the adult equivalent of the little boy proudly displaying his erection. It adorns and announces a level of power or prestige.

We love to be admired! Within every human being is a need to feel important, special, one of a kind. And we are. Human variations exceed those of any other species. Other species, exposed to the differing conditions of Antarctica and Africa, will form subspecies. The human being, with his capacity to accommodate his environment to his physiology, has remained a single species of all sizes, shapes, and colors.

Despite our variability we are also cognizant of some likeness to our fellows, and we have a need to assert our individualism—to stand out in a crowd. Generalizations offend us. And rightly so. In common speech they are a means of diminishing an individual. People (other than sociologists) who generalize about blacks, Jews, Hispanics are generally ignoring the individual and stereotyping him. We do not want to be conceived of as "typically" anything. We want to be respected for ourselves.

In the Western democracies we have the most individualistic societies ever created. These societies compound the psycho-biological need to establish a "sense of self" by generating values in which autonomy and the individual are often dangerously placed above the society or the common good. Probably the most individualistic creature evolved is the twentieth-century American.

This individualistic society is a mixed blessing. The unlimited conditions available for achievement and advancement make it harder, not easier, to stand out. *Everyone* is racing forward. If everyone is breaking away, then one must run hard to simply keep pace. We are left with a steady measure of insecurity about our own special worth. To stand out, to emerge, to sustain self-respect requires prodigious effort.

Beyond the need to feel important is the need for respect. We require reassurances that our particular value is recognized by others. We need means to announce our importance and to receive acknowledgment of it in the respectful glances of our cohorts. To these ends, we human beings have invented the status symbol. We have discovered "jewelry" and its multiple variations.

All of these props—the jewelry, the trophies, the metaphors, the uniforms, the signs, signals, and symbols—are desperate attempts to achieve status. They are all signs of the fragility of the male ego.

Well before the discovery of bronze, silver, gold, and various forms of wrought jewelry, such materials as nuts, berries, seeds, stones, shells, feathers, animal teeth, bones, and ivory were used for adornment. The wearing of jewelry actually antedates the wearing of clothing. It is likely that the first users were men, not women, since the primary purpose of such adornment was to make an announcement. Jewelry was then, as now, a "fashion statement." It advertised the affluence and position—and by implication the power which accrues from these—of the wearer.

Over the centuries, cycles of fashion have changed. In certain periods men adopted the role of the finely feathered, heavily adorned gender.

This alternated with periods in which it was considered "unseemly" or "unmanly" for men to adorn themselves. But even in puritanical periods of self-effacement, men found a way. They invented the metaphorical jewelry of titles, honors, orders, and badges. Still it is worth examining what real jewelry men in our culture are prepared to wear as a guide to understanding the wheres and whys of fashion. The need for stature and public respect is an inborn part of male psychology, and the more disadvantaged one feels, the greater the pressure to establish "presence."

Rich men do not wear gold chains and bracelets; the poor do—or aspire to. In a world of poverty, there is no disdain for expensive material goods. The real thing is still more important than the symbol and more is always better. Jewelry here means real jewelry, although the poor will also add a symbolic value to the real. Some material things speak louder than others. It is the heavier gold chain that carries clout—it is so outrageously self-indulgent. Children in inner-city schools are literally killed for the gold chains around their necks or their "Oakleys" (sunglasses), "Eightballs" (jackets), and Air Jordans (sneakers at $200 a pair). Fashion dictates each year's luxury symbol. Where they get the money for these items is a sociological question that warrants asking. *Why* they spend this amount to establish status is intrinsic to understanding the male ego.

There were other eras in which men spent lavish fortunes on themselves. One thinks of the court of Louis XIV, *Le Roi Soleil*, in which the extravagance of Versailles was so great that it bankrupted a significant number of the nobility. Here indulgence and wealth were essential to maintain the fashion set by the king. This required crass materialistic outlay for men, women, children, and households. It was important that your liveried servants be dressed almost as elegantly as yourself; a horse's harness became a form of reckless display and advertisement of station. So great was the damage done to the nobility that some historians have theorized that this was a stroke of genius on the part of Louis XIV. By such fashion he kept the nobility on the verge of bankruptcy, maintaining the balance of power in favor of the monarchy over the ever-threatening nobility and landed gentry.

Even today we have examples in our adult population of peacocks of glorious display. Liberace, Mr. T., and Sammy Davis, Jr., would not have dreamed of appearing in public without first adorning themselves with the traditional trappings of jewelry: gold, sequins, feathers, and furs. To look at them one would have thought these were the wealthiest men in the United States. But none of them ever made the Forbes 500 list. They were representatives of a subculture with its own standards, denizens of the demimonde of entertainment.

In the business community, material things are also a sign of wealth. But they must be articulated in a softer tone; they must be more subtle, more tangential, less obvious. The entertainers address the public at large, including large populations of the poor and aspiring. They are symbolic representatives of what poor men think riches mean.

The bourgeoisie and the affluent disdain the standards of hoi polloi but just as desperately seek approval of their own kind. They also wish to announce the ease with which their wealth permits them to divert energy and funds toward totally useless things. But they must find a less blatant way of "showing off." There was a time when one did not have to announce the manufacturer or designer of one's clothing. The cut of cloth spoke for itself. But men, following the lead of women, have begun to be insecure enough to wear their labels on the outside. A little Polo player attached to a knit shirt allows for a one hundred percent premium in the selling price, and announces to the world at large that you have been willing to spend double the shirt's value because you have the money and don't care. This public announcement is a significant digression from practices of even fifty years ago. Sooner or later, a host of men eager for status will show up with the little Polo player insignia on their breast. When the "club" becomes crowded, it loses its exclusivity. Finding status symbols that will "sit still" is difficult. Gradually the masses encroach, and one is driven ever forward in a quest not only to keep up with the Joneses but to surpass them.

Prestige is composed of a number of different values, noble or contemptible, depending on which groups are involved. But one aspect common to all is that the label must imply a limited number of members, it must suggest a concept of exclusivity. It must elevate the man above the common host. Expense would seem to set a boundary for exclusivity. Everyone can stretch to afford a Polo shirt, but not a gold Rolex. A careful course must be steered, however, between the Scylla of popular usage and the Charybdis of ostentation. A Piaget and a Porsche are acceptable; yet in some circles either one of these might be considered excessive. Surely the Piaget should not be embellished with diamonds; and when the Porsche becomes a Lamborghini or a Rolls-Royce, one is skirting the border of excessive display. It is not easy for the rich.

Since women are often still treated as adornments, a safe alternative is to lavish jewelry on one's wife. If a wealthy man cannot wear a mink coat, and up until very recently he could not, his wife certainly could. So sables, lynx, and fishers; emeralds, sapphires, and rubies; sequins, laces, and gold lamé were conveniently draped on one's accompanying wife or lady friend.

Clothing can be a form of adornment for men, but designer shirts and sweaters represent a very limited wardrobe. Dress does not have to be an extravagant embellishment whose intrinsic value represents specific dollars of outlay. A uniform can establish status in a different way. There has always been a uniform defining each social sphere. A certain amount of individuality—even kookiness—is allowed, but always within the boundaries set by the peer group. Everyone pretends to a streak of nonconformity because nonconformity has traditionally been accepted as a virtue. But the limits of nonconformity are as precisely defined as parochial school uniforms. One need only look at the cabinet meetings of any modern President to see the pitiful conformity of these men. Who knows where they went to school? Who cares? Texas Tech, Princeton, Alabama, Stanford. The men around the President adapt to his image.

Uniforms may be made of cheap, inexpensive material and common design, but if they are "old school ties" they are beyond purchase. Precisely because no amount of money can buy the school or club tie, it establishes the ultimate status—an unpurchasable rank.

Clearly, in the military, uniforms denote rank. The admiral's dress blues are made of the same material as the ensign's, and except for the additional gold bars and scrolls may cost no more. The purpose of the uniform is to establish immediate presence. One salutes the uniform, not the man in it.

Our world is filled with appropriate uniforms often only identifiable to that small and exclusive population who "count"—those who share the same values and the same environment. Each culture designs its own uniforms. Dress of any sort can advertise the social status of the individual and can be a powerful instrument of socialization.

There are types of "uniforms." The first is the objective, actual dress code of the military or the school. The second is a uniform imposed by rigid social mores within the group. The dress code of peers is as rigidly enforced as the formal one. The parent who tries to buck the styles inherent in the high school culture of his son or daughter is fighting a losing battle. In that world, the child knows what is de rigueur, and humiliation follows that child who either does not know or is forced to violate the standards of his or her subculture.

One of the more enduring memories of my youth was my exposure to the "dress code" at Harvard. One place where "proper" dress was publicly announced was the dining hall. The wearing of coats was mandatory. I remember arriving in mid-February, being a "mid-semester" boy during the war, and reading outside the dining room of Eliot House a sign saying: "Coats will be worn at all meals." I misread the word "Coats." In Ohio, we called them "jackets," and while I had one, it was arriving later with my "fancy clothes" rather than my every-day dress. The language barrier was quickly overcome, but since I didn't have a coat by their definition, in order not to break the rules or be humiliated, I wore the coat I had—a heavy winter overcoat—to every breakfast, lunch, and dinner during a weekend of misery. This was the only official dress requirement; the unofficial ones were more extensive. This was not a parochial school where little navy jackets and white shirts were required. Here was, presumably, a sophisticated, democratic, heterogeneous community whose purposes were beyond the mundane vanities of fashion. Or so one would have thought. The indecently rapid transformation of a polyglot group of seventeen-year-old boys from the farms of Iowa, the cities of Chicago or Detroit, and the suburbs of San Francisco into the image of the children of Boston Brahmins proved otherwise.

We arrived not knowing the rules. The acceptable fashions were set at Exeter, St. Paul's, and Groton—schools of which I had never even heard. The fashion established in those eastern prep schools would very quickly influence my own dress.

I came to Harvard as a freshman, with little money but an adequate wardrobe of Shetland sweaters, white shirts, trousers, a pair of brown shoes for everyday and a pair of black shoes for dress, the "uniform" of my high school. That was it. Very quickly it became apparent that in order to meld with the crowd I would have to change my plumage. Surprisingly, it was not always upward.

No one seemed to have heard of either black or brown shoes. The shoes to be worn were white bucks, the dirtier the better, with red gum soles. The distinction between dress shoes and everyday was unknown. Proper pants were chinos: they were cheap. No one wore sweaters and the "coat" of choice was a beat-up Harris Tweed jacket with patches on the elbows, worn with chinos during the day and dark gray flannel slacks for fancier occasions. A suit was necessary and this was an expensive item. It had to be gray, very dark gray, single-breasted, and purchased either at Brooks Bros., J. Press, or Chips, the only firms at that time designing suits with the loose fit then known as "Ivy League."

Through hardship, by scrounging and cadging, after four months most students assembled a proper "uniform," and one could not tell, by haircut or dress at least, the hick from the haute monde. Every man can define the "dress code" of his own school for his own time.

Beyond clothes, there are other signs that reveal money and status. Strip a man of his clothes, put him on a beach in bathing trunks, and there will still be ways in which one can tell.

I recall an incident in Colorado during a series of academic meetings. After a particularly hot summer session, I went to a public swimming pool. The area was close to a large military installation and it was clear that most of the men at the pool were military men. This was apparent by the age—all were young—and the haircuts, which tended to be much shorter than the styles of the time. What was equally apparent was that this was a place visited primarily by enlisted men, not officers—they were blue collar in background.

The number of gold chains worn around the neck were not a sign of affluence but of poverty. They were the uniform of a working-class group. The presence of tattoos, another form of adornment, indicated a greater class distinction. But beyond that, other less tangible indices were present. Bad teeth and bad complexions tend to be more numerous in the poor than the rich. Dental care is expensive and prophylactic— future-oriented. The future is always a luxury of the wealthier classes. The poor are too trapped in the present to worry about the future. Orthodontia, caps, all the paraphernalia of modern dentistry give way among the poor to missing teeth and cheap fillings. A clear complexion is somewhat more confusing to me. I presume it is a matter of care and nutrition, and it may be a less reliable guide. Farmers' sunburns, on the other hand, red necks and red arms below the elbows, tend to be a giveaway for the man who labors with his hands and out of doors. This is in contrast to the year-round Palm Beach tans that adorn the jet-setters. Even in the so-called "classless society" of the United States there are indices of the class from which one comes.

Unlike poor boys, the rich do not kill each other for jewelry, but rich men often kill *themselves* for items of material standing. There are material possessions that are permissible within the bounds of conservative "good taste." There are approved things to own that announce one's wealth. The beach house in East Hampton or Newport; the ski lodge in Aspen, Sun Valley, or St. Moritz; the villa in Tuscany or Provence; and the staffs to fill all those places. And the private planes to get there. All can become a burden, even for the very rich. They demand a leveraged existence. Debt becomes a legitimate part of that way of life, and subjects even the Donald Trumps of the world to the extreme vulnerability of financial ruin in the midst of splendor.

We must leave the world of material things, however, to see the most pervasive evidences of male jewelry in our culture.

In 1682, Peter, the youngest child of Czar Alexis, was named czar of all the Russias. The next ten years saw turmoil, political struggle, coups, and treachery. Peter's life was in constant danger, and for at least half the period he was in virtual exile or a prisoner in a suburb of Moscow.

For these fourteen years Peter was surrounded by a group of European advisers—Dutch, Scots, French, and Swiss—who tantalized him with visions of a world only hundreds of miles away but centuries away in manners and forms. Peter learned from these foreigners. From the Dutch, he developed a fascination with ships which led him to establish his great seaport in the north, St. Petersburg. And from Louis XIV (through French representatives) Peter learned the enormous power of vanity and the value of narcissistic rewards.

Russia was in a state of almost continual warfare at the time. Political intrigue was rife. Enemies must be punished and friends must be rewarded. The rewards exacted by triumphant generals were enormous: thousands of acres of land, sable skins by the hundreds, emeralds and rubies, and, most valuable of all, thousands of serfs might be given to a successful general in appreciation for his victories and payment for his future loyalty.

Louis XIV had little money to spend on his minions. More important, he did not wish to make them rich. In fact, he wished to enslave them by poverty. What Peter learned from Louis is that material goods are treasured mainly as adornment—a self-advertisement of affluence and power. Louis solved the problem of conserving his wealth and flattering his nobles by the ingenious device of creating orders and decorations in lieu of sharing his actual wealth. Thus Peter the Great, too, learned the power of the symbol: the Legion of this and the Order of that. All could be achieved with minimal expenditure, yet all would confer a *visible* distinction on the bearer. One had only to see the anointed to know that he was a favorite of the king and therefore a power. Why waste money? Jewelry could be purchased independently by others not privy to the czar's favor. The new rewards were ranks and honors: the blue sash, a crimson rosette, a medallion or even, simply, a title. Dukes and counts were created by Peter at a rate equivalent to the expansion of vice presidents at an advertising agency or radio network or bank.

Modern society abounds in such trophies and honors. A Nobel Prize in science is coveted by every researcher, and would be sought as zealously if it paid only a token number of dollars or none at all. It is the most exclusive of clubs, and it is exclusive in the way that defines its value, i.e., the recipients are perceived as being the most distinguished of their peers.

From this "sublime" one can descend to the "ridiculous" as represented by the legions of officers in clubs, lodges, and fraternities, whose primary purpose may be the creation of such hierarchies.

With children it is easy. Gold stars on school papers, listings or honor rolls will say the equivalent of "Bravo." Sports trophies are particularly prized. Dinky though they may be, they will rest in a place of honor on the bookshelves of hundreds of thousands of boys. Tennis, soccer, chess, spelling, even attendance awards are marks of superior effort recognized.

By the time everybody becomes a member of the club, the club is seen as not worth joining. Two common stories illustrate this: Groucho Marx's famous line that he would never join a club that would accept someone like him as a member is further amplified by the apocryphal (I dearly hope) British lord who, on approaching middle age, despaired of the corruption of the class system in England. "Everybody" could now gain access to the patronage lists of the queen and the once exclusive clubs of England. To rectify this, he devoted the remainder of his life to the establishment of a club for true aristocracy. He combed the ranks of his acquaintances from the ancient families with the bluest of blood and came up with a potential membership list of twenty. Studying the list over the years, he began slowly to eliminate one name after another, reaching for perfection. Finally, after years of effort, he found his list reduced to but one name—his own. Contemplating his own name and his own life just before his death, he reluctantly drew a blue pencil through this final entry.

The concept of exclusivity is eminently corruptible by snobbery. If a man cannot measure his superiority by actual achievements, how is he to establish that he is better than those around him? He does so by creating an artificial measure. He creates the "in-group." He establishes a club. What, after all, is the benefit of a membership in a snobby, exclusive, and bigoted organization like the Bohemia Club in San Francisco or the Meadow Club in Southampton? The food is not necessarily better than the local restaurants or the other clubs around; the surroundings are not any more lavish; the facilities are no more sybaritic than in less exalted places.

In these establishments one is assured that only one's "own kind" will be present. Is this truly to protect yourself from the contamination, the fear, the threat of a Jew or an Afro-American? Not really. One may do business with a Jew, work with an Afro-American, actually take orders or borrow money from a man of Italian descent. It is not for protection from the contaminating presence of minorities that these clubs are created. Rather, they are an announcement of caste and position. By exclusion, they create an illusion of superiority for the in-crowd.

Many people of "lower caste" are "friends" but they must not become members of the club. William Paley was excluded from the North Shore country clubs in his neighborhood. His stepchildren, genetically bearing blood as blue as the bluest North Shore family (Mortimers and Cushings), were contaminated by his Jewish link and could only attend the local club when invited by their cousins, in-laws, and next-door neighbors, the Whitneys.

In a world that challenges self-importance, that undermines self-esteem, that terrifies by the threat of egalitarianism, and that eventually leads to the devastating common denominator that is death, some prop to the ego must be afforded. Exclusivity allows for that. It is an exclusivity based on prejudice and bigotry, since the very definitions that determine who is excluded from the group will be the artifacts of a vulgarian mind.

These clubs are in form nothing but an extension of the kids' gangs that exist in junior high schools and high schools across the country—the Black Diamonds, the Enforcers, the Dragons. Children would seem to have better reasons for joining such clubs than adults. In childhood, there is a hunger for belonging, an anxiety at being adrift with no identity, a need for security, and a fear of the expansive unknown where dangerous enemies lurk. These anxieties should pass with the security and status of adulthood. That they often do not indicates the insecurity of many adults. There are men with memberships in golf clubs too numerous for them to play at. It is the membership list, rather than the opportunity to play, that is important.

Men originally joined clubs for other reasons than ego props. The initial purpose may have been, like the child's, a desire for male companionship, which then became adulterated for the purposes of ego enhancement. Golf clubs are not terribly different from bowling leagues. Their intention was to bring together a group of men who shared a common interest.

But golf clubs became country clubs, a place where one could bring one's family. Tennis courts and swimming pools were built and became the center of social life. Then, beyond the purpose of male bonding, the concept of "our kind" was introduced—and all the biases of the culture streamed forth. Recently, with the commercialization of golf on television and the vulnerability of advertisers to manipulation, pressure has been exerted to open up these bastions of bias.

There are clubs and associations defined to identify true merit, and to honor such merit with public recognition. I am using the term "clubs" loosely here to include organizations like Phi Beta Kappa or its predecessor in high school, the Honor Society; membership in the Academy of Science, Institute of Medicine, or Academy of Arts. These are presumably honors in recognition of achievement. That these, too, are corruptible, purchasable, and the product of politics and fashion is only too apparent by examining those who became Nobel Prize winners in literature as distinguished from science. Where are Tolstoi, Proust, Joyce, and D. H. Lawrence? Replaced by Mommsen, Eucken, Carducci, and Spitteler!

Exclusivity and exclusive institutions are artificial means to counter the assaults on our ego by the implacable forces of modern society. At least temporarily, in an isolated and mean-spirited way, we can feel superior. We build a wall and a gate and pass out keys to a limited number; then we look over the gate, feeling that somehow or other those on the outside are disadvantaged or deprived.

Sadly, those outside often see this to be the case too, and will struggle to get inside, unaware that one carries one's insecurities within one's head and heart wherever one goes. Exclusivity can eventually deteriorate into overt bigotry. Jean-Paul Sartre said in his brilliant essay on anti-Semitism: "If the Jew did not exist, the antisemite would invent him."[1]

The hated person is not really the bigot's problem, but part of the solution to a problem he has with himself. Some people—frustrated, angry, and feeling impotent—have to find someone to look down on and to hate. The despised group must not be perceived as simply an object of anger but understood as an instrument for release from painful tensions within oneself. One expert expressed it well: "The hatred of the out-group serves the function of supporting the person who entertains it. However spurious the relief that comes from this type of defense, it is a vitally important function in the psychic economy of the insecure person. It is easier to reject others than to reject oneself."[2]

Bigotry is one of the many devices used for handling impotent rage and fear of inadequacy. No man can go through life distrusting and loathing himself. He is dependent on that self from whom he can never escape. So he must find some means of denying the inadequacy and self-contempt that he contains. By projecting them onto others, he rids himself of self-loathing and elevates himself at the expense of the other.

Gordon Allport, in his pioneering treatise on the nature of prejudice, stated that "The net effect of prejudice . . . is to place the object of prejudice at some disadvantage not merited by its own misconduct."[3]

The purpose of prejudice expressed in the necessity of finding scapegoats is to protect the bigot's damaged self-image and fragile self-respect. By creating a despised minority, he can adopt the fallacious assumption that someone else must be responsible for everything. If your life is miserable, if you feel weak and helpless, you can create not just one person but a whole class on whom you can blame all the miseries of your existence. We protect ourselves by assigning the guilt to some group of others before they can assign it to us, or before we ourselves are forced to look into that abyss that is our internal soul. To do this, we create a deprecated or despised minority. Of course it doesn't work. It really solves no problems. A man will still carry within himself, only somewhat disguised, a clinging anxiety about his own capacities.

What we now call "sexism" is not traditional bigotry. It is not the same as our attitude toward a despised minority. Sexism starts with the need for a boy to detach himself from things that are womanly; girls and girlish things are treated with contempt, and boys who like to do girlish things are taunted and truly despised. The spillover from the woman's activity to the woman herself is almost predictable. This is, however, complicated because underneath the activities that lead to the rejection of womanly things lies a deep, abiding affection for women— which must accommodate to the fear of her reasserting her original authority. Men find it easier to control and then diminish women in their eyes rather than confront their own latent anxiety.

The same men who may be the most condescending to women in public may defer to the authority of their wives in private. A caricature of this is seen in the Japanese culture, where women are ignored or even excluded in social settings. Traditional Japanese women were trained to be deferential in the presence of men. Yet in the privacy of the household the woman is often the unquestionable authority.

Most men continue to have difficulty with their relationships with women, juggling the awe and reverence indoctrinated in early life with the contempt and disdain necessary to assert their rejection of womanly things. The adoption of a typically male attitude toward women must be seen as the misdirected adoption of a mantle of authority.

Even in American life, one sees the rituals. The liberated women in the suburbs who commute with their husbands, often to equally important jobs, will almost inevitably sit in the passenger seat while their husband occupies his position, literally and figuratively, "in the driver's seat." At commuter stations one sees women who do not work, driving to the station to meet their husbands, and then, awkwardly, maneuvering themselves to the opposite side so that the husband can drive the three minutes from the station home.

In the business world a whole vocabulary of jewelry equivalents exists. As is appropriate for a phallic symbol, size is always important. Every square inch added to a man's office is seen as an acknowledgment of his superiority to the pack. We are back to the tape measure, seeing, in the language of Salomon Brothers, how "big a dick" we can swing. There are all sorts of subtle variations. A corner office is a major statement. How many corners are there on a floor? If not a corner office, how many windows? Is there carpet on the floor? A key to a private executive bathroom? A private bathroom itself? A secretary, who by the fact that she is a reflection of the self, must herself have more space, a bigger desk, a choicer location than others' secretaries?

But the preeminent symbol of love and approval, of respect and admiration in the business, is a batch of "pink roses." A man can be kept happy if when he comes to work in the morning, he finds a display of a dozen or two roses on his desk. But these roses are not cut from the bushes and delivered by florists. They are the little pink notes on one's desk announcing the telephone calls that must be returned. Men will bitch and moan about the fact that they "can't clear their desks," but the man who comes in and fails to find a quantity of notes on his desk begins to feel unwanted and unpopular. There is nothing more reassuring than observing a grand display of messages announcing people who want to reach you, who are waiting to hear from you, who need something from you. The sign of the failing executive is the diminished number of tributes on his desk.

The standard way of humiliating a man who has a powerful fixed contract and therefore must be either paid off or forced to resign is to clear his desk of "roses." We do not load him up with odious duties. A member of the executive committee cannot be asked to clean the toilets—that would be unseemly. We cannot compromise the status of the position he holds. That would threaten those who survive by virtue of the fear and respect in which such positions are held. He is, after all, a member of the club, and one must protect all members from even indirect public humiliation. What can one do, then, to get a chief financial officer to resign? You can cut off his balls—not literally, of course. We don't live in a society uncivilized enough to express things so directly. We find a metaphorical way to castrate him, we "cut him out of the loop." Meetings are held to which he would normally be invited; he receives no notification. Memoranda are sent directly from his superior to his underlings. Those who normally reported to him now report to someone else, and if it is someone who formerly held a somewhat lower ranking position, there is an added humiliation. One leaves him in his large office with the four windows, the carpeted floor, the big desk—and a sense of total isolation and emptiness. The "pink roses" are withdrawn. All his calls are shunted. He has no responsibilities except to pick up his monthly paycheck of $50,000. But no amount of pay is sufficient to make such utter humiliation endurable. The feeling of uselessness, of being passed by, is usually sufficient to soften up any man for renegotiation of his termination agreement.

The ultimate status symbol for men has always been women. In primitive times, one knew the power and station of a chief by the number of wives he could afford. Women were, after all, luxury items. They had to be fed and properly clothed. In addition they were breeders, and a man with many wives would have many children, all of whom must be fed, clothed, and protected.

More flamboyant countries than ours continue to maintain this tradition. In *The New York Times*, Philip Shenon described how the general who led a military coup in Thailand was

> finding his position undermined in a wife-vs.-mistress scandal that has offered a rare, very public glimpse of Thailand's system of near-legalized polygamy. . . .
>
> Mistresses are to some degree a demonstration of wealth, and as a rule, the more mistresses, the wealthier the man. A handful of Bangkok's flashier millionaires are said to have 10 or more extramarital companions. . . .
>
> What is usually required in these relationships, and what has been entirely lacking in the romantic triangle involving General Sunthorn, is a sense of decorum.[4]

We in the West live in a monogamous culture. Nonetheless, women still remain a narcissistic embellishment for men. In high school, just as the football player is the epitome of the desirable male, the cheerleader or her equivalent is the prestige item for the boy. Later, men may find supports for their ego through infidelity, but the nature of infidelity is that it must be kept quiet. Infidelity is not technically an adornment. Jewelry must be worn and displayed. The adult equivalent of the cheerleader can be seen in the role that models play in the life of the successful bachelor. A beautiful hooker will not suffice. She can be purchased at a price too many other men can afford. There exist a demimonde of women who cannot quite be labeled as prostitutes since they are bought for non-fixed prices at a very elevated level. They exist to be beautiful and dated by wealthy men. Some of them through marriage may even gain entry to the world of respectability. Above them are the starlets or the beautiful creatures of the "social" scene: models, actresses, self-made or media-made, semi-public figures. These women are the ribbons, sashes, rosettes that men love to "wear" in public places.

In New York, at least, a peculiar phenomenon seems to epitomize the woman as decoration—the "tall blond shiksa" syndrome. In New York during the seventies and eighties there was a rash of short, powerfully affluent, often Jewish men who shed their wives of twenty-five or thirty years to become involved with younger women. This event is hardly unique and occurs all over the country. What struck people as statistically odd was the number of short men that were involved, and the fact that the women were not only twenty or thirty years younger but also tended to be blond, preferably WASP, and six or seven inches taller. The assumption here was that a man advertises his virility by showing that he can attract a woman much his junior. He can deny any stigma to his height by displaying the tall, stunning, and therefore conspicuous woman on his arm. Here is a woman, he announces to the world at large, who is younger, taller, whom a man would fight for. She has chosen me. Or, more to the point, I have chosen her—and prevailed. Such is my power and appeal. Do not, therefore, judge my "stature" by my height.

The phenomenon goes well beyond short Jewish New York men. The tall blond shiksa may be considered a metaphor for the second wife, whose primary purpose is to reassure an aging man that he is not losing his sex appeal, publicly to state that he is still sexually attractive, still desirable, and finally, to deny the awareness of the end of life and impending death that is insinuating itself into his consciousness.

The women who enter such relationships seem to be abandoning sexual appetite and sexual pleasure for material possession. It seems to me a poor trade-off. But time and again I have heard women deny the mercenary calculus I had placed on the event. There was no trade-off, they insisted. What I failed to understand was that, to some women, power is an aphrodisiac. A powerful man is as "sexy," though in a different way, as a powerfully built man. These women claimed to be truly attracted to such men, and while not unaware of the luxuries that came with the package, they were not selling themselves. They were having their cake and eating it too.

We should be grateful to those who use their wealth for the public good and decency. Generosity is a virtue we ought to respect. There is much honorable motivation underlying philanthropic and charitable contributions—everything does not have to be unconsciously motivated, and even when unconsciously motivated, acts should be judged on the basis of the consequences of the action. Nevertheless, the underlying dynamics at work here are worth examining.

Death cannot be denied. With aging, individuals—particularly those of wealth—begin to look for forms of immortality. The assumption is that Andrew Carnegie the steel magnate might be forgotten, but one cannot forget the Carnegie Institutions or the Carnegie Libraries. The "name" will be perpetuated. Not only will his name be immortalized but it will be associated with the trait of benevolence. If the name is on a public building, whether it is Zeckendorf Plaza, Duke University, or the Millstein Hospital Wing (advertised by gigantic illuminated letters that shadow its subservience to the Columbia-Presbyterian Hospital group), a certain immortality is presumed to be guaranteed. Of course, it does not necessarily work out that way. People riding up Madison Avenue do not normally think of James Madison any more than people walking down Houston Street in any way feel the glorification of Sam Houston. The number of plaques in the Metropolitan Museum are beyond tallying and beyond notice. The poet Shelley described the futility of such immortality:

> "My name is Ozymandias, king of kings:
> Look on my works, ye Mighty, and despair!"

> *Nothing beside remains. Round the decay*
> *Of that colossal wreck, boundless and bare,*
> *The lone and level sands stretch far away.*

If the statues do not disappear, the names may become unrecognizable on the markers; or, if recognizable, may be dissociated from the person for whom they were supposed to produce eternal glory.

For a genuine image of power that supports his self-esteem, a man cannot accrue assets selfishly. Since part of one's ego must be built on a sense of one's own decency, goodness, and beneficence, philanthropy becomes a means of transforming us into the good person we wish to be. Throughout history the great earner, the great accumulator of fields and properties, was not the most respected; rather, it was the provider who was respected. One of the limits set on the desire for power, and one of the respectable boundaries to greed, is the need to be seen by others and ourselves as generous. The virtue of generosity and the fact of generosity are deeply embedded in our culture.

This can of course lead to freewheeling spending, where extravagance becomes foolhardy. Yet most of us tend to respect the reckless provider more than the prudent miser. Many crimes are worse than stinginess, but few character traits are more insufferable. The parsimonious, un-giving, anal-retentive individual, who measures out his life in coffee-spoons of giving and receiving, is an almost intolerable companion. The check grabber is still preferable to the slow-handed protester.

One of the most bizarre cultural evolutions reflecting the relationship between generosity and manliness is the potlatch, a ceremony associated with the Pacific Coast Indians of Canada. The entire society is based on the public disposal of wealth. Status in the community demands that one must be a giver of extraordinary means. In a great potlatch celebration, the host will give his guests—who may include his enemies—his most valuable possessions, possessions for which he had labored for years. In the same vein he may take treasured copper plates and conspicuously destroy them. This is carried to such ludicrous lengths that a lifetime of savings may be destroyed or given away in one potlatch, totally impoverishing the individual.

In a corruption of its original intention, the potlatch became a means of destroying one's enemies. Since reciprocity is the fundamental principle of the potlatch, no recipient was allowed to refuse a gift, and every receiver of gifts was expected to hold his own potlatch and to return presents *in kind*. This became a clever means of bankrupting your enemy by giving him more than he could afford to give back without completely devastating his household. Nonetheless, the potlatch signifies that respect is gained in this culture through the disposal of wealth rather than its accumulation. One can infer that a contempt for material things was seen as a form of nobility, particularly when it was combined with the other virtue of generosity.[5]

A contempt, or pretended indifference, for material things is part of a Puritan strain that runs through many cultures, parallel to materialism and acquisitiveness. An extreme example can be seen in Henry James's *Portrait of a Lady*. Isabel Archer, a naive and beautiful young American, is exposed to the vagaries of the European culture. Awed but repelled by society's elaborate enslavement to fashion and fashionability, she falls in love with Gilbert Osmond, who represents to her the epitome of the independent man, disdaining public fashion and living by his own values rather than others. So attracted is she to the purity of this emotion and the virtuous adherence to standards above the need to impress that she enters into a disastrous marriage with Osmond. Shortly after marriage, she realizes that his manner represented the ultimate pose: "Under all his culture, his cleverness, his amenity, under his good-nature, his facility, his knowledge of life, his egotism lay hidden like a serpent in a bank of flowers."[6] Osmond's entire life had been devoted to creating this image of superiority and independence, ironically revealing the ultimate narcissist who gains awe and approval by establishing an identity as a man above any need for approval.

This phenomenon is the basis of all reverse snobbism—of the love by the wealthy for old clothes and beat-up possessions. In the fine gradation of automobile possession one can trace the fall of the Cadillac as the car of the rich and affluent. It became suspect when a glitziness began to suggest that it was a car of the parvenu. The rich then embraced the conservative and (then) unostentatious Mercedes. Even at a lower level of affluence there is the nonchalant disregard "for public opinion" that ends in slavish adherence to the opinion of a smaller public.

Narcissistic pleasures almost always serve to relieve anxiety or insecurity. They include most of the quick-fix pleasures of modern life. Male jewelry—in all of its forms—is the product of narcissistic pleasure. A compliment, an honor, even a good review can give a momentary sense of well-being and self-enlargement, but these are not the stuff of real security or real pleasure.

Every adult knows a small child who drags around his so-called "security blanket." Or he may have had a pacifier stuck in his mouth to make him feel safe and comfortable. The adult man, just like the child, has his "passies" and "blankies." The "pacifier" may be as simple-minded as a cigar (large and expensive) or as complicated as the special deferential treatment accorded in restaurants that are only available to a man of his means. The "security blankets" are more often than not bank books and stock holdings. In the competitive world of high rollers, everything is measurable in terms of relative power: the private plane, the size of the plane, the role of club memberships, the collections of "things." There are tilt points in our lives where reassurance, support, reward, all of the so-called "positive reenforcements," are helpful. But if they are to be effective in the long haul, they must operate by encouraging the *activities* or the *relationships* that are the true materials out of which we build the sense of self.

Narcissistic pleasures are inevitably the extras. Put the maraschino cherry on top of the ice cream sundae if you must, but do not confuse either with the true nutrients of life. As adjuncts, narcissistic pleasures may serve a purpose by temporarily rescuing us from self-doubt, but they cannot build true self-esteem or self-confidence. Used as alternatives to genuine pleasures, they inevitably deprive us of those aspects of experience that truly nourish pride. When we sacrifice true pleasure for the pleasures of status and reassurance, we are striking an abysmally bad bargain.

The narcissist is a cracked vessel that can never be filled. No amount of applause, status symbols, or external rewards will ever fill the leaking cistern that is the ego of the narcissist. Too many men will wake in the twilight of their lives, surrounded by the products of their narcissistic pursuits, and wonder, not only what joy or passion remains for them, but whether any ever existed for them. Men must not, in their anxious pursuit of such pleasures, ignore the true pleasures that alone lend significance to the existential life; that alone are capable of supporting a male ego that remains under constant assault in this maladaptive society we have been constructing.

10 ▸ PLAYING THE GAME

Games are never simply fun and games. At least not for men. Men will play games—organized and otherwise—all of their lives. So will women. But the nature of the games, their rules, their purposes, and their symbolic meanings will be significantly different. To understand the games men play—both on and off the playing field—observe the games boys play.

Before there were child psychiatrists or cultural anthropologists or emerging experts in childhood development; before the participant observers or professional pundits of any sort—there were knowledgeable mothers. From the earliest recorded observation, literature, mythology, and the spoken tales of childhood, we know that parents realized that girls and boys played different games; they played according to different rules; and they played for different reasons.

Consider the following familiar scene: Two five-year-old boys are enjoying the traditional "pissing contest." They unzip their flies and manipulate their penises to see who can project the stream of urine furthest. One seems clearly to have a longer range than the other, but both of them, laughing and clowning around, claim victory. The seeming loser takes delight in the fact that he goes for "longer" than the one who went farther, insisting he won. In the process, although both are giggling, both are equally determined to win, and a playful aggression insinuates itself into the activity. One waves his penis around, trying to splash the other boy with urine. The other does not find it funny, but grins nonetheless. Then one gets an erection. They both start laughing hysterically. The one with the erection unashamedly drops his pants and starts strutting around in military fashion, proudly displaying his penis at full mast.

This is not a game that little girls are likely to play. Beyond equipment, it is unlikely that such *direct* competition, abuse, and assault would be acceptable. Men play this same game throughout their lives —in different versions. We never outgrow the games of childhood. We simply reinvent them in different playing grounds.

The social scientists have now confirmed what was already known. One of the most recent and influential observers of children is Carol Gilligan. At the very opening of her book *In a Different Voice*,[1] she comments on the differences in children's play documented by such distinguished researchers as Jean Piaget, and George H. Mead, and Janet Lever.[2]

Lever set out to discover whether there are sex differences in the games children play. Studying 181 fifth-grade, white, middle-class children, ages ten and eleven, she observed the organization and structure of their playtime activities. From this study, Lever reports sex differences: boys play out of doors more often than girls do; boys play more often in large and age-heterogeneous groups; they play competitive games more often, and their games last longer than girls' games.

The last is in some ways the most interesting finding. Boys' games appeared to last longer not only because they required a higher level of skill and were thus less likely to become boring, but also because, when disputes arose in the course of a game, boys were able to resolve the disputes more effectively than girls:

During the course of this study, boys were seen quarreling all the time, but not once was a game terminated because of a quarrel and no game was interrupted for more than seven minutes. In the gravest debates, the final word was always, to "repeat the play," (Lever, p. 482). In fact, it seemed that the boys enjoyed the legal debates as much as they did the game itself, and even marginal players of lesser size or skill participated equally in these recurrent squabbles. In contrast, the eruption of disputes among girls tended to end the game.

Thus Lever extends and corroborates the observations of Piaget in his study of the rules of the game, where he finds boys becoming through childhood increasingly fascinated with the legal elaboration of rules and the development of fair procedures for adjudicating conflicts, a fascination that, he notes, does not hold for girls. Girls, Piaget observes, have a more "pragmatic" attitude toward rules, "regarding a rule as good as long as the game repaid it" (p. 83). Girls are more tolerant in their attitudes toward rules, more willing to make exceptions, and more easily reconciled to innovations.[3]

Gilligan apparently affirms the observations of all these people, particularly Lever, and even endorses the sociological conclusions that they prepare each gender for a *different* role. Men must learn to control large groups. To do so, they emphasize rules (law) and learn to play according to the rules of the game. Girls are more involved in intimate relationships. The play of two is often more important than the play of the team, even in team games. Gilligan interprets this phenomenon as signifying that play replicates and prepares one for the differing roles that men and women will play throughout their lifetime. Thus Gilligan, either directly or inadvertently, brings a feminist sanction to the ideas that from infancy on, boys and girls have different modes of adjustment.

The imprimatur of a leading feminist supporting sexual differences —provided that those differences do not suggest or imply a male superiority—may be the most valuable contribution of Gilligan's work. Although the more radical feminists severely attacked Gilligan for even suggesting or validating the differences, Gilligan has now made it "safe" to believe what every mother has always known; we can now accept

Piaget's careful observation that boys are more concerned with rules while girls are more concerned with relationships, without leaping to any judgments as to the moral superiority of either position.

Anthropological data support the constancy of that difference in its essentials. Boys organize their play into games, later to be called sports. These games have rules, and the way one adheres to them may be more important than the game itself. The purpose of the game is winning, but the rules of the game must be clear, even when the rules will be violated.

I have gone out of my way to observe children at play, knowing that there is no substitute for the intimate, almost day-to-day examination of a child with whom one is involved to illuminate adult behavior. My own two children are girls. While I saw huge and inexplicable differences between these two children, born of the same set of parents only fourteen months apart, the similarities—at least in terms of play and its meaning for identification—were even greater. My daughters conformed in their play to what I had expected from my patients, and what I had seen in direct observation of other children. Relationship was everything; friendship and attachment were crucial. Fantasy and imagination were driven toward anticipation of direct adult relationships which they observed. Dolls became their children. Stories were generated about how their "children" behaved or misbehaved.

What was most impressive about these games was how imitative they were. They mirrored life situations that existed in the girls' own lives —or at least the way the girls interpreted them. These games were preparations for a real adult life, even though, ironically, the conditions of women's existence would be radically changed by the time these children reached their adulthood. They played with dolls. The dolls were little people—real people they encountered and people they might expect to become: mommies, daddies, babies, teachers, doctors, and nurses. The rules were simple: "You be Mommy and I'll be Lynn (or Mary or Jane)." From then on a scenario emerged that was often a hilarious parody of the adult relationship they had observed. This is authentic "play" as first defined: playing at adult roles and relationships in preparation for the real thing.

Technically, little boys play with dolls as much as little girls do. That is, they play with small replicas of human beings. But the difference is enormous. The little girl's doll must look like a normal human being, or a caricature of one (as in the case of Barbie). Most dolls are baby dolls, cuddly dolls that are extraordinarily amenable to the imaginative and fantasy life of caring, comforting, and relationships.

If a boy is given a "doll," it dare not be so labeled. He will be attracted to something called an "action figure," in which the person-hood and humanity of the subject are diminished. The doll or action figure has value only in terms of its capacity to enter into a fantasy of epic nature: heroic, unrealistic, and otherworldly. It must be a "GI Joe" (a figure who ceased to exist thirty-five years before this child was born), or a "He Man," or the mechanical apparatus known as a "trans-former" (little devices that are converted from tanks into creatures of humanoid form and then back to tanks again); or a Teenage Mutant Ninja Turtle, who looks like a turtle but dresses in a bandit uniform that reveals its Ninja arts capacity.

These action figures are superhuman, or better yet, not human at all. Here the human is subverted to the cause and purpose of the game—a heroic confrontation of good and evil, good guys and bad guys, with an emphasis on victory, conquest, and triumph.

As important is to recognize how trivial, indeed irrelevant, are the truly human elements of these toy figures. They are not people with whom the child can identify or play out his future roles. They are extensions of his fantasy and expressions of specific modalities—mus-cular strength, capacity to vanquish, tools of power. Video games such as Nintendo distill these concepts even further, making the three-dimensional figures irrelevant.

My first and most intense observation of the gender difference in games occurred with the birth of my first grandchild, who happened to be a boy. Preceding play with humanoid figures was the game of "cars and trucks." This was primarily a solitary game for the two- to three-year-old. I was only an observer. But very early on, I learned that if I desired to participate in the game, I had to learn the rules. Somehow this barely articulate child knew the distinction among very similar construction vehicles: backloader, forklift, back hoe, names that even now elude me and that looked, in replica, extraordinarily similar to my presbyopic vision. Everything had to be referred to by its proper name. Playing, it seemed, was serious business, and even if the rules were not explicated, they seemed to be understood.

When I watched him play with another little boy at a slightly later age, the rules again were not articulated in advance, but any arguments were likely to be over infractions of some implicit rule they both seemed to understand. "You're not supposed to go there." "I sneaked in behind." "You're dead." "No, I'm not, I was only wounded." Major arguments often arose over who broke the rules. "Setting the rules" often took as long as playing the game.

The distinction between the rule-oriented behavior of boys and the more spontaneous nature of girls' play suggests some possible purposes. If the girls are preparing for traditional biological roles which involve all that goes under the name of domesticity, then surely this play prepares them for such roles. The virtues of the maternal role are empathy, a capacity to conciliate and accommodate, unselfishness and flexibility. In their games, girls are in training to deal with people. More important, they are practicing dealing with people they love and that they will live with. Traditionally, when women left the home to work they tended to be directed into professions where interpersonal relationships dominated. They were teachers and nurses. Their play even prepared them for this.

Boys play according to the dictates of their traditional roles: warriors and hunters. These roles took them outside the community of caring. They dealt not with empathy or conciliation but with power, antagonism, conflict, and attack. I remember one evening with my grandson when he wanted to watch a television program that I thought inappropriate. I suggested a video cassette that he might enjoy. His first question was: "Are there any bad guys in it?" This is not a child who liked violence or demanded brutality or sadism in his entertainments. What did he mean by "bad guys"? In order for there to be bad guys, there would have to be good guys. In other words, he wanted conflict. He did not want a story of development, of relationship and life. He wanted action. Winners and losers meant challenge, courage, heroics, victory —and justice. He did not want *Little Women* or *Heidi*; he wanted *Robin Hood* or *Treasure Island*.

Children have always played. So have animals. Play—unlike work —is not a specifically human phenomenon. Some animals not only play, they "keep score." The rough-and-tumble play of litter mates will quickly establish a pecking order that may endure through a lifetime. Lions play and in their play learn to establish territories, to assert their priority among males (presumably in anticipation of the more serious confrontations that will occur during mating periods), and to prepare for the essential aspects of the hunt. Animal play prepares the young for those elements necessary for species survival: competition with fellows; establishment of territory; mating and hunting.

While it is undoubtedly an oversimplification, one can also view children's play as a preparation for fundamental biological adult roles.

Male and female animals, human and otherwise, are genetically conditioned to take specific roles in life. The difference between human beings and other animals is that we are free to modify (but not deny) our genetic directives. We are soft-wired. We can do things that nature never intended us to do except by implication in supplying us the freedom to change our nature.

There is a basic difference between the sexes in the directives toward aggressiveness and nurturing. It is impossible that direct confrontation and aggression could be as central and biological a component of a woman's makeup as it is a man's. Being physically smaller and slighter, a direct conflict with a man would be suicidal. Built into the woman must be some checks on direct expression of aggression that reflect this obvious differential. Similarly, since the mother must be encouraged to nurture and nurse her young child, there must be a powerful reenforcement in women of the normal caring and protective tendencies that I assume are inherent in *both* sexes. Since play is intended as a training ground for the serious business of adult life, the play tendencies should therefore be different and express the differences between the genders. Boys' games are different from girls' games because boys are different from girls, with a different biological mission implied in this early unacculturated, unmodified behavior.

No one need be frightened of biological "determinism." Children may be taught to conform to gender stereotypes or may be conditioned to resist them. The play of boys seems biologically directed to high action, high aggression, high confrontation activities. The play of girls centers on caring, loving, tenderness, relationships. All of this can be changed if we choose to do so, because none of it is fixed. Only a genetic vector exists. If we decide to alter these roles or to mitigate the differences between them, so be it; pliability is also a biological fact of human nature.

It will not be easy. The aggressive gender-specific activities that prepare the boy for a life of physical conflict and assault, and is manifest in his play, is biologically driven. But we see in the use of cars and trucks, guns and tanks, the readiness to use current cultural artifacts to satisfy directives that pre-date these specific activities.

With ingenuity, we can use the play of childhood to rechannel masculine aggression into more socially acceptable patterns. We can set new models that will define a new masculinity. To do this we need a less individualistic, more communitarian approach. We could use all of the assertiveness, all the drive for mastery, all the energy and redirect these into any number of current social problems desperate for attention. If we had a tradition of service to employ these for the common good, instead of social aggrandizement and individual assertiveness, the individual male could fulfill his needs for conquest, achievement, and self-esteem through service to others.

Play starts spontaneously, driven by biological directive, and is then shaped by the adults of the community. We can read clearly from an examination of boys' play what nature intended and society expects of the boy when he becomes a man. Boys' play—particularly the kind of play that is encouraged by the adult population—supplies the keenest index of the meaning of manhood in the society.

Playing the game is an essential metaphor in the life of a man. The early rules of the childhood game are still evident in the rules of the adult male "game." It is still important for the average adult to be "a player," a term that is used not for an activity on a baseball or basketball team but for the world of business and finance. To be a player means that you count, that you are involved in the game, whatever the major game may be. The rules of business often are an amalgam of two things: the need to earn money and the need to establish male status.

I remember a young woman interviewing Harry Helmsley before his difficulties with the courts. At the time, he was certainly one of the richest men in New York. The reporter asked him why at his age (he was already well into his seventies) he continued to enter into deals and expand his real estate holdings. Surely it could not be simply to make money? He insisted that he was still very much interested in making money. She then inquired how much money he had; he demurred, according to the rules of the game, modestly suggesting that to state the amount would be boastful but that it was hefty indeed. She said, "I have a feeling that if you bought everything you personally wanted, there is no way you could possibly spend all of your money. Is that true?" He agreed that that was probably true. She then asked, "Then what in the world do you want to do with even more money?" His reply was: "You don't understand. In the game I play, money is the way you know that you have won." (Sports metaphors continue to be used by Presidents, astronauts, and business leaders. Sports remains the only common ground for men to relate and communicate with each other.)

In the world of business, the rules of the game are as vital as they are in playing "cars and trucks." You are free to test the limits by going to the edge. After all, winning is crucial. Still, the rules are broken with peril.

A friend of mine was visiting the great bazaar of Istanbul. This was a man who managed to combine a certain expansiveness with a pathological tightness. It stemmed of course from his fear of being taken advantage of, his feeling of vulnerability. He described a stay in Istanbul that was spent almost exclusively in the Souk in conflict with a jeweler. He had seen a bracelet he wanted for his wife, bargained the jeweler down to less than half the price, at which point the man said it would be impossible for him to go further and make any profit, whereupon my friend nonchalantly began to leave, assuming he would be called back. To his absolute surprise and horror, he was not called back.

To save face he left, then came back the next day to continue the combat. He succeeded in getting the price down further. Again my friend tried the ploy of leaving and again the man let him leave. Chagrined, he had lunch, then decided to return and buy the bracelet. But, on confronting his adversary, he could not resist insisting on yet another reduction. Finally, in consternation and rage, the vendor gave him the piddling extra discount, stating it was worth the money to get rid of him. He wrapped the package and sullenly handed it to my friend.

My friend then described the absolute sense of triumph that he felt when in the airport at Rome, while waiting for his connection, he noticed the identical bracelet in a shop designed to wring the last lira from the departing tourist. He asked the price eagerly, just to heighten his sense of victory. After translating liras into dollars, he realized that it was precisely what he had ended up paying in the Souk! Here we see the game played out according to the rules. Both men left the field of battle feeling macho and victorious. Except for the unhappy incident at the airport, both would have continued to gloat.

On his last day before returning from North Africa, a patient of mine was truly out of money, and was determined not to cash yet another check at the hotel. Killing an hour in the bazaar before going to the airport, he saw a particularly beautiful Bedouin necklace. It was not something he would ever have bought, nor would anyone he knew have worn such a flamboyant piece of workmanship. But he made the error—truly out of curiosity—of examining the work. Whereupon the game started. The vendor asked if he was interested. He answered, "Absolutely not!" He further stated that he had no money, that he would not consider it at any cost (the necklace was priced at about $375). The vendor insisted he name a figure, but the American explained that at any figure he could not take it. Supposing he took $100 off, the vendor asked. He followed my patient with the necklace and a pencil and paper, saying, "Just name your price." On the paper was $375, and my patient made the fatal error of crossing off the 3. The vendor looked at him with consternation and outrage. "You mean $75?" The American nodded and walked away, thinking he had gracefully eluded the situation. But the vendor followed, shouting after him, continuing to lower the price until finally he came down to the $75. At that point my patient continued to walk away, literally having no money.

My patient, by bidding for but not buying the necklace, had not played according to the rules and the invective he received was deserved. Had he played by the rules he would have left feeling victorious. And the vendor for his part would have felt he had been in a tough battle but, having emerged with some profit, he too could feel victorious.

Both these stories of male "shoppers" illustrate the social rules that keep such competition from getting ugly.

When games are socialized and the rules published, we enter the formal competition of the world of sports. Sports have a disproportionate influence on the lives of boys and adult men. This is one of the more distressing aspects of our modern culture. The progressively earlier age at which we now encroach on the informal world of boys' games to impose the formal world of sports is one of the least desirable modern developments in child rearing. Baseball, football, and basketball leagues that were considered postpubescent activities are now being forced on younger and younger boys.

The spontaneity and freedom that mark children's early games are lost. In addition, the presence of an adult audience at sporting events thrusts public and social approval into the foreground, converting play into performance. With the presence of adult spectators, the fear of failure is enhanced. Losing now becomes public humiliation.

Sports are defined in most dictionaries as physical activity of a competitive nature that conforms to established rules. The rise of organized sports in the twentieth century has led to many fanciful theories analyzing the athletic experience and its role in the development of male identity. None of them is completely convincing or satisfying. The sociologist Michael Messner has summarized some of these theories.[4]

During the first two decades of this century, according to Messner, American men feared that the closing of the frontier, along with changes in the work place, the family, and the schools, was having a "feminizing influence" on our society. One result of the anxiety men felt was the creation of the Boy Scouts of America as a separate sphere of social life where "true manliness" could be installed in boys *by men*. The rapid rise of organized sports in roughly the same era can be attributed largely to the same phenomenon. As socioeconomic and familial changes continue to erode the traditional basis of male identity and privilege, sports became an increasingly important cultural expression of traditional male values—organized sports became a "primary masculinity-validating experience."[5]

In the post-World War II era, the bureaucratization and rationalization of work, along with the decline of the family wage and women's gradual movement into the labor force, have further undermined the "breadwinner role" as a basis for male identity, thus resulting in a "problem of masculinity" and a "defensive insecurity" among men. . . .

How have men expressed this need to "amount to something" within a social context that seems to deny them the opportunities to do so? Again, organized sports play an important role. Both on a personal-existential level for athletes and on a symbolic-ideological level for spectators. . . . It is likely that the rise of football as "America's number-one game" is largely the result of the comforting *clarity* it provides between the polarities of traditional male power, strength, and violence and the contemporary fears of social feminization.[6]

Well, I don't know. The frontier was a uniquely American phenomenon, and yet the rise in sports existed equally in European countries. Perhaps not with the same organization that it did in America, but certainly with the same degree of passion. One need only observe the animalistic behavior at soccer matches of the normally civilized English to see a kinship with the American passion for football. England not only had no frontier but is an island, an ocean-locked country with precisely the antithetical attitudes and psychology of a constantly expanding America.

In the United States, Little League has become an institutionalized alternative for the hunt. The young boy is now being trained in the rules of manhood, not in the quasi-real area of the hunt, which was a preparation for the very real hunt he would have to join as a man, but in a game. The purpose of the game might once have been to train the boy to fulfill both the practical role of a man and the ideal of manhood; today, with the changed role of men, it simply preserves certain social values inherent in an obsolescent idea. Life, itself, will not often test the specific aspects of these ideals. The game becomes a substitute for the real thing in childhood, and the metaphor of the game becomes more real than reality in adult life.

Play for adult human beings has an obvious function beyond preparation for life roles. It also serves as an alternative to, or simulation of, competitive areas of life that may now be too distressing or dangerous. As in the tourneys of the medieval world, we can joust with blunted spears while savoring victory or nursing defeat that is less than life-threatening. We can test ourselves against limits without the humiliations and risks inherent in such activities in the real world—although some of the humiliation remains, as we can see by observing men walking off the tennis court after a particularly disappointing set.

Cultural anthropologists have observed the play of various tribal groups around the world, and now they are beginning to use the same participant techniques on our own society. One of the most helpful for our purposes is Gary Alan Fine's study of prepubescent boys in Little League baseball.[7]

In this book, Fine attempts to analyze the purpose of organized sport and to draw some conclusions about the nature of training a boy to become an adult. He points out that four elements of Little League suggest the basic elements of adult work. It is serious, "it really matters"; it is goal-directed; it is intense and characterized often by outbursts of extreme emotion; and lastly, like the work place, it is common for injuries to occur, and in fact these are expected.

The last is a somewhat strange inclusion since it is known that fewer men are injured in their work place than they are in play or extracurricular involvements. The leading cause of Allied injuries during the Iraqi invasion was sports. Nevertheless, Fine is a marvelous observer and recorder. He notes that boys of that age have short attention spans and if left to their own devices are liable not to take the game as "seriously" as their coaches, adult males, would like them to. So attention is demanded; "hustle" is one of the attributes most frequently called for. They must not "screw around" too much. They must "pay attention" when sitting on the bench. They must demonstrate appropriate emotions to indicate that this is "serious" business.

And what is it they are expected to learn? Fine divides the expectations into adult concerns and peer concerns. Coaches tend to be self-deludingly moralistic. They want to feel they are doing more than simply playing with boys, that they are contributing to moral development, so they emphasize the importance of "effort." He quotes one coach: "I believe in taking Little League baseball seriously. There's a time to horse around and a time to be serious. I take the Little League pledge of doing your best seriously. If we play good ball and lose, you'll never hear a cross word from me. You will hear from me if you play bad ball and win. That's as bad as losing."[8]

Or, from another coach, "Whenever you guys are inside the fence I want to see you hustle. The name of the game is hustle. I promise you if you hustle, you're going to win this year."[9]

While coaches say that winning or losing doesn't count, they tend to interpret defeat as lack of effort, not a lack of ability. Fine corroborates that winning transcends sportsmanship: "Although a coach may praise his team for good effort in a losing cause, this is rare and often occurs when a poor team almost vanquishes a superior team."[10] Coaches are constantly emphasizing "sportsmanship." Being a good loser and being a good winner is repeatedly idealized. This is interesting, this pure concept of morality. Nonetheless, in the actions of the coach there is clear evidence that if excessive sportsmanlike behavior leads to a loss, the coach is not happy. The young boys are faced with the traditional problem of children in the company of adults: should one attend to what they say or what one knows they want?

More important at this age is the role of peer pressure. Here morality is enforced by the most brutal mechanisms possible: scapegoating, exclusion from the group, and public humiliation. Peer pressure is exerted at its most extreme when the boy's behavior is deemed inappropriate. "Inappropriate" has clear meanings that directly relate to the thesis of this book. The term "Mama's boy" once again comes to the forefront: a "sissy", a "wimp," or a "dork" is somewhat effeminate, inept at sports, perhaps fat or small, unaggressive, cries readily, behaves like a girl, behaves like a child. Appropriate behavior is defined by distinguishing it from the behavior of a girl, of a "fag," or a "baby."

Thus, in Little League the negative models whereby the criteria of manhood are established are everywhere manifest. A man must not be a baby; a man is not a woman; a man is not a homosexual—which represents his loss of phallic power and is usually the ultimate expression

of humiliation. These criteria persist through preadolescence into adolescence, through maturity to senescence. They are the essential judgments of all men about each other.

Fine defines various standards of behavior imposed by the peer
group. They must show appropriate emotions: "Terry Hays, an eleven
year old on the Expos, is generally scorned for what others consider
his immaturity and social awkwardness. One Expo says that Terry is
'daffy.' Another says, 'He sucks.' Brian Nash, the Expo's starting
catcher, mocks Terry, saying with spastic gestures, 'I've got cerebral
palsy.' Harvey Gregg, another eleven year old, says, 'Hays takes birth
(control) pills.' (i.e., he is a girl)."[11]

One must be tough and endure pain "like a man." Tears are rarely
acceptable. "A player on Jamesville Lumber is hit on the knee with a
pitch, but not so hard that he must leave the game. Their opponents
yell, 'Make them pay their dues' instructing their pitcher to bean an
opposing player. Injuries are a part of the game and the capacity to take
injuries are a sign of a man."[12] One must demonstrate stoicism.

Fear is a part of almost any contact sport. Young boys of ten or
eleven often are not prepared for the fast ball pitching present in Little
Leagues. When this is combined with the lack of control of the typical
child pitcher, serious injury can occur. One of the essential differences
in skill between boys of roughly the same natural talent is in their
capacity to control fear. A boy who crouches at the plate, unafraid of
the ball, or stands still for the line drive driven at him simply becomes
the better player. Fear is much less acceptable than anger. Anger is a
direct product of frustration, and frustration is an acceptable aspect of
any competitive sport—anger is a tough, aggressive male emotion.

But all the rules are flexible. Behavior considered "bad" may be
accepted if it comes from an admired boy. There are established heroes
and natural leaders, and their behavior, even when idiosyncratic and
against the rules, will define the permissible. Crying and moping depend
in great part on who is doing the crying and moping. If a low-status
child cries, he is a Mama's boy and a sissy; but when done by a boy

who is a powerful athlete and team leader, it is interpreted as a sign that he is taking the game seriously—not that he is a sissy.

The emotions and attitudes expected of adult males—by themselves and by their peers—are brutally and explicitly spelled out by these Little Leaguers. Nowhere is the peculiar role of the preadolescent boy more contradictory, paradoxical, and illuminating than in his attitudes about sex and gender. For the most part, sex at this age is all talk. There may be some "making out." Some of the boys are at the very early stage of pubescence, and will have masturbated to ejaculation. But most have experienced none of this. They are typically prepubescent. This does not mean that sex talk is not everywhere. The boys do talk about girls, but to admit the importance of a girl is only permissible in a very strong, dominant male. Girls must never be more important than the other fellows, otherwise the boys are severely criticized. Everywhere Fine sees the double standard at work, even though he is writing in a period where the parents of these boys are part of the post-feminist generation. With numbing predictability boys gain status by being judged sexually potent, exaggerating their sexuality; whereas girls lose status by having the same reputation.

While the opposite of a "man" is a "woman," to these boys the opposite of being a sexual man is being a homosexual. Fine points out that most of them have not met anyone they believe "really" is a homosexual, and they actually do not know how to define homosexuals, other than to say there are boys who "like other boys" or "the guy who wants to marry another guy." Despite this, homosexuality is a central theme in preadolescent male talk. In each League, boys used expressions like "you're a faggot," "God, he's gay," "he's the biggest fag in the world," "he sucks," "what a queer."[13]

Often the concept of homosexuality gets merged with the concept of being a baby or a girl. " 'Goody goody' boys or teacher's pets are considered 'queers.' "[14]

The most popular boys inevitably were the best athletes. The true meaning of friendship is almost unknown here. When Fine asked his boys who were their "best friends," the only correlation was with good athletes. Almost everybody named the top two athletes on their team as their "best friends," and nobody named the poorest. They named a boy they would have *liked* to have as their best friend, i.e., the boy they most valued or most esteemed.

Later in adolescence a boy can redeem his manhood in the face of physical ineptitude or physical cowardice. Generally, by the senior years of high school, power other than physical or athletic prowess begins to be recognized; the editor of the paper, the "brain," the actor, the orator, the business manager, the entrepreneur become alternate modes of achieving peer approval. With puberty, not only do different roles of masculinity emerge, but that central aspect of manliness, sexual success, also comes to the fore. Only after puberty do boys have another arena besides sports in which they can prove their manhood, and that is in their relationships with women.

Women are conditioned to adopt the values that men place on themselves, so that prepubescent girls will often also be attracted to the athlete. But this is much less constant and stereotyped than it is with the boys. Relationships have real meaning to girls, and they will be attracted very early to boys who are funny, smart, clever, or physically attractive. These latter virtues become increasingly important to boys only later, in postpubescence.

As boys, too, begin to realize the proper locus of power in the adult world, status and prestige are transferred from muscle to money. Those attributes which are likely to produce money are readily recognizable as indices of power. The presence of money, itself, becomes power.

Personal skill in the world of games, while less dominant in late adolescence, still represents power and status. There is honor for the football hero and adoration for the basketball star. As reality intrudes, we see some gradual dilution of respect for sports. This varies markedly with the socioeconomic facts of life within different communities. In an urban black ghetto, athletic prowess will still be revered, for it carries with it not just the symbolic trappings that it has for the prepubescent, but also the very real significance it may have for entering into the otherwise inaccessible world of money and status. In most high schools, however, success with women, a fast track to an Ivy League school, or a sports car are easy and ready substitutes for athletic prowess. These boys are getting ready for adult games. They now also begin to play the adult sports which are part of the world of successful men. They learn tennis, skiing, sailing, and golf. But these rarely have the status-garnering aspect of the contact sports.

The power of contact sports is sustained in adult life in the peculiar institution of spectator sports. For many men, spectator sports represent the last arena of the heroic. It is identification of the most bizarre nature. We pick a team and we invest it—like a gladiator—with our manhood. The team members are our surrogates: in their victories we feel victorious and in their defeats we feel humiliated. The distance between the spectator and his surrogate is grotesque. They are not our colleagues, companions, or community. When we root for the New York Yankees or the Los Angeles Rams, the people on the team are not even the geographical compatriots that the name suggests.

Sports watching is passive. The relationship of spectator sports to real sports is the equivalent of masturbation to sexual intercourse. Fantasy plays an enormous role; very little happens except in our imagination, and as with masturbation, the substitute often becomes an excuse for not pursuing the real thing. For too many men the competitive action of sports involves lying on a couch and watching others play the game. The love of brutality is made greater by the fact that it is vicarious and we spectators risk little. We have returned to the Roman arena and the battle of the gladiators.

Identification with sports heroes starts early in life, though it is purer in the way it is played out in boyhood. After all, the boy cannot be the full man, but he imitates him in actions. In his games, he needs some models.

I am not a sports fan anymore for a variety of reasons. First, I have little patience with passive entertainments; secondly, I had no sons, and my daughters did not identify with institutional sports as some women do these days. Still, I can remember the anguish that identification with sports caused me as a prepubescent. I can remember shedding tears, real tears, over the Cleveland Indians—always a contender and never a winner during my youth. I can remember putting my fist through a screen door in anguish and despair when at the end of a close season —with everything at risk—they blew a close game in the final innings. Yet another opportunity for glory gone down the drain. And I can remember the ecstasy, the elation—the actual sights and sounds—when in 1948 the Cleveland Indians finally (several years after I came into manhood) came into *their* manhood and won the American League Pennant!

The significance of spectator sports to the adult has recently received considerable attention, sometimes of a somewhat idiosyncratic sort. In answer to an article by William Aaron in which he described football as "a male preserve that manifests both the physical and cultural values of masculinity,"[15] Allen Dundes offered a countervailing view of the meaning of professional football.

Aaron saw professional football as a caricature, an exaggeration of maleness. The uniform "accents the male physique with shoulder pads expanding the breadth of the natural shoulders and making the waist look even slimmer," while the lower body is "poured into skintight pants extended only by a metal codpiece . . . dressed in this manner, the players can engage in handholding, hugging and bottom-patting which would be disapproved of in any other context, but having which is accepted on the gridiron without a second thought."[16] These men, having proved their manhood in the most brutal way, are now free to demonstrate overt affection to other men.

Dundes, however, offers an alternative explanation of professional football:

I think it's highly likely that the ritual aspect of football, providing as it does a socially sanctioned framework for male body contact—football, after all, is called a "body contact" sport—is a form of homosexual behavior. The unequivocal sexual symbolism of the game, as plainly evidenced in folk speech coupled with the fact that all of the participants are male, make it difficult to draw any other conclusion.[17]

He cites David Coppe, one of the few professional football players who acknowledged being gay, in supporting his thesis that the game of football is simply a metaphoric acting out of sexuality:

> The whole language of football is involved in sexual allusions. We were told to go out and "fuck those guys"; to take that ball and "stick it up their asses" or "down their throats." The coaches would yell, "knock their dicks off," or more often than not, "knock their jocks off."
>
> The trust one has for one's own teammate is perhaps signalled by the common postural stance of football players. The so-called three point stance involves bending over in a distinct stooped position with one's rear end exposed. It is an unusual position (in terms of normal life activities) and it does make one especially vulnerable to attack from behind, that is, vulnerable to a homosexual attack.[18]

Dundes makes the point even more explicitly later on when he says: "In symbolic terms, I am arguing that the end is a kind of backside and the end zone is a kind of erogenous zone."[19]

Dundes's article is essentially a response to the classic traditional "Freudian" interpretation of the game of football by Adrian Stokes. In the somewhat embarrassing, high-falutin' language of traditional psychoanalysis, Stokes says of the running back: "Ejected out of the mother's body, out of the scrum, after frantic hooking and pushing, there emerges the rich loot of the father's genital." Then ensues a major fight to see which of the teams will inherit the Oedipal role, displacing the father and claiming the phallus for himself. Here it is necessary to "steer" the ball as phallus through "the archetypal vagina, the goal."[20]

Dundes buys the sexual elements of the Stokes analysis, but thinks a better case can be made for a homosexual analysis. On the other hand, in attacking Stokes, he falls into the same hyperbole, by making the psychoanalytic assumption which sees in every non-sexual aspect a covert sexual meaning.

What Dundes neglects, like Freud before him, is to acknowledge that sexuality itself may not be an end but a means. One may fight a man for sexual reasons—to get a woman. Or one may take a woman for non-sexual reasons—to assert one's supremacy over men. In our culture, where manhood is so fragile, even sex may be subverted to serve a failing masculinity. Even using Dundes's own data, one can draw alternative interpretations. Homosexuality is seen as the negative of the powerful male. Homosexual language refers to weakness and power, not just sex. What may be symbolically happening on the field is that male supremacy is asserted by reducing the opponent. The losers feel "screwed." They do not feel sexually titillated; they feel humiliated, emasculated, and impotent. What Dundes is observing is not homosexual desire, but the homosexual imagery of macho men, where, as with the prepubescents of Little League, the victor becomes a man by "screwing" (humiliating) his opponent.

Still, any male affection, even freed from homosexual desire, may only be acceptable on a field of battle as brutal as a football or rugby field can be. These men have nothing to prove to any other man. They have beaten each other up, literally, for well over an hour, exposing their bodies to pain and punishment. They have proved themselves men in the most physical sense of the competitive beast. Only with such dramatic reassurance are they free to embrace, caress, show their affection and love for their fellow men without the dread fear of homosexuality. Tenderness and affection do not come easily to men in our time and our culture.

Leonard Kriegel has pointed out that

It is curious to see how sports help shape our ideas—not just the sexuality, but also of manhood. Participation in sport—and this, I suspect, is true even for the beer-guzzling overweight crowds that roar their approval of Ohio State's football team on autumn weekends—affirms values that are both more immediately productive and simpler than those from other areas of American life. Sport is not a training ground for success in life, nor is it the sole determinant of the responsibilities of manhood. Still, sport *is* absorbed into our need for autonomy, for an existence in which skill conditioned by discipline creates a sense of adventure for both participant and observer. It may very well be that America's fascination with sports activity is what actually saved us from becoming a "jockocracy." The body's demand for excellence is perhaps one of the few remaining areas of an autonomous existence. It certainly fulfills a need for the kind of potency which is absent in so much else in the world.[21]

While acknowledging Kriegel's point of view, I find it only part of the explanation as to why spectator sports so dominate modern life. Identifying with sports—and even participating in sports—becomes an alternative support for an ego that inevitably fails under the crushing demands on manhood placed by our peculiar society. Torn between conflicting demands of biology and culture, the adult male must struggle to maintain self-respect, to support his ego in both senses: his identity as a man and his pride in being a man. Both of these are powerful structural elements in his pride in being a person. Involvement with sports becomes a way of avoiding and evading the implications of everyday life. In a peculiar way, it is the equivalent of male jewelry. Sports become an illusory reassurance. We are important. We are successful. We are strong—if only in the battlefield of games, and even when the battlers are only distant surrogates.

The failure of traditional values—those emphasized in the games men play—is particularly evident at the top. One of the greatest deficits in the business world is men who are adequate managers. Men arrive at the middle-top of their professions on the basis of technical skills, competition, and aggressiveness. They are tough engineers, aggressive bankers, compulsive reporters, driven researchers; but at the very top of their professions—and this is true whatever their profession—they must give up their technical expertise and become managers of people. The skills needed to run a giant manufacturing company are not essentially any different from those needed for running a giant university, hospital, or money management firm. The expertise and compulsive competitiveness that drove a man to the top will no longer be helpful. The company will now rise or fall on his capacity to do "human engineering," a skill for which these successful men are woefully ill-trained and ill-suited temperamentally. The constant problem of all businesses is to find men who understand human nature and human behavior and can create a team—men, in other words, with a domestic frame of mind! Inflexibility, rigidity, compulsiveness may be marvelous attributes for a tax lawyer or accountant. They do not help in being the managing director of a giant law firm.

The love of the heroic, and the hunger for it, is a tragic feature of male development that leads inevitably to the frustration of the vast majority of men and may indeed—as many authors have suggested—lead to the glorification and even the need for war. The burdens of manhood are crushing the masculine populations of the Western world. We deny our own sense of failure by using narcissistic pleasures as a device for reassurance. But identification with athletes, along with phallic substitutes, big cars and young women, are inadequate protections against a sense of personal failure.

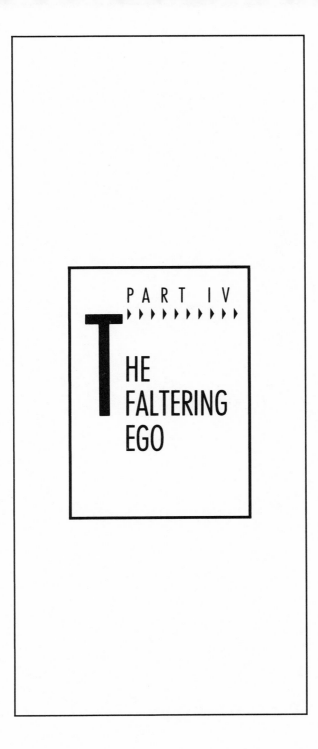

PART IV
▶▶▶▶▶▶▶▶▶▶▶

THE FALTERING EGO

11 ▸ FEELING SCREWED: "PSEUDO-HOMOSEXUALITY" AND PARANOIA

There are two models of failure for a man. He can feel he is inadequate in the broad competitive world of men, impotent and vulnerable in the face of superior competitors. Or, independent of competition with other men, he can feel himself an unreliable executor of his own affairs, inadequate to the tasks of survival. In this chapter I will deal with the first model.

Why do so many adult heterosexual men who have never in their conscious active life evinced any homosexual tendencies produce dreams during the course of therapy with homosexual imagery? The answer was "obvious" to the traditional analyst a generation ago: homosexuality is a stage in every young man's development; all neuroses involve regression, so when we are frightened by conflicts in everyday life, we go backward in time to an earlier state. With anxiety, a man regresses in his dreams particularly to a homosexual "fixation point." These dreams represent the earlier *desires* of the patient, now experienced in regression. When the patient panics at the thought of "being" truly a homosexual—and he does—the therapist has the ready reassurance that all human beings have this "latent homosexuality" within them; it is foolish to be anxious about something that is part of the normal development of every human being.

This interpretation implies that what appears in a dream is a latent desire, although what the patient expresses is *anxiety*. But all anxiety was presumed by early Freudians to be a product of our desires. If you are frightened of homosexual assault, it means that you "truly" want it.

During the same period that I was being indoctrinated by my therapist to this point of view, I was being supervised by a teacher of great talent, Dr. Lionel Ovesey. He questioned the premises of the entire libido theory, i.e., that the only drive is the sexual one and that fear always masks a hidden wish. Ovesey considered the frequent homosexual imagery in the dreams of straight men and, working on the simple Freudian assumption that anything may be symbolic, he wondered why the "anything" always had to be symbolic of sex. Why could such imagery not be also symbolic of power? He readjusted the relationship, establishing a kind of parity. Symbols can work both ways—non-sexual things could be truly sexual; sexual things could be truly non-sexual.

Does it make any difference whether you are concerned with power cast in sexual terms or sexual things cast in power terms? Can't you just get to the underlying insecurity in either case? You can, but the process was often disastrous for the patient. Desire for homosexuality has an entirely different implication for the patient from fear of homosexuality. The patient was expected to come to grips with his homosexual desires, not an easy thing for a frightened man to do—particularly when he truly had no homosexual desires.

The fallacy of this concept is patent: it denied the primacy of fear as an authentic biological mechanism, and it implied that the unconscious is a truer view of a man than his actual conduct. Ovesey rejected out of hand this concept and invented the term "pseudo-homosexuality" to describe those homosexual fantasies in heterosexuals, where the primary function was clearly other than sexual.[1]

Unencumbered by the imposition of psychoanalytic theory, most men would simply have *assumed* that their dreams of homosexuality, like the homosexual symbols in their speech, were metaphors for the "fuck-or-be-fucked" nature of everyday life. The fact that you are being screwed in a dream does not necessarily mean that you are having "latent homosexual needs" gratified, any more than if you say to a friend in your conscious life, "I really got fucked today," you are expressing the delight at consummation of a homosexual affair. In both cases, common sense points to the correct meaning. The inserted penis is a symbol of humiliation.

Like dreams, homosexual fantasies are as richly endowed with non-sexual meanings as sexual ones. Homosexual fantasies may be "regressions" to an early developmental phase. But at that earlier age any power play among boys involves *avoiding* being either a sissy or a Mama's boy. The homosexual is the ultimate "wuss." He is the non-man, half woman, half man. When a boy's ego is threatened, he begins to wonder about his identity—he will wonder if he is really a man or simply a Mama's boy or sissy.

Young boys are often terrified of homosexual dreams or fantasies, particularly if such fantasies occur in the early adolescent period when their heterosexuality has not yet fully developed and been confirmed by behavior. During this period, they are also aware of the strong affectionate bond they feel toward their buddies; sometimes certain disquieting sexual feelings toward their pals may emerge. False labeling in these ambiguous relationships can be disastrous in creating confusion about gender identity in many boys who are not homosexual. During adolescence particularly, the ego is constantly being assaulted by various daily blows to our self-confidence. When identity is still in the making, a permanent injury may be inflicted on the self-image. The groundwork for later sexual problems will be laid.

The ego or self is difficult to examine directly. The ego is the instrument by which we generally examine all other things. Like breathing, we are unaware of the ego when it is functioning properly. When the machinery breaks down, when sexual failure threatens our sense of self, self-examination is demanded, for it is then that anxiety intrudes. Anxiety is like the wheezing of malfunctioning lungs. It manages to seep into the total reservoir of the self, commanding attention and contaminating all other functions. A sexual failure threatens our confidence in work, in play, in every area. Think of self-esteem as a series of connected pools. Anything that alters the level of water in one of the pools affects the level in all the others.

This anxiety is revealed directly through the language of dreams, which characteristically uses puns and metaphors. Consider the following dream: Someone had tampered with a man's favorite automobile—not insignificantly a high-powered sports car. He was on his way to a date with a woman whom he had been wooing away from another man. He had gone all-out in the pursuit, and was succeeding. The other man was "closer" to her, but he was secure in the knowledge that his car would get him to his "prize" first. He stepped on the accelerator, only to find that the car clattered along like a "cheap four-cylinder Yugo." He could not believe this was happening and became frantic, pressing down harder. Nothing would make the car move. He began to have a sickening awareness that he simply would not be able to make it, and he frantically pumped up and down on the accelerator. He woke from the nightmare in a sweat of frustration, exhaustion, and anxiety.

Never mind the specific symbols in this dream. There is a lot of stuff of a phallic nature we could play with—the long, sleek sports car, the frantic pumping to no avail in an "attempt to get it up" to speed. The dream suggests in sexual terms feelings of inadequacy, if not impotence, and inevitable failure. The precipitating *cause* of the dream, however, was clear, and was not sexual at all. It was a response to an affront in his work. The patient had suffered a significant but hardly death-dealing narcissistic injury on the job. A choice assignment that he had been hoping for had been passed out to another. His job was not threatened, but he was humiliated. And a teasing wisecrack by a friend of his alluding to the Tortoise and the Hare—with specific mention of his sports car—may have focused his attention on the car as a symbol.

In dreams, we draw on those aspects of the day's events that have particular symbolic meaning because of past or ongoing tensions. They are the building blocks which focus on ongoing problems. The man who had this particular dream was competitive and insecure in his male role. He had come into treatment because of anxiety on the job, but it quickly became apparent that his primary anxiety (which was spilling over into his work) was connected with women and commitment. The concept of male competition so dominated his desire for attachment that it became the transcendent goal. When the woman (the trophy) was won, she had no further value. He was ready for another contest.

In this dream, we see a common link that connects homosexual imagery and general vulnerability: insecurity in the job or an affront at the office brings into question the patient's ability to compete as a man. This is still short of homosexual anxiety, but it is a crucial connection. First cast all humiliation in terms of sexual humiliation; then the successive step that leads to pseudo-homosexual panic will follow.

As a psychoanalytic candidate, I began collecting dreams with explicit or implicit homosexual meanings in heterosexual males. The following is a dream of a thirty-year-old executive. He came into treatment because of mounting anxiety at his work, irritability and difficulty in getting along with people, particularly male authority figures, and a tendency to experience panic attacks at odd and unpredictable moments when he was alone. During a period in analysis when this patient was focusing on his aggressive mother and her anger with him, he was dating an acerbic and angry woman, in every way like his mother.

He had the following dream: "I was driving my car and I skidded on some dog shit. I swirled around and around. Sally was next to me. I was having a good time and enjoying it. Then I hit a lamp post and it broke in two and the top part broke off. The bottom shot up through the floorboard, right under my seat, and I was in danger. I woke up in a terrible panic."

The dream followed an argument with his girlfriend, Sally, in which he had refused to be passively browbeaten and answered her back. A vicious argument ensued. He began to feel frightened and returned to his previous pattern of withdrawal into himself. To the patient, the homosexual imagery was immediately apparent. He felt frightened of Sally and felt that she could "break my cock off" and hand it back to him. He felt humiliated, castrated, and homosexual.

The following night, after a particularly bitter battle at work, the executive had a dream the specifics of which he could not remember, but it ended with his being anally raped by a gorilla. Here he moved from the fear of the aggressive, castrating woman to the fear of the competitive man. When he did so, the imagery of anal penetration as a form of humiliation became even more direct. His fear of male competition was thus compounded by a panicky feeling that he was indeed inadequate, that he was not a man, that he was a "queer."

The therapist has a choice of interpreting this as the emergence of "latent" homosexuality or as a typical case of pseudo-homosexual anxiety. The course of analysis will differ drastically. The concept of pseudo-homosexual anxiety allows one to move quickly to the underlying damaged male identification.

Despite the massive progress that has been made in accepting human differences; despite the pleas for tolerance and the urgency for acceptance, the readiness of organized psychiatry now to view homosexuality as "an alternative lifestyle" rather than a perversion or sickness; despite the compassion generated by the AIDS epidemic and the heroism displayed by members of the gay community confronted with this, it is my belief that little or no progress has been made in male attitudes about homosexuality. The ultimate threat to a man, his ultimate degradation and his most extreme contempt, remains the "castrated male," which is still the image that the typical straight male has of the typical homosexual male. The prepubescent boys studied by Gary Alan Fine only ten or twelve years ago are as vehement as their parents' generation was in their insistence on seeing anybody who doesn't measure up as a "faggot," "cocksucker," "queer," "woman," or "wuss." The universal statement of disrespect is: "He sucks."

In the adult world it is the same. The language of the streets is filled with expressions of contempt and aggression cast in homosexual terms:

"Stick it up your ass"; "Fuck you"; "Boy, did I get fucked over"; "He got shafted"; "Up your ass with [fill in the blanks]"; "Did I get screwed." The traditional expression for being exploited, taken advantage of, humiliated, or used, is "getting screwed." A man must not allow himself to be bested in any contest. When he is, he is left limp and vulnerable, an object of derision.

This is everywhere evident in the two most modern novels that I have used as prototypes of masculine literature, *Deliverance* and *Why Are We in Vietnam?* I could have picked any number of other sources. Hemingway is paradigmatic. In what many feel is his quintessential novel, *The Sun Also Rises,* Hemingway presents the impotent man as the ultimate tragic hero. Fear of impotence seemed to plague Hemingway his entire life. Norman Mailer is our current equivalent of Hemingway.

The apotheosis of Mailer's concern with manhood and male affection is found in the final scenes of *Why Are We in Vietnam?* Here the two boys, having proved themselves men by such foolhardy acts of courage as only adolescents could contemplate, finally view themselves as *real men*—but alone against the world. And yet, even between comrades (a universe of two) competition arises. There can be only one lion on the mountain.

Mailer fuses this competition with his feeling that love between men may ultimately be expressable solely in sexual terms. This has been interpreted by many as Mailer's own "latent homosexuality," a concept I find mischievous and irrelevant. One is free to interpret it in any way. The fact is that these two boys so close to each other, both having established their manhood in a rite of passage so powerful and dangerous that their pride is swelling, feel attracted to each other and threatened by that attraction.

God was here, and He was real and no man was He, but a beast, some beast of a giant jaw and cavernous mouth with full cave's breath and fangs, and secret call: come to me. They could have almost got up and walked across the pond and into the north without their boots, going up to disappear and die and join that great beast. In the field of all such desire D.J. raised his hand to put it square on Tex's cock and squeeze and just before he did the Northern Lights shifted on that moment and a coil of sound went off in the night like a blowout in some circuit fuse of the structure of the dark and D.J. who had never put a hand on Tex for secret fear that Tex was strong enough to turn him around and brand him up his ass, sheer hell for a noble Texan but . . . temptation made him weak at the root of his balls and he always swelled to be muscle hard around Tex so that Indian could never get it up his ass . . . and D.J. . . . knew he could make a try to prong Tex tonight, there was a chance to get in and steal the iron from Texas' ass and put it in his own and he was hard as a hammer at the thought and ready to give off sparks and Tex was ready to fight him to death, yeah, know it was there, murder between them under all friendship, for God was a beast, not a man and God said, "Go out and kill—fulfill my will, go and kill."[2]

To Mailer all manhood is rage and all life is fuck or be fucked. Not so with Dickey. Yet, even with Dickey one senses that coming to grips with one's own manhood means coming to grips with homosexuality and the power of the phallus. The civilized man respects that power and learns to keep that dangerous instrument sheathed. But he must be prepared to face an assault on his manhood, and this is often visualized in terms of penetration.

Deliverance represents a delayed rite of passage, a proof of manhood in a world where manliness is held tentatively and must be reappraised daily. *Deliverance* starts out with the same simple premise as Faulkner's "The Bear." To prove oneself, one must leave the trappings of civilization and face the wilderness with the simpler tools of a previous time. In Dickey's story, unlike Faulkner's, one is surrounded everywhere by the symbols of the phallic man. The tools of death and destruction, dramatized by Dickey, are penetrating instruments, the bow and arrow and the knife.

Dickey feels that the time is past when men could prove their manhood against the forces of nature. A real rite of passage in our day will inevitably be visualized not in relationship to a bear or even a lion—but in terms of another man. *Deliverance,* therefore, shows a hunt of a different sort: one group of men pitted against another group, with the stage set for the most primitive challenges to manhood.

In *Deliverance,* four city men set out into the wilderness: Ed, the narrator and modern-day Everyman; Lewis, the ultimate Hemingway man; and two other less relevant friends, Drew and Bobby. To bring these civilized people to a point where they are prepared, indeed eager, to kill the mountainmen they confront, something more than simple abuse must happen. A humiliation, a direct confrontation to manhood must strip the veneer of civilization and expose the beast presumed to be within every man. This can only be accomplished by homosexual rape.

Ed and Bobby are temporarily separated from their two companions when they confront two ominous mountainmen. These two rednecks, armed with rifles, are filthy, crude, obscene. They start by verbally humiliating both city men. Then they single out Bobby: pudgy, smooth-skinned, and hairless. The shotgun is held to his mouth, he is forced to pull up his shirt, pull down his pants, and crouch over a log with his naked buttocks exposed. The white-bearded redneck pulls off his pants, and, naked to the waist, crouches over Bobby. Ed describes what happens next:

I struggled for life in the air, and Bobby's body was still and pink in an obscene posture that no one could help. The tall man restored the gun to Bobby's head and the other one knelt behind him.

A scream hit me, and I would have thought it was mine except for the lack of breath. It was a sound of pain and outrage, and was followed by one of simple wordless pain. Again it came out of him, higher and more carrying. . . .

The white-haired man worked steadily on Bobby, every now and then getting a better grip on the ground with his knees. At last he raised his face as though to howl with all his strength into the leaves and the sky, and quivered silently while the man with the gun looked on with an odd mixture of approval and sympathy. The whorl-faced man drew back, drew out.

The standing man backed up a step and took the gun from behind Bobby's ear. Bobby let go of the log and fell to his side, both arms over his face.[3] (p. 100)

Then the two men force Ed to his knees to perform fellatio on the tall redneck, holding the gun up under his nose.

He said to me, "Fall down on your knees and pray, boy. And you better pray good."

I knelt down. As my knees hit, I heard a sound, a snap-slap off in the woods, a sound like a rubber-band popping or a sickle blade cutting quick. The older man was standing with the gun barrel in his hand and no change in the stupid, advantage-taking expression of his face, and a foot and a half of bright red arrow was shoved forward from the middle of his chest. It was there so suddenly it seemed to have come from within him. (p. 111)

(At the moment before Ed's humiliation Lewis shot an arrow that penetrated the chest of the mountainman.)

This scene is essential to establish the motivation that will drive Ed, the civilized narrator, to kill with passion and joy, free of conscience or remorse. The scene is set by the differing relationships between Ed and Lewis, his savior, and, more shockingly, his changed attitude to Bobby. Ed is now prepared to accept Lewis as his leader and model. Bobby, the innocent victim, is never again seen as a full member of the team. Bobby has become a pathetic non-person.

The assurance with which he [Lewis] had killed a man was desperately frightening to me, but the same quality was also calming, and I moved, without being completely aware of the movement, nearer to him. I would have liked nothing better than to touch that big relaxed forearm as he stood there, one hip raised until the leg made longer by the position bent gracefully at the knee. I would have followed him anywhere, and I realized that I was going to have to do just that. . . .

Bobby got off the log and stood with us, all facing Lewis over the corpse. I moved away from Bobby's red face. None of this was his fault, but he felt tainted to me. I remembered how he had looked over the log, how willing to let anything be done to him, and how high his voice was when he screamed. (ibid.)

The rest of the book is a protracted metaphor of a man reestablishing himself and his identity through combat with other men; fulfilling his ego and his destiny in the hunt for the enemy, an elaborate paradigm of man's fate on earth.

Ed proceeds to his moment of truth, confident and ecstatic. Waiting in ambush, he sees his prey:

Everything around me changed. I put my left arm between the bowstring and the bow and slid the bow back over my shoulder with the broadheads turned down. . . .

My heart expanded with joy at the thought of where I was and what I was doing. There was a new light on the water; the moon was going up and up, and I stood watching the stream with my back to the rock for a few minutes, not thinking of anything, with a deep feeling of nakedness and helplessness and intimacy. (p. 137)

Dickey then plays out the universal fantasy that haunts every man's dreams: the terrifying drama of impotence at the moment of trial. Ed is in the tree, exhilarated, waiting for the man he will kill, playing with the bow and arrow, feeling the tension, sensing its power. But he falls asleep and drops his good arrow to the ground.

There was no arrow in my bow. My God, I thought, I've done it now. I don't think I can get this crooked one even clear of the tree. Without a weapon I knew I would huddle helplessly in the tree, praying he wouldn't notice me . . . it was as dark as it had been, even darker. I hung the bow on a limb and went down the trunk. The arrow should have been on the ground probably sticking up but it was not. I crawled around in the needles, sobbing with fear and frustration, feeling everything and everywhere I could with hands, arms, legs, body, everything I had, hoping the broad head would cut me, anything, but just be there. (p. 159)

Every male patient I have ever treated has produced a similar dream at one time or another. Granted the metaphors will change, but the ubiquity of the dream is evidenced by the fact that it has become a standard feature in suspense dramas on television and film: As the enemy is approaching one must flee in the car, but the car won't start. A choking, gasping, helpless grinding occurs. Then, at the very last minute, when the familiar panic is completely absorbed by the audience, the car leaps forward with newfound strength. The gun that jams, the blow that doesn't stun, the baseball bat made of limp rubber; the running through molasses; the swinging fist through water so that the blow seems to have no strength; the discovery of oneself in a canoe without a paddle, the current getting swifter and the waters foaming white; the reaching for the pull cord on the parachute, only to find it swing off in your hand or it won't pull or that you can't locate it. All these are the stuff of both melodrama and the dreams of men.

Sexual imagery infuses the language of almost all male activities. We have already looked at the language of football, with its emphasis on deep penetration and getting into the opponents' end zone. Carol Cohen undertook a study of nuclear language and felt that this, too, was loaded with sexual imagery:

. . . Another lecturer solemnly and scientifically announced, "to disarm is to get rid of all your stuff." A professor's explanation of why the MX missile is to be placed in the silos of the newest Minuteman missiles, instead of replacing the older less accurate missiles, was "because they're in the nicest hole—you're not going to take the nicest missile you have and put it in a crummy hole." Other lectures were filled with discussion of vertical erector launches, thrust to weight ratios, soft laydowns, deep penetration, and the comparative advantages of protracted vs. spasm attacks—or what one military adviser to the National Security Council has called "releasing 70 to 80 per cent of our megatonnage in one orgasmic lump."[4]

She continues: "A former Pentagon target analyst, in telling why he thought plans for 'limited nuclear war' were ridiculous, said, 'Look, you gotta understand that it's a pissing contest—you gotta expect them to use everything they've got.' This image says most obviously, that this is about competition for manhood, and thus there is tremendous danger."[5]

The language of power and the language of male competition utilizes sexual imagery because all power is ultimately experienced as a form of male potency. It is not surprising therefore that the dreams and fantasies of men are occupied with fears of homosexuality, still the most direct statement of a lack of manhood.

Any increase in paranoid homosexual anxiety is a sure sign of an eroding self-confidence and a diminishing ego. One sees an increase in sullen paranoia with many aging men. In senile dementias and Alzheimer's disease, it erupts into irrational and often obscene accusations. In earlier life, whenever such behavior increases, it is a warning to those around that something is happening to make this man feel diminished and less secure. It serves as a plea to nurture this ego, or be prepared for the irrational thrashing and flailing of someone who feels he is about to be submerged.

The breakdown of the male confidence structure is seen at its most dramatic within the fragmentation of self which occurs in psychoses. Homosexual imagery is the most graphic metaphor for degradation, social humiliation, and the ultimate feeling of being used, one man to another. It is the central fantasy of the male paranoid schizophrenic. So closely tied is homosexual imagery to paranoia that in the early days of psychoanalysis, paranoia was seen as being caused by denied and repressed homosexual impulses. Paranoia was described as the "alternative" to homosexuality, i.e., the price one paid for denying one's homosexuality.

But paranoia is not directly related to homosexuality. Rather, both are related to the fear of social humiliation. The delusional systems of paranoia are metaphorical expressions of our waking nightmares. The symptoms of the illness are protective devices we mobilize against these fears. In our culture the average man equates castration, impotence, and homosexuality with his most dreaded humiliations. That is why even in our presumably enlightened time the vast preponderance of male paranoid delusions still involve accusations of homosexuality.

In the nineteenth century, a German jurist, Justice Shreber, published an autobiographical account of his paranoid illness. Freud, in one of his most brilliant conceptions, analyzed this literary fragment and on this brief evidence built his theory of paranoia.[6] Freud assumed that paranoid delusions were simply projections of a person's unconscious homosexual wishes, which were foisted on others as a way of denying them in himself. The theory may have been wrong, but it was based on accurate observation. The fact is that to this day the preponderant delusion of paranoid psychotic males is that they will be exposed or used as a homosexual. Their hallucinations inevitably involve voices calling them "perverts," "faggots," or "queers." The delusional paranoid woman rarely if ever hears such terms. The whispering voices that she perceives will always be labeling her a "whore." This clearly establishes the differing roles of sexuality in the ego system of men and women. A woman's sexuality is still seen as demeaning her, whereas a man's is seen as elevating him. Perhaps this will change, and the paranoid delusions of both will be liberated from their sexuality.

In Freud's libido system, neurosis involved the denial of early sexual "perversion." The assumption was that if the paranoid simply came to terms with his homosexuality and experienced it directly, he would not need to go through the elaborate procedures of projecting his own wishes on others and creating delusional systems. It is simply not true that paranoia is an alternative to homosexuality, as Freud believed. We now have ample evidence of overt homosexuals who still suffer paranoid breakdowns; and paranoid psychotics (many women, for example) who have absolutely no homosexual wishes.

In some way, then, any assault on power, any humiliation, any sense of impotence, whether physical or non-physical, raises questions for a man about his sexual identity and therefore the worthiness of his "self." Few of us face physical humiliations in everyday life. Rather, we suffer psychological humiliations in the work place, where we must swallow our anger and frustration because our economic survival demands on it. But we will be left with a sense of impotence which may demand some catharsis. Suppressed anger will unfortunately be expressed in self-loathing or directed against those whom we do not fear. A wife will be assaulted, if not physically, then verbally. A subordinate will be humiliated, a child abused. Much child abuse and battering of women can be understood as the frustrated rage of a frightened and impotent man.

James Joyce describes this situation painfully and poignantly in his collection of short stories, *Dubliners*. In one story, "Counterparts," Farrington, a clerk, has been "obliged to offer an abject apology" to his boss for an "impertinence." It was a day of discontent, and "he was full of smouldering anger and revengefulness. He felt humiliated and discontented." His wife, "a little sharp-faced woman who bullied her husband when he was sober and was bullied by him when he was drunk," is not at home. He is greeted by his little boy, Tom:

. . . "Where's your mother?"

"She's out at the chapel."

"That's right. . . . Did she think of leaving any dinner for me?"

"Yes, pa. I—"

"Light the lamp. What do you mean by having the place in darkness? Are the other children in bed?"

The man sat down heavily on one of the chairs while the little boy lit the lamp. He began to mimic his son's flat accent, saying half to himself: "At the chapel. At the chapel, if you please!" When the lamp was lit he banged his fist on the table and shouted: "What's for my dinner?"

"I'm going . . . to cook it, pa," said the little boy.

The man jumped up furiously and pointed to the fire.

"On that fire! You let the fire out! By God, I'll teach you to do that again!"

He took a step to the door and seized the walking-stick which was standing behind it.

"I'll teach you to let the fire out!" he said, rolling up his sleeve in order to give his arm free play.

The little boy cried, "O, pa!" and ran whimpering round the table, but the man followed him and caught him by the coat. The little boy looked about him wildly but, seeing no way of escape, fell upon his knees.

"Now, you'll let the fire out the next time!" said the man, striking at him vigorously with the stick. "Take that, you little whelp!"[7]

Displaced rage or self-directed rage is the inevitable result of our biology, which urges us to attack, and our cognition, which knows we live in a time when attack is more likely to destroy us than to save us. Dickey's sodomized Bobby is a good example. His sullen rage is directed toward his friend as well as his attackers—and most destructively against himself. He ceases to be regarded by them and himself as one of the men, a member of the group. He becomes instead a pathetic outsider, a source of embarrassment, a frightened symbol of their own vulnerability.

Competitive threats from other men are inevitably felt by most men as a challenge. Those who are particularly insecure will find challenge even where none is offered. These vulnerable men, who have emerged from childhood with the sense of having been always given the dirty end of the stick, or less than their fair share, will cast all relationships in terms of that same childhood constellation. The emotions of these men are filled with feelings of deprivation. They are always being used badly, given less than their fair share, or taken advantage of. They envy all of those who seem more blessed by the gods.[8] There is a serious danger in this form of paranoid adaptation for the individual and for those who share his environment.

Sibling rivalry is visualized by the child as a struggle for survival. Aware of his own vulnerability, the child sees parental love as the ultimate measure of safety. In the child's mind, the sibling who seems more successful, who garners more approval, is more likely to be cherished and protected. All competition will then be exaggerated in the unconscious mind of this insecure child, who will view even slight umbrage as a threat to his very survival—and act accordingly. He need not become a paranoid psychotic. He may deteriorate into a sullen state of chronic envy; in other words, a paranoid way of life.

Envy can become a way of life, converting the envious person into a grievance collector who masochistically embraces situations that confirm his sense of deprivation and exploitation. If necessary, he will go beyond this and will actually create the situation, unaware that he is the designer of the event that leads to his own humiliation. Further, he will take every ambiguous situation as a judgment against him: his lane at the toll booth is always the slowest to move; his theater seat is always the worst in the house; his piece of pie is always the smallest.

Grievance collecting is a step toward paranoia. These damaged creatures tend to become litigious, suing at slights or threatening to do so. Since an envious person is always measuring himself up against the other—always with a panicky feeling that his stick is a little shorter and he is therefore vulnerable—it becomes apparent that he need not be in direct competition to feel threatened. He need not be defeated. Other people's successes are enough to make him feel diminished. Their failure, on the other hand, will give him a certain amount of added security.

Obviously, all of us get some pleasure in the fall of the mighty—those we feel deserving of some humble pie. Cheers went up from the crowd at Yankee Stadium when the news was broadcast that George Steinbrenner was to be deposed. The grievance collector, however, takes pleasure in bringing down any other. The "paranoid" loves to find fault. He is a born iconoclast, who thrives on the exposure and the defect of heroes. He takes his greatest pleasure in the fall of angels. He is always delighted when the "goody-goodies"—who somehow or other have achieved success through wile, ingratiation, politics, luck—are defeated. When those undeserving others get their comeuppance, justice is done.

We see this character adjustment in many guises: he is the physician who never has a good word for another physician; the attorney who acknowledges no competence beyond his own; the new dentist who frowns when he examines your teeth and politely restrains himself from the verbal criticism (of the previous dentist) that he so eloquently portrays in his expression. This range of competitive emotions is part of the character structure of many men.

The level of paranoia is as good an indicator of the vulnerability of a society as any of the economic measures of gross national product. A society that leaves a significant minority, not to mention a majority, of its population feeling insecure and unfairly treated is a dangerous one. We live, I believe, in such a society.

The political opportunist works to create two distinct groups: "us" and "them." The idealogue is always casting the "us" against the "them." Generalizations can fall along tribal lines as they do now in Africa; religious lines as they have done traditionally in India and Ireland; racial lines as they have been in the United States; and now gender lines as they are with the rise of the feminist movement. In the early days of a revolution the easiest way to mobilize the masses is through manipulation of their paranoid fears, regardless of the merits of the movement.

The non-psychotic paranoid individual is volatile and subject to manipulation. An appeal to paranoid fears is an effective and major instrument of the rabble rouser and the political agitator. Any disenfranchised or underprivileged group, aware of their own impotence and helplessness, is ready to be exploited by those who can give voice to their paranoid fears. Paranoid feelings abound in the mean streets of our mean cities. But still men function. We are not yet at war.

A flawed ego diminishes both security and pleasure, yet it is rarely crippling except at its most extreme form in a paranoid psychosis. But there are means other than paranoia by which a diminished ego can affect our self-respect. The self can be reduced to a point where we lose confidence in the coping capacity of the ego; when we distrust the self as a reliable instrument, we approach the borders of depression.

This source of despair also differs markedly between men and women, even though in both genders the marks of depression are identical—an overwhelming feeling of hopelessness and helplessness. Once again, the specific despair of men illuminates the special nature of manhood.

12 ▸ HELPLESSNESS: DEPENDENT, BORED, TIRED, AND DEPRESSED

In the previous chapter I focused on the feeling of *vulnerability* that leaves a man feeling disarmed and open to assault and humiliation. In this chapter I will focus on the phenomenon of *helplessness* that comes, not from the competitive struggle, but from a primary sense of diminished self-pride and self-confidence. The endpoint of losing the competitive struggle against a strong opponent is paranoia. The endpoint of losing the battle against a diminished sense of confidence in the self is depression.

In paranoia, you are exposed to the shame and scorn of a public that "recognizes" your emasculation. No longer a man among men, you are a wimp, a sissy, a fag. In depression you are beyond concern for public judgment. You know it is "all over." You cannot cope; you are reduced to the helplessness of infancy. In this state of abdication of male responsibilities, no public voices offend your ears with reproach; you are judging and condemning yourself. Self-loathing and self-denigration are the hallmarks of depression: I am not dependable; I am a fragile reed. Indeed, I must depend on you.

The response of men in dependent modes is evident in a variety of responses short of depression. One of the most illuminating is physical illness. Common wisdom has it that men make poorer patients than women, particularly when faced with trivial illnesses. In conversations among women the anecdotes fly fast and furious about how helpless, clinging, and childlike, not to mention irritable, demanding, and irrational, men become when they are sick at home. Conventional wisdom usually has at its core some truth and, while I know of no statistical studies of minor illnesses, I am inclined to believe that men do make worse patients.

With some men, illness becomes the only legitimate way to achieve dependency gratification. A prototype exists in the duodenal ulcer, a predominantly male disease, which before modern medications could be fatal. Early observations had shown that a peptic ulcer victim was likely to be what today we would call a "Type A" man: driven, success-oriented, with little tolerance for his own dependency cravings and needs to be cared for. Rough to a point of being macho, these patients were usually good providers, beneficent and generous people, who often accumulated a great many dependent figures around them, but who allowed themselves very little show of weakness and very little indulgence of what dependency cravings they had. The elaborate independence and assertiveness of these patients were interpreted by many psychoanalysts as either "projections" of their unconscious desires to be childlike and taken care of, or a "counterphobic" device to protect against the same threatening dependencies they desired.

The life-threatening nature of a bleeding peptic ulcer demanded that the individual be hospitalized. Hospitalization is a totally infantalizing experience. Your clothes are taken away from you and you are given a garment (or were in those days) that resembles nothing so much as the kimono of the newborn baby—a thing with ties that always manage to come undone and a looseness of design that permits your vital parts to be exposed, despite whatever clutching you might do. You were put on a rigorous schedule, told when you had to go to bed, when you had to get up, and when you could eat. You were bathed against your will, also on schedule, by the tender ministering hands of nurses. Pillows were propped, beds were made, you were often referred to in the third person. The nurse might say, "He's been a very good boy today, Doctor." If the patient asked, "How am I doing?" he would often be condescendingly told, "Don't you worry. We're taking good care of you." A patient in those days, even if he was himself a doctor, was forbidden to read his own chart. If the patient attempted to do so, his hand might be gently slapped like a naughty boy's reaching for a piece of pornography. "You don't want to know about that." He was reduced to a state of total, utter dependency.

While many patients griped and bitched, for the ulcer type there was a certain comfort in knowing that he would be taken care of and need feel no guilt about it. This dependency was not a condition sought but rather an imposition demanded by the authorities. Also it was in the service of your health, not your comfort or your desires. It was an ideal condition for satisfying all unconscious dependency needs while simultaneously asserting contempt for such dependency. The patient was free to grumble about the important things that were being neglected, while reveling in the situation.

Men have difficulty with dependency for the same reason they have problems with handling cowardice and fear. These feelings threaten the fragile construction of the male ego. Men must constantly shore up the sandcastle that is their ego. They are continuously vigilant against the encroaching waves that daily erode another section of this structure. Supporting the male ego in our current culture is a building process that is endless, the ultimate labor of Sisyphus.

To be a man, one must free oneself from the attachments to the mother. One must not cry. One must not show tenderness. One dare not even be demonstrative. Surely one cannot *want* to be taken care of. Men are the caretakers.

Physical illness is a reduction to a state of dependency that is threatening even while it may unconsciously be desired. Peptic ulcer is a notorious psychosomatic disease, but the problem for men extends to any disabling or activity-inhibiting conditions, accidents, and deteriorative illness.

Disabling illnesses have a profound effect on women as well as men. But with men they pose the additional threat of emasculation. They do not seem to have a—and here one gropes for an equivalent word— "defeminizing" effect on women. Women bear illness with less distortion of self-image than do men. I know of no scientific study to back up this observation, but physicians confirm that men are more likely to be driven to psychiatric treatment as a result of reduction of mobility and activity than women. Mobility has a disproportionate meaning to men. From the early emphasis on cars, and before that bicycles and scooters, getting off, getting away, getting out fast, running and leaving have been central to male activity. We know that a teenage boy can no more visualize life without his legs than he can life without his head. He will overvalue ambulation. With maturation and age one presumes this will lessen, but the residual persists.

Cars and vehicles in general appear to an extraordinary degree in men's dreams, and almost always represent the man (the self). For one of my patients, the automobile always represented his dependency. He was never the driver, always the passenger—in the back seat. And always a back seat driver, I might add. This prototypical dream became the focus of his transference, i.e., it was his indirect way of expressing his anger and dissatisfaction with me. The driver was going too fast, endangering him, taking him around hairpin turns; the driver was taking him where he didn't want to go; the driver was ignoring his instructions; the driver was lost; the driver was more interested in himself, taking care of his own business, and despite his passenger's urgency dawdling along the way doing his own errands; the driver seemed more attentive to other passengers in the car, dropping them off at their destinations before him.

This patient had developed a powerful dependency transference to the analyst, whom he saw as a surrogate father and a role model in his own career. I found these dreams invaluable for exposing his unconscious angers, frustrations, resentments, and disappointment with me. This was a man who had great difficulty with direct confrontation. He was the youngest of three brothers. The two elder, being considerably older, could demolish him as a child. Politics and ingratiation were his chief way of handling male competition. His passive-aggressive qualities were expressed throughout the therapy.

His role as the passenger symbolized the overarching problem that endured beyond the everyday vicissitudes of his attitude toward me. His conflicted wish that I would lead and he would follow was independent of the specific interpretations inherent in these dreams. I would never allow him to leave the dream without his once again acknowledging that he was the passenger and I was the driver. And that he, not me, made it so.

With progress in his therapy, he gradually began to move into the driver's seat—in life as well as in dreams. Despite this, at times of anxiety the dreams always returned to the image of dangerous vehicles with another man in the driver's seat.

Even a less dependent man will be forced to confront the ambivalences and threats of dependency. Illness will do this. But so will the simple passage of time. Aging ultimately reduces us all to a state of helplessness. The pattern and impact of aging are changed both by the different sociological roles assigned men and women and by the different foundations of the self. Women are most likely to become depressed in post-menopausal periods. There are massive hormonal changes during menopause which make a woman more vulnerable to depression. Still, the psychological sense that she is past childbearing age makes a profound contribution to these depressions. Even in our times, the role of the childbearer is an essential part of a woman's core identity. Given the longevity of men and women today, this is a heart-breakingly early phenomenon. A woman may enter into menopause in her forties and fifties with a life expectancy now of eighty-two.

Men are capable of being fathers at a much later age than women are capable of being mothers, but it matters less to most men. Very rarely is a sixty-five-year-old man concerned about whether he can produce offspring. He is much more likely to be concerned with potency than fertility: as long as he can get it up and get it in, he tends to be indifferent to whether the sperm is viable and capable of producing a child. Although there have been men who delight in having children in their sixties, here one suspects other mechanisms. What they are proving is that somehow or other they have defied the rules of aging and remained the potent young stud.

Men are likely to enter depression as they go into retirement or business eclipse. The average man identifies himself primarily as a worker. If a man is asked "Who are you?" he rarely answers by saying, "I'm the father of three," or "the husband of Mary," but almost inevitably, "I'm a plumber, a doctor, a lawyer with such-and-such a firm." To be a man is to be a worker and provider, and there is no way around that. The man who is deprived of the opportunity of working feels a disdain from society that is nothing compared with his own self-contempt. Expulsion from the work place is the male equivalent of barrenness.

Some men struggle desperately to avoid enforced retirement. A man of sixty-four years of age, chairman of the board of a major corporation, is besieged by invitations to speak; complimented by fawning and sycophantic inferiors; heralded with pomp and circumstance wherever he goes. His office desk is a litter of "pink roses." On the day that he retires as chairman of the board, he becomes a non-person—not only in his own business but within the business community at large. It is a shocking, disgraceful, and cruel announcement that he never was someone to be cherished for his own sake, but only as an instrument of power and a conduit of goods. Once the flow stops, he ceases to have value.

Aging is only the most common cause of sudden reduction in power. An athlete "ages" during his youth. There are other cases of abrupt withdrawal of power. One dramatic example from politics involves young men who surround the President of the United States. These wielders of power, who in their twenties and thirties make senior senators and foreign diplomats quake because they guard access to powerful presidents, will find that in the post-term period they are reduced to nonentities. Many prepare for this by planning their careers while still in a position of power, but there is no adequate preparation for such a fall. Whatever awaits them is seldom as glamorous and heady as the days in the Oval Office.

When our egos become sufficiently battered that we feel useless, hopeless, and helpless, we may deteriorate into a state of depression. But well before depression there are certain borderline areas which warn that we are spending our ego resources at a more rapid rate than we are expanding them. Often, they are dismissed by a minimizing labeling. We say that we are "tired," "have no appetite for life," are "bored." When any of these three become chronic, they are warning signs to be taken seriously and may constitute a condition that some call "chronic depression."

Emotions until very recently did not interest psychoanalysts, and when they did, they tended to be only the grand passions of rage and fear. One of the few psychoanalysts who devoted himself to a small passion, the question of boredom, was Ralph Greenson. To this day his definition of boredom commands attention. He describes it as "a state of dissatisfaction and a disinclination to action; a state of longing and an inability to designate what is longed for; a sense of emptiness; a passive expectant attitude with the hope that the external world will supply the satisfaction; a distorted sense of time in which time seems to stand still."[1]

Implicit in Greenson's description, although never articulated, is a sense of passive resignation that one no longer has confidence in his own ability to satisfy his needs and desires. In boredom we wait passively hoping that luck, chance, the benevolence of others will give us some pleasure in life. This kind of boredom may seem similar to that of the dependent child looking for entertainment and outlet for his restless energies, who turns to his mother asking, "What can I do now?" Although it looks the same, it is not. The child's boredom stems from impatience not with the self (which is expanding at an alarming rate) but with the environment, which is too small for his appetites, too constricting for his energies. With the chronically bored adult, it is exactly the opposite—the world is too much with him, and too much for him to cope with.

The literature of boredom reveals a sense of emptiness and abandoned hope in the self that underlies this emotion. In the autobiographical "The Love Song of J. Alfred Prufrock," T. S. Eliot has Prufrock bemoan the loss of potency and the coming of senescence.[2]

Incredibly, the poem was written by a twenty-three-year-old man already anticipating a life of ennui, boredom, and unfulfillment. Beneath the language of boredom and ennui lies the hidden hand of depression. Another modern poet, C. P. Cavafy, expresses much the same thought in "Monotony," seeing his future as an unfulfilled extension of the present:

> One monotonous day follows another
> identically monotonous. The same things
> will happen to us again and again,
> the same moments come and go.
> A month passes by bringing another month.
> Easy to guess what lies ahead:
> all of yesterday's boredom.
> And tomorrow ends up no longer like tomorrow.[3]

The similarity is even more precise in another of Cavafy's poems, "The City":

> This city will always pursue you
> You'll walk the same streets, grow old
> in the same neighborhoods, turn gray in these
> same houses.[4]

No great stretch of the imagination is necessary to extend such ennui into the concept of real depression.

Another way station on the road to depression is a feeling of exhaustion or "tiredness." Many depressed men misread the psychologic signs of depression as physical complaints. Depressed patients often come in complaining of chronic "exhaustion," "lack of energy," "tiredness." But feeling tired is a long way from feeling hopeless and helpless. Those primary emotions of depression require an erosion of self-confidence over an extended period of time. Depression represents an exhaustion of psychic resources. Feeling tired should be a transient physical feeling; a warning of lowered reserves. Feeling chronically tired and bored should alert a man to the fact that he is "spending" more psychic energy than he is "earning."

By using a physical term—"feeling tired" (when in our unconscious, at least, we know better)—we attempt to reassure ourselves that there is nothing wrong psychologically. We are only tired. If we use our body hard physically, we have the comforting reassurance that with rest and nourishment there will be a renascence of strength and energy.

When we begin to recognize what is going on, when we consciously feel an erosion of our self-confidence, we experience "discouragement." The feeling of discouragement is specific and task-oriented. When we are unaware of our diminishing confidence and it seems to relate to our entire life endeavor, we will "somatize" the feeling: we will convert our sense of emotional exhaustion into a physical feeling—and we will "feel tired."

Because the source of the tired feeling is hidden, the mechanism may be compared to a thermostat rather than an alarm. If it registers at a discomfort threshold, the feeling automatically triggers corrective maneuvers. Even if we mistakenly interpret "tired" as a physical phenomenon, the cures directed toward it are similar to what is necessary when we know we are dealing with the exhaustion of psychic energy. For both conditions, we need spiritual and psychological nourishment; it is time to be cared for, and to be self-caring; it is time to indulge our desires. We are ready for some reward.

When we feel tired too often and too unremittingly, it may represent a prologue to the oppressive exhaustion that constitutes depression. Psychological strength is based on self-confidence and self-esteem. These in turn are built on the prideful awareness of worth that evolves from doing, giving, loving, achieving—and the rewards inherent in love and work. This reservoir of strength can be drawn on to help us endure the depleting aspects of daily drudgery, the dry seasons of our endeavors. We must restore ourselves through prideful activities in order to underwrite the unrewarding labors of necessity. The balance is important and precarious in modern life. Most men lead lives with psychic reserves as minimal as their economic ones.

The shift in the balance—predicated on pathetically small differences—effects antithetical results. As Dickens's distinguished nineteenth-century economist Wilkins Micawber said: "Annual income twenty pounds, annual expenditure nineteen ninety six, result happiness. Annual income twenty pounds, annual expenditure twenty pounds nought and six, result misery."[5]

And as Micawber's colleague, David Copperfield, reminded us: "Trifles make the sum of life." We must watch the pence of pain and pleasure.

One peculiar aspect of emotional currency is that it operates on a different cash-flow principle. When a man feels tired or depressed, what is needed is *more* activity, not less—or, to be more precise, more activity of a different quality. Energy must be used, not conserved, but used for loving, playing, and doing. Here, spending is saving. We build our reserves through our actions.

Often the feeling of tiredness is specifically directed toward an activity, thing, or person, and we then use that particular idiom, "tired of." We may say that we are tired of travel, tired of television, tired of our job, tired of our marriage. Here the meaning is clearly that we are bored, impatient with the specific activity or person. But we do use the metaphor of fatigue and exhaustion—and not by chance. "Tired of" feels different from "bored with." It does literally mean that we no longer have confidence that our involvement with that person or activity will nourish or enrich us. When we say that we are tired of a relationship, it means that the sum total of the involvements has slipped into deficit. It is expenditure, not earning. And it is time to leave—or change the conditions of involvement.

If we modify the conditions and the feelings still persist, we must begin to question whether we are not simply projecting our internal dissatisfactions onto a convenient external scapegoat. This nagging and persistent internal sense of dissatisfaction may be prelude to depression. When we feel tired, then, we are feeling temporarily used up; when we feel depressed, we feel permanently used up.

A man may feel tired when, for a moment or even a day, he has doubts of his capacity to ensure his survival, or his capacity to guarantee the quality—in terms of pleasure and usefulness—of that survival. When we feel tired, we are having doubts. When we feel depressed, we are no longer having doubts; we are convinced—and convinced in the negative. Tiredness is transient; depression is rigid and fixed. There is absolute conviction that there is no exit.

The conviction of hopelessness is wrong—but it dominates our perception. When we are depressed, we are, of course, tired of life in all of its available forms and with all of its potential pleasures. Usually, in depression we abandon hope prematurely. It is not truly life and all its potentials that we have exhausted, only the narrow segment of our particular lifestyle. We are only tired of certain conditions of our current existence, but narcissistically we confuse our universe with the universal.

There is a polar relationship between aspects of depression and pride. We build pride on achievements. With pride we raise our levels of self-confidence and self-esteem. Depression is the absolute bankruptcy of the ego, the ultimate failure of the self.

The clinical state of depression does more than merely increase the quantity of suffering from feeling tired. The experience is different because the constancy of the emotion converts it from a warning to a way of life. The chronicity adds an agonizing dimension to the suffering. Hopelessness compounds the despair. Those of us who are spared its experience can never imagine the pain. No number of slaps, bruises, cuts, or abrasions prepare one for the chronic pain of certain malignancies. No accretion of "downness" prepares one for depression.

The very term "depression" is a difficult, confusing one. When one asks a patient who comes for psychiatric help whether he feels depressed, he is likely to look at the interviewer as though he were an idiot. To the patient it goes without saying that if he feels bad, he is "depressed." To the psychiatrist, however, clinical depression is not an emotion, but a specific disease. One of the ironies of that disease is that *feeling* depressed—i.e., dejected, blue, down—is not necessarily an indication of *being* depressed. The true "feelings" of clinical depression are hopelessness, helplessness, agitation, despair, self-loathing, a sense of the corruption and degeneracy of the world, a constriction of feelings, or worse, anhedonia—no "feeling" at all.

"Depression" is a relatively new word for what had been traditionally called "melancholia." In the nineteenth century, psychiatry was almost completely a descriptive discipline, but its descriptions were very good indeed. At the turn of the century, psychoanalysts began to probe the mechanisms of "melancholia." An early analog was drawn between the signs and symptoms of melancholia and the traditional mourning pattern.

Grief has traditionally been viewed as a healthy response to the death of a beloved. Anyone who has mourned or even shared grief with a good friend will certainly recognize its common features. Generally there will be a deflation of mood—a sense of sadness and dejection—and an accompanying withdrawal of interest from the outside world and the activities that normally occupy our daily life. The image of the mourner sitting hunched over, rocking, perhaps fingering an article in his or her hands or simply staring into space, is prototypical. Depressives also look this way. Melancholia produces similar behavior, despite the fact that no loss may have been suffered. Another common sign of both grief and depression is a general inhibition of physical activity. Finally, in both one sees a lack of capacity to feel or relate in a loving way.

While one may carry the sense of loss for a loved one over a lifetime, we are expected to pass out of the intense symptoms of mourning in a reasonably short period of time. We may continue to bear our grief, but we should be prepared to resume normal experiences and activities, reenter the active life of responsibilities and relationships. When one does not, the grief reaction has slipped into a depression. One of the leading causes of depression is the loss of a loved one.

Originally, the brilliant German psychoanalyst Karl Abraham proposed a direct relationship between grief and depression. This crucial analogy dominated psychoanalytic thinking for at least sixty years, and it was presumed that all depression represented at least symbolically an unconscious loss of a loved object. Explicitly what was lost may have been a job or even just a job opportunity, but the assumption was that the individual was grieving as though he had lost a loved person.

Early in my career, I began to question this dynamic. None of my first set of depressed patients were ever mourning a loss of love. I was then at a Veterans' Hospital, and all of my patients were men. Men rarely are driven to suicide by a real loss of love. How strange, then, that the symbolic representation should be so much stronger than the actual loss! That more men commit suicide over the loss of a job than the loss of a wife or child does not suggest that a man values his job over his wife or child; it would be monstrous to judge it so. What it means is that the mechanism of depression had been misunderstood. The grievous loss which cannot be borne, which leads to despair, is not love, but the loss of our sense of confidence in our future.

Depression is a macabre and grotesque parody of grief. It persists too long; it becomes self-destructive; and to the traditional forms of grief it adds a few irrational emotions. The depressed patient seems almost masochistic in demeaning himself, in blaming himself, in finding fault with his life, his functions, and his persona. He seems devoid of all self-esteem and is excessively involved in self-accusations. He has passed beyond the sense of *a* loss into a state where *all* is lost. When Hamlet says: ". . . I have of late—but wherefore I know not—lost all my mirth, forgone all custom of exercise; and indeed it goes so heavily with my disposition that this goodly frame, the earth, seems to me a sterile promontory, this most excellent canopy, the air, look you, this brave o'erhanging firmament, this majestical roof fretted with golden fire, why, it appears no other thing to me than a foul and pestilent congregation of vapours" (Act II, scene 2, lls. 300–309), this is despair, this is depression.

Depression occurs whenever we lose confidence in our own coping mechanisms. We become depressed when we are depleted of self-esteem and self-confidence, when we no longer have the sense of our own capacities to ensure either our actual survival or the value of the life which we can sustain. With women, most depressions and most suicide attempts do emanate from the real loss of a loved one, either through death or through rejection or abandonment. The fact that women so frequently are driven to depression by loss of a loved object is because in our culture a woman's future and her value were fused in her mind with the figures on whom she is dependent. Kierkegaard, in trying to understand morbid depression, has said:

Despair is never ultimately over the external object but always over ourselves. A girl loses her sweetheart and she despairs. It is not over the lost sweetheart, but over herself-without-the-sweetheart. And so it is with all cases of loss whether it be money, power, or social rank. The unbearable loss is not really in itself unbearable. What we cannot bear is that in being stripped of the external object, we stand denuded and see the intolerable abyss of ourselves.[6]

The two major causes of depression, then, are loss of confidence in ourselves as executives of our futures, and loss of respect for ourselves as suppliers of pleasure in the life that may remain for us.

It becomes obvious that the loss of *whatever* we overvalue in terms of our pride system will be a potential source of depression. Women invest their pride and security in their capacity to be lovable and to love; men equate ego with strength, respect, and power.

Normally, whenever we feel threatened, we become angry or anxious. These two emotions trigger mechanisms to prepare us to meet the threat. When we become depressed, however, we abandon both emotions and reserve what anger we have for ourselves. We accept our defeat as inevitable. Depression is not primarily a defensive maneuver, as most neuroses are; it is rather the absence of such maneuvers. It represents the bankruptcy of the individual as announced to himself and the public at large. It is his acceptance of his dismal fate. He sits there helpless and hopeless, beyond reassurance, beyond comfort.

It is the tragedy of our time that the evolving social structure, built by men to serve their purposes, has conspired to make them feel ever more insecure. We men are hoisted on our own petards. We have created a male-dominant society, but a society in which the very nature of our dominant role becomes increasingly difficult to fulfill. We live in a world of insecure men. We live in a society in which success is becoming an impossible dream.

13 ▸ WHY THERE ARE NO SUCCESSFUL MEN

I have never met a man—among my patients or my friends—who in his heart of hearts considers himself a success. When I ask a man in the intimacy of a one-on-one conversation if he is satisfied with himself, or if I explore his dreams, how few of them have a sense of exultant pride and achievement; how many have a wistful sense of having missed the mark. Not failing completely, but also not succeeding—"just short," "not quite what I expected," or, "something gone astray, something lacking."

I believe that the changing social structures in modern Western democracies have conspired to make the male ego the fragile and vulnerable vessel it has become. It is not just the failures of our society but its successes that undermine the self-respect of the modern male. Those aspects of Western democracy which we cherish the most may have contributed the greatest amount to the erosion of masculine pride.

Failure is always tied to aspiration levels. When men are particularly tenacious in clinging to overly ambitious, adolescent goals, they are most vulnerable to that overwhelming failure represented by depression. The exaggerated disparity between our unrealistic expectations and our reality is what destroys our confidence. Our despair is the ashy residue of our hope. Compare us now at the end of this twentieth century with our forebears at the end of the nineteenth century. We can trace the roots of our own destruction to the beginning of the technological and scientific age, spawning democratic ideals and the upwardly mobile society. The nineteenth century was the century of great expectations. No man hoped for more or expected more of himself than the nineteenth-century man. Certainly, there were voices of pessimism then, too, but the general sense of the time was one of anticipation and expectation; of dazzling achievements to come and prideful accomplishments to follow. At the turn of the century, Western man appeared to himself as the master of the world. He had control of the forces of nature and he was about to solve all of the problems of his existence by the application of his intellect.

This nineteenth-century man saw himself as a godlike figure, with almost unlimited potential powers, who must merely avoid the pitfall of hubris, overweaning pride. By the end of the nineteenth century, technology had surpassed even its own expectations. There was nothing that technology would not eventually solve. Man began to realize that he need not fear God. He could replace Him. The whole of history at that point seemed to be contrived to serve the purposes of and glorify the name of *Homo sapiens*. Contrast this with our modern view of ourselves. No longer arrogant and self-confident creators, potential rivals of God, we now perceive ourselves as—if anything—the destroyers of the world. We view ourselves as trapped in a society which, while necessary for our survival, is peculiarly unnourishing.

Examining just a few of our areas of success will indicate how they have perversely led to a decline in our self-esteem. Certainly, the success of science has proved to be a mixed blessing. The Frankenstein myth is the central metaphor of the modern human condition. It indicates how our success has reduced, rather than enhanced, our self-image. In 1818, when Mary Shelley first published her story, the scientific domination of society was at its very beginnings. The idea of one human being fabricating another was purely metaphorical. The capacity to do so was presumed to be an impossibility, simply a grotesque exaggeration which enabled the author to examine her philosophical concern about man's constant reaching for new knowledge and control over the forces of nature cast in the form of a Gothic tale. In her own words, it was "a ghost story," a fantasy used to frame a poetic truth. But by the twentieth century the inconceivable had become conceivable. We now find ourselves patching human beings together out of parts of other human beings or manufactured substitutes.

It is grossly unfair that so short a time should have produced so precipitous a fall. The tragic irony is not that Mary Shelley's fantasy is still relevant. The tragedy is that it is no longer a fantasy, and that in its realization we no longer identify with Dr. Frankenstein, the creator, but rather with his monster. Our anxiety has mounted with the giant strides of the new biology of recent years: genetic engineering, in-vitro fertilization, and surrogate mothers are already part of the landscape; artificial body parts and artificial organs are created and new ones anticipated; no natural end of life is now definable. We are left with agonizing decisions about when life begins and when it ends, and what the purposes are in between.

Our technology offered too many promises that were left unrealized. Where is the promise of the nineteenth century to remove pain, hunger, suffering? A general disillusionment has developed with our capacity to manage our affairs, invoked in part by a recognition of continuing social injustice in the face of the successes of science. Where are the balancing successes in the social or political sciences?

On a cultural level, it is disquieting to find that our most staggering and profound achievements of imagination only add to our insecurity. It was not the biological revolution that initiated or created our most intense self-doubts. That honor is reserved for the world of physics. The image of the frightened, guilt-ridden scientist achieved its greatest credibility with the explosion of the first atomic bomb. The ecology disaster is yet another recent shattering blow, forcing us into a new sense of humiliation. The unexpected side effects of our new technologies are not simply incidental and casual accomplishments of our new necessities. They are serious—deadly serious. The vehicles and discarded wrappings of our conveniences are killing us. We do not know how to handle the efflusion, the offal, the noxious fumes and silent poisons of industrialization that fill the very air we must breathe, the very water we must drink, the very land we must till. There is no scientific formula to cure these ills. In a world where even success leads to increasing anxiety, in what can we take satisfaction? From what can we draw nurture? Where is a source of pride and sustenance?

The triumphs of modern science are not the only double-edged sword; so is the glorious discovery of democracy, equality, and freedom from feudal destiny. Masculine self-doubts and insecurities have risen precipitously as a result of the unanticipated effects of an upwardly mobile society. These are evident in all the Western democracies, but are epitomized in the rough-and-ready traditions of twentieth-century America.

In the traditional Old World society, a person knew that he could not leave the role, station, or even locality that was defined for him by the accident of his birth. He generally accepted his social class as he accepted his height. It was a part of him not to be questioned. The same was true for the activities of his life. He was a slave of birth, true, but he was freed of the terrors of choice. A boy whose father was a baker, became himself a baker. Indeed, often in the same shop as his father.

This was a constricted life, but constriction with constancy. It recreated in a technical world the tribal life in preindustrial societies. A man did what he had to do. There were limited goals and one knew when one had achieved them. Constricted it certainly was, but it had its compensations. To be a success in life, to have achieved his goal in such a society, all a man had to do was to be a good baker.

In an upwardly mobile society, unlimited opportunities seem to be present (albeit less than meets the eye). The carpenter's son is free to become a cabinetmaker or even a manufacturer of furniture. To be a successful man means, not as it did in the old days, "succeeding," i.e., following in the footsteps of the father, but surpassing him. What does this do to the models?

In the old society, one would compliment a man by telling him that he was almost as good a baker or a carpenter as his father had been. In the upwardly mobile society it is a different story. The preceding generation is never the symbol of success. If anything, it is the paramount symbol of failure. The irony is that this is not only so in the eyes of the son but also in the eyes of his father. The immigrant father characteristically insisted that his child work harder lest "you end up like me." The father then is an accomplice in redefining himself, not as a model to be emulated, but as a failure to be distanced from. The son's success will be judged by the degree to which he exceeds his father's achievements.

The advances in technology have compounded the problem even further. In most areas it has meant that even the methods of the father are no longer transferable to the son since they have, in fact, become inferior. In many fields, the methodology of even a few years ago seems archaic today. For generations we learned to write, and to write in the same way. Very few of us in my generation mastered the elegance of nineteenth-century script. Then came the typewriter, making penmanship obsolete. This technology remained in place through one or two generations. Sure, the electric IBM was quicker and niftier than the old L.C. Smith—but not essentially different. It is impossible, at least for me, to keep up with the new computer technologies. No sooner is one complicated computer set bought for an outrageous amount of money than a cheaper and superior product emerges: more compact, more rapid, more "memory." For someone like myself, uninitiated in youth to the magic of the computer world, each step is an agony.

The field of medicine is another example. No physician would be willing to follow earlier models of practice. We might want to retrieve some of the ideals of the nineteenth-century physicians and recover some of the humanity we seem to have lost along the way, but certainly nobody—neither our teachers, our patients, nor ourselves—would want us to use the techniques and tools our predecessors used in treating specific conditions. Technology *has* made the past irrelevant, and worse, even foolish. These factors are real, not just psychological, and they make it difficult for a son to identify with his father or to identify him as a success.

The ideal of upward mobility implied that each generation of men not only had the opportunity but an obligation to surpass the previous one. Ever-increasing opportunities demanded comparable increases in achievement to obtain self-satisfaction. But we still live in a society which has very limited room at the top. This inevitably leads to a feeling of never quite arriving; an erosion in self-confidence and an ever-enlarging sense of one's own inadequacy. Sure, a man can move up the ladder of success; this is not a myth. Horatio Alger does exist, and with a vengeance. Young computer geniuses and film makers achieve international status and power in their early thirties. We know it can be done, and if they can do it, so could you. Whatever your level, you can look up the ladder and find a higher station. If you move up a notch, why not the notch above that? Men always define success as the notch above—the notch we occupy is the position of failure.

Furthermore, in this wonderful land of opportunity, failure must always be of our own making. Whose fault is it? Not God's. Many of us don't believe in God. Not a feudal society that oppresses us from above—although certain minority groups may with some justification ascribe their failures to oppression from the top. For the most part, however, it is visualized by the individual man as something lacking or wanting in himself. Current literature is filled with the sense of masculine inadequacy and despair, which bears a remarkable similarity to the self-deprecation of the depressed patient.

This discussion may strike some as too theoretical. Do we really suffer from the existential *angst* of the human condition? Are we not, most of us, at least, more concerned with the mundane world of everyday events: of waking in the morning, going to work, going to dinner, of watching television and going to sleep? What of this workaday world of ours?

Anything in our society, in our daily life, or in the broader existential facts of life that makes an environment seem more threatening to our survival increases anxiety and threatens our security. Anything that diminishes a man's self-confidence and raises questions about his strength, value, or worth—in other words, his capacity to cope—also invokes self-doubt. The vital balance between the power of "them" and the power of "us," the differential between the obstacles raised and our sense of our strength to meet them, will ultimately determine our confidence in the self that must sustain us.

For the most part we do not live in a tribal society of vigilance and preparedness for physical assault. When a man tones his muscles these days, it is for narcissistic reasons, not survival; a gun is a better means of defense than sculpted pectorals and bulging biceps. Physical violence is not the central source of current insecurities for modern man. Still, when a direct physical assault, or even a physical confrontation occurs, it can have the most profound influence on a man's self-image.

When a man does not meet a physical challenge, he experiences something that goes beyond fear. He is humiliated and diminished in his sense of himself as a man. This is perhaps the closest equivalent to what a fear of rape means to a woman—a sense of degradation as a person. But if a woman feels guilty or somehow defeminized after being raped, we try to comfort her with the knowledge that she had no role to play in her humiliation. She was indeed the victim. It is more difficult to say this to a man who has been bullied by a street thug; he feels he *should* have had a role to play, and not a passive one.

We are not yet at a point where every individual in New York City has been mugged, but I have yet to meet an individual who does not have a relative or acquaintance who has gone through this experience. One authority estimated that before the age of sixteen, 25 to 50 percent of New York City children would be accosted in some way.[1]

Allan Stone, a former president of the American Psychiatric Association, concerned about the growth of crime, reported that according to one well-known statistical study, in 1940 a citizen in Manhattan had one chance in ten of being a victim of a serious crime in the course of his lifetime. By 1970, the risk had gone to only a little better than one chance in ten of *not* being a victim.[2]

Beyond the direct consequences of such threats of violence, a man is particularly susceptible to the symbolical implications. To feel frightened, especially in the presence of someone he loves and who may be dependent on him, is to feel humiliated and enraged with those responsible for his humiliation: these include the authorities who have failed to protect him; the population from which the attackers are drawn, even when this constitutes an unjust and falsely perceived generalization; and himself for not having the balls to confront his tormentors. I do not wish to overestimate the amount of violence and physical confrontation that the average man experiences in urban life, but one must not underestimate the leverage of such violence, or the impact it has not just on the individual and his own pride system but ultimately on the social and political milieu. The constant sense of violence—threatened or actual—could tip the balance of trust to distrust, of security to danger, of congeniality to rage.

There are many sources of "direct assault" on our survival beyond the physical. One is an attack on our financial base. The modern world operates on an elaborate system of metaphor, and money is one of the preeminent symbols. Those who devote their life to the accretion of money are often as concerned with the meaning of the wealth as with its purchasing power. It can corrupt a congressman, seduce a sexual partner, purchase health, pleasure, and even survival; it can buy space, security, and that which passes for love.

The person who destroys me financially, who takes my money, is the modern equivalent of the person who, in a previous age, extinguished my fire, raided my cave, contaminated my well, ravaged my food supply, burned my barn, or stole my horse. They used to hang horse thieves. That seems incredible these days, but not to the frontiersman who knew that the survival of his family might depend on that horse. The greatest perceived threat to a man's sense of security (with the possible exception of an attack on his sexual pride) is an assault on his financial structure.

The rage at the thief who steals his wallet is less than the rage at the office colleague who threatens his job—because what the thief takes is only a finite quantity, whereas the colleague threatens his livelihood. Threats to economic survival are perceived as life-and-death matters.

I recall an event from the days when I was still unknowledgeable in the ways of New York City. On the southwest corner of Madison Avenue between 95th and 96th Streets was a small luncheonette, the "Soupburg." The border of fashionableness then extended only as far as 86th Street. When I opened my office in this block, having little choice, the Soupburg became my standard base for morning coffee and lunch. It had a limited bill of fare. Coffee, Danish pastry, soup, and hamburgers pretty much exhausted the menu. It was a small place, with perhaps twelve stools. Because the 96th Street area in those days was still a low-rent district, yet close to the fashionable 70s and 80s, it abounded in private schools. The luncheonette was operated by a man in his early fifties and his son. The man seemed tough, mean, and angry all the time. I was appalled by his behavior. I would see anger mounting as he watched two polite adolescents sitting on stools next to me lingering over coffee and lighting cigarettes. He would eventually explode, telling them, "Get the hell out, this is not a goddamn lounge!" I had not yet adjusted to the tempo and abrasiveness of New York, and found myself disgusted and defensive in his presence.

After three months of eating every breakfast and every lunch in that Soupburg, I began to know that man and to appreciate the extraordinary amount of labor that went into his efforts. Beyond that, I became aware of what time and space meant in New York. He had only two peak periods in which to make the bulk of his money, the morning breakfast hour and the lunch period. He had twelve seats, and only twelve seats. His livelihood was dependent on rapid turnover.

He did his part, but it was not enough. If anyone chose to loiter twenty minutes over a hamburger that could be consumed in five minutes, his business was doomed. Those polite but casual teenagers were robbing him of time and space. That seat must turn over every five to eight minutes for him to meet his bills. In New York City, people physically fight over time and space.

The man's behavior never changed. But my attitude toward him did. I began to like him, and feel compassion toward him. He was a man working hard to support his family in an honorable way. What surprised me was not my changing attitude toward him but my changing attitude toward "them." I began to see the students as "the enemy," and to my chagrin would find myself seething as I gulped down my coffee and hamburger while watching two of them chatting away, while prospective customers waited for space. In identifying with this beleaguered worker, I felt his anxiety and adopted his anger.

To this day I am ambivalent about my life in New York. Whenever I evaluate the cost of city life, the price I pay for its pleasures, I do so not in terms of external danger, what someone might do to me, but rather in terms of what is happening to me, to my internal self. I have become less patient. I find myself somewhat brutalized and coarsened, less considerate of the needs of others, less polite. At one time I took the essential me out into the public space. Now there is another me, and I do not much like him. I see him occasionally when I travel to distant, less corrupted places (becoming progressively fewer in number).

In such a way men will be enraged by those elements which become symbolically equated with their survival. If money is survival, then time is money, and space is money. The connecting line extends from survival to things only indirectly involved. While the line may be attenuated and devious, in men's minds it is continuous and direct. The number of things that seem to endanger them is constantly expanding through symbolic elaborations; and therefore the number of perceived threats to a man's survival increases.

In modern life, no new element of danger need be introduced to make a man feel less secure, less manly, less worthy. Simply raise doubts about his strength, his ability or stature, and you will diminish his self-respect or self-confidence. The same environment is then perceived as more hazardous.

The extremely insecure man in today's society will receive any criticism as a threat. There need not be rejection, humiliation, abandonment; it is enough for someone to raise questions about his essential worth to produce a sense of stress, introducing either a frightened or an angry response. In the ghettos of our cities, "disrespect" is offered as an excuse for "wasting" an opponent, and "turf" is a leading cause of gang wars. Any criticism can be interpreted by a man as questioning his power and his competence.

In addition, we live in a complicated world where image is often more important than reality, where the way people view you may determine the respect with which they treat you. If we are viewed as having power, we are treated with awe and respect. This is the equivalent of vesting us with that power; more often than not the validity of that assessment will never be tested.

Within the last fifty years or so we in America have managed perversely to maintain our deprived minorities while making our privileged majority *feel* deprived. A sense of deprivation thrives on the sense that others have what we feel entitled to but do not have. A man may be able to endure the fact that he does not have what he feels he has earned. However, when he feels that his rightful reward has been taken from him and given to the less deserving, then he will experience a sense of violation. This usurpation is an assault on his powers, which will ultimately be experienced as denigration and castration. The smoldering rage that comes from feeling cheated is always present in deprivation.

We know deprivation when we see a disparity between what we have and what we assume we are entitled to. A man who feels unfairly treated carries with him a resentment that may be contained but will eventually spill over from those who have cheated him (whom he may not know) onto those innocent but proximal and handy victims he perceives as accomplices in his deprivation.

The feeling of deprivation, in our society particularly, derives from the fact that the system seems constantly to promise more to almost everybody than it is capable of delivering. Perhaps it is promising too much. It doesn't matter. Whenever a man feels he has played according to the rules and a reward is not forthcoming, he will feel duped and deprived.

We live in a world of embarrassing disparities. The sybaritic life of the affluent advertised incessantly on television and on the front pages of the tabloids is an affront to conscience. The man out of a job cannot have much sympathy for Donald Trump, who is limited by the courts to $500,000 a month in subsistence allowance.

But the average man's feeling of deprivation goes beyond the material. If it were only in the material area I think it would have a limited effect, particularly in a society such as ours where the worst off are better off than the majority in other places. But even when we get the "good stuff" of existence—the twenty-nine-inch television set that displays only drivel—and it still does not bring the pleasure it was supposed to, then we feel deprived of the very promise of life.

Americans have managed to establish a somewhat pleasureless existence. If we feel deprived of pleasure, we may question the very value of ourselves and our existence. Not knowing how to account for our dissatisfaction, we focus on material objects. If only we could afford a Mercedes, a house in East Hampton, a trip to St. Moritz, we would be happy. We keep assuming that in the acquisition of material success we will finally locate pleasure high up there among the accumulated trappings of the material life.

But the same lack of pleasure dominates the beach clubs and watering places of the rich. The penthouses are as lonely and sterile as the tenement flats. Our ignorance of these areas allow us to romanticize them and maintain the illusion that somewhere in this society pleasure is abundant.

I am not a fool. I am aware that money does buy good things. It is a lot pleasanter to eat at Lutèce than the local bistro. The food is better for one thing. But the regular diners at Lutèce suffer from the same dispirited ennui, no, I would say more ennui than the diners at the local restaurant. To the man eating at the diner with his family, an evening out is still an occasion.

A man can tolerate the pain and joylessness of work. For many, work is not expected to be its own reward. It helps avoid disaster; and with sufficient diligence he will eventually be able to buy "things," which will supply the enjoyment that his daily work did not provide. But by the time most men achieve middle-class status, this expectation proves false. Money does not buy pleasure, even though its absence can surely generate pain.

By the time a man discovers that he has been driving himself down a path that leads nowhere, he is often too frightened, too discouraged, too exhausted to look for other roads to pleasure. He has already sacrificed his youth, his pleasure in the company of his children (who are no longer children and no longer surround him), his imagination, and his undeveloped resources. Then, approaching middle age, he feels deprived at the most fundamental level. He feels robbed of the very meaning of existence. He feels betrayed and impotent.

In boredom we turn to the narcissistic pleasures—and we know how unsatisfying these have proven to be. We have created a culture with no rites of passage, no markers, no clearly achievable goals, no guaranteed rewards, no safe havens for the male ego. And who can we blame but ourselves? For it is we men who have been empowered over generations to shape the world we live in; we men who have been entrusted with the value systems of our culture; we men who have been privileged to define our own role and place in society. We have managed to take this trust and responsibility, and without design or awareness create a jury-rigged culture, alienated from our biological directives and inimical to our pschological needs. Our bodies rev us up for combats that never occur. We do not require the physical mobilization for which our endocrine system and our autonomic nervous system prepare us.

We have freed ourselves from the everyday need of vigilance against marauding enemies; we have liberated ourselves from the daily search for food. What must we then do to prove our manhood, to feel fulfilled as creatures of purpose, insight, and self-worth? The liberation from the daily struggle for survival should have left us freer to pursue pleasures and activities that enhance the ego and enrich the soul. But we have created a society which seems to corrupt true pleasure, and we contaminate all of our activities with the insistence that somehow or other even play, even love, must be subsidiary to supporting our manhood. Of course, in so doing, we corrupt the primary nurturing values of both love and play. Everything is subjugated and abased in the service of supporting the fragility of the male ego.

In the last generation we have seen women struggle to overcome the oppression of gender stereotyping; to unshackle themselves from the labelings of femininity; to liberate themselves from men's view of their proper place. Many women have deluded themselves into feeling that only they had been given the dirty end of the stick. They assume their sufferings will end when they seize the initiatives, the roles, and the identities that have been exclusively a masculine preserve. They are rushing into the world of men. Be cautioned! It is a world with its own variety of humiliation and its own brand of grief.

We have created a society in which there are no victors, only victims. The role of man in our culture may be the role of privilege, but it is not the role of pride. Because men have been vested with the power over the fate of our culture, indeed our planet, the thrashing of a male ego in decline may destroy us all. We must begin to redefine manhood in terms that are achievable; with conditions that will nurture and sustain us all, men and women. Our civilization may depend on it.

NOTES

INTRODUCTION: METHODS AND MADNESS

1. Virginia Woolf, *A Room of One's Own* (New York: Harvest/HBJ Book, 1929), p. 94.
2. Abram Kardiner and Lionel Ovesey, *Mark of Oppression: Explorations in the Personality of the American Negro* (Cleveland: World Publishing Co., 1962).
3. Nathan Glazer and Daniel Moynihan, *Beyond the Melting Pot: The Negroes, Puerto Ricans, Jews, Italians and Irish of New York City* (Cambridge, Mass.: Massachusetts Institute of Technology Press, 1970).
4. Since I admire the general scholarship of this book, I prefer not to cite it here for its rare lapse in judgment. Any doubting Thomases are free to write me for the exact citation.
5. Immanuel Kant, *On History*, edited by L. W. Beck (New York: Bobbs-Merrill, 1963), p. 55.
6. Jean-Jacques Rousseau, *The First and Second Discourses*, edited by R. D. Masters (New York: St. Martin's Press, 1964), pp. 113–15.
7. Primo Levi, *The Drowned and the Saved*, trans. by R. Rosenthal (New York: Vintage Books, 1989), pp. 183–84.

PART I: DEFINING MANHOOD

CHAPTER 1

1. Quoted in David Hamburg, *et al.*, "Anger and Depression in the Perspective of Behavioral Biology," in L. Levi, ed., *Emotions: Their Parameters and Measurement* (London: Oxford University Press, 1973), p. 137.

2. Ibid., p. 237.
3. Willard Gaylin, "On the Borders of Persuasion: A Psychoanalytic Look at Coercion," *Psychiatry*, vol. 37, no. 1, pp. 1–9, Feb. 1974.

CHAPTER 2

1. For a full discussion of the unique nature of the human animal, see Willard Gaylin, *Adam and Eve and Pinocchio: On Being and Becoming Human* (New York: Viking Press, 1990; paperback published as *On Being and Becoming Human* (Viking/Penguin, 1991).
2. John Cheever, "Journals" (Part 2), *The New Yorker*, Jan. 28, 1991, p. 49.
3. Gilbert Herdt, *Guardians of the Flutes: Idioms of Masculinity* (New York: Columbia University Press, Morningside ed., 1987), p. 203.
4. Ibid., p. 204.
5. Ibid., p. 217.
6. Nancy Chodorow, *The Reproduction of Mother: Psychoanalysis and the Sociology of Gender* (Berkeley: University of California Press, 1978).
7. Ibid., p. 174.

CHAPTER 3

1. Philip Shenon, "War Notebook," *The New York Times*, Feb. 19, 1991, p. A6.
2. Deborah Tannen, *You Just Don't Understand: Women and Men in Conversation* (New York: William Morrow, 1990), p. 240.
3. Barbara Lloyd, "Rules of the Gender Game," *New Scientist*, Dec. 2, 1989, p. 62.
4. Ibid., p. 64.
5. John Williams and Deborah Best, *Sex and Psyche* (Newbury Park, Calif.: Sage Publications, 1990), p. 183.
6. Michael Herzfeld, *The Poetics of Manhood: Contest and Identity in a Cretan Mountain Village* (Princeton, N.J.: Princeton University Press, 1985), p. 124.

CHAPTER 4

1. David Gilmore, *Mankind in the Making: Cultural Concepts of Masculinity* (New Haven: Yale University Press, 1990), p. 11.
2. Arnold Van Gennep, *The Rites of Passage* (Chicago: University of Chicago Press, 1960).
3. Ray Raphael, *The Men from the Boys: Rites of Passage in Male America* (Lincoln, Nebr.: Bison Books, University of Nebraska Press, 1990), p. xi.
4. H. I. Hogbin, *Kinship and Marriage in a New Guinea Village* (London: Athlone Press, 1963), pp. 30–31, cited in Raphael, *op cit.*, p. 11.

5. Once again I am indebted to David Gilmore for bringing to my attention the work of Paul Spenser. The elegant pioneering work on the Samburu people may be found in P. Spenser, *The Samburu Study: Gerontocracy in a Nomadic Tribe* (Berkeley: University of California Press, 1965).
6. All citations are taken from William Faulkner, *Uncollected Stories of William Faulkner*, edited by J. Blotner (New York: Random House, 1979).
7. Norman Mailer, *Why Are We in Vietnam?* (New York: G. P. Putnam's Sons, 1967), p. 12.
8. Thomas Wolfe, *Look Homeward, Angel* (New York: The Modern Library, n.d.), p. 505.

PART II: FEELING MANLY

CHAPTER 5

1. Robert Stoller, "Overview: The Impact of New Advances in Sex Research on Psychoanalytic Therapy," *American Journal of Psychiatry*, 130:3 (March 1973), pp. 244–45.
2. E. Reynaud, *Holy Virility: The Social Construction of Masculinity* (London: Pluto Press, 1983), p. 40 (translated from the French by R. Schwartz).
3. Ibid., p. 79.
4. Ibid., p. 98.
5. See Thomas Gregor, *Anxious Pleasures: The Sexual Life of an Amazonian People* (Chicago: University of Chicago Press, 1985).

CHAPTER 6

1. See Robert Graves, *Hercules, My Shipmate* (Westport, Conn.: Greenwood Press, 1979).
2. Gilmore, *op cit.*, pp. 106–07.
3. Ibid., pp. 134–35.
4. All citations are taken from Stephen Crane, *The Red Badge of Courage* (New York: W. W. Norton, Norton Critical Edition, 1976).
5. Mailer, *Why Are We in Vietnam?*, pp. 175–76.
6. All citations are taken from James Dickey, *Deliverance* (New York: Laurel Books, 1970).
7. Leonard Kriegel, *On Men and Manhood* (New York: Hawthorne Books, 1979), p. 199.

CHAPTER 7

1. Sigmund Freud, *Three Essays on the Theory of Sexuality* (1905), 7:125.
2. Sigmund Freud, *Totem and Taboo* (1913), 13:1.

3. E. O. Wilson, *On Human Nature* (Cambridge, Mass.: Harvard University Press, 1978), p. 140.

4. Ibid., p. 141.

5. Roberto Unger, *Passion: An Essay on Personality* (New York: The Free Press, 1984), p. 176.

6. C. S. Lewis, *The Four Loves* (New York: Harcourt Brace Jovanovich, 1960), pp. 134–35.

7. William Aaron, *Straight* (New York: Holt, Rinehart & Winston, 1973).

8. Larry Kramer, *Faggots* (New York: Random House, 1978).

9. Gilmore, *op. cit.*, p. 32, summarizes the works of three distinguished anthropologists of Mediterranean masculinity: J. Pitt-Rivers, *Mediterranean Countrymen* (Paris: Mouton, 1963); J. Davis, *People of the Mediterranean* (London: Routledge & Kegan Paul, 1977); and Herzfeld, *The Poetics of Manhood: Contest and Identity in a Cretan Mountain Village.*

10. Gilmore, *op. cit.*, p. 33.

11. Ibid., pp. 40–41.

12. Ibid., p. 41.

13. N. Masters and V. Johnson, *Human Sexual Response* (New York: Bantam, 1981).

14. Sigmund Freud, "Contributions to the Psychology of Love," I (1910), 11:163; II (1912), 11:177; III (1918), 11:19.

15. Sigmund Freud, "Analysis of a Phobia in a Five-Year-Old Boy" (1909), 10:3.

CHAPTER 8

1. Pope John Paul II, "Laborem Exercens," *Origins*, vol. II, no. 15 (Sept. 24, 1981), pp. 225–27.

2. Hannah Arendt, *The Human Condition* (Chicago: University of Chicago Press, 1958), p. 124.

3. Ibid.

PART III: SUPPORTING THE MALE EGO

CHAPTER 9

1. Jean-Paul Sartre, *Antisemite and Jew* (New York: Schocken Books, 1948), p. 13.

2. M. Jahoda, *Race Relations in Mental Health* (UNESCO: The Race Question in Modern Science, New York: Columbia University Press, 1961), p. 64.

3. Gordon Allport, *The Nature of Prejudice* (New York: Addison-Wesley, 1954), p. 9.

259
NOTES

4. Philip Shenon, "Irate Wife, Talky Mistress, Shellshocked General," *The New York Times*, Aug. 1, 1991, p. A4.
5. See P. Drucker and R. Heizer, *To Make My Name Good* (Berkeley: University of California Press, 1967).
6. Henry James, *Portrait of a Lady* (New York: Bantam Books, 1983), p. 378.

CHAPTER 10

1. Carol Gilligan, *In a Different Voice* (Cambridge: Harvard University Press, 1982).
2. See, for example, Jean Piaget, *The Moral Judgment of the Child* (New York: The Free Press, 1965); Margaret Mead, *Mind, Self, and Society* (Chicago: University of Chicago Press, 1934); and Jane Lever, "Sex Differences and the Games Children Play," *Social Problems*, 23 (1976), pp. 478–87.
3. Gilligan, *op. cit.*, p. 10.
4. Michael Messner, "The Meaning of Success: The Athletic Experience and the Development of Male Identity," in H. Brod, ed., *The Making of New Masculinities: The New Men Studies* (Boston: Allen & Unwin, 1987), pp. 193–209.
5. Ibid., pp. 195–96.
6. Ibid., p. 196.
7. Gary Alan Fine, *With the Boys: Little League Baseball and Preadolescent Culture* (Chicago: University of Chicago Press, 1987).
8. Ibid., pp. 62–63.
9. Ibid., p. 63.
10. Ibid.
11. Ibid., p. 80.
12. Ibid., p. 82.
13. Ibid., p. 114.
14. Ibid.
15. William Aaron, "The Great American Football," *Natural History*, 84 (1975), p. 77.
16. Ibid., p. 79.
17. Alan Dundes, "Into the Endzone for a Touchdown," *Western Folklore*, 37 (1978), p. 87.
18. Ibid., p. 83, citing D. Coppe and P. D. Young, *The David Coppe Story* (New York, 1977), pp. 53–54.
19. Ibid., p. 81.
20. A. Stokes, "Psychoanalytic Reflections on the Development of Ball Games, Particularly Cricket," *International Journal of Psychoanalysis*, 37 (1956), pp. 185–192.
21. Kriegel, *op. cit.*, p. 124.

PART IV: THE FALTERING EGO

CHAPTER 11

1. Lionel Ovesey, *Homosexuality and Pseudo-Homosexuality* (New York: Aronson, 1969).
2. Mailer, *op. cit.*, pp. 202–03.
3. All citations are taken from Dickey, *op. cit.*
4. Carol Cohen, "Nuclear Language and How We Learn to Pat the Bomb," *Bulletin of the Atomic Scientist* (June 1987), p. 18.
5. Ibid., p. 19.
6. Sigmund Freud, *Psychoanalytic Notes Upon an Autobiographical Account of a Case of Paranoia* (1911) 12:3.
7. James Joyce, "Counterparts," in *Dubliners* (New York: Viking Press, 1961), pp. 97–98.
8. For a more detailed description of such emotions as feeling used and aggrieved, see Willard Gaylin, *Feelings* (New York: Ballantine Books, 1979).

CHAPTER 12

1. Ralph Greenson, "On Boredom," *Journal of the American Psychoanalytic Association*, I (1953), p. 8.
2. T. S. Eliot, "The Love Song of J. Alfred Prufrock," in *The Complete Poems and Plays of T. S. Eliot* (London and Boston: Faber & Faber, 1969), p. 16.
3. C. P. Cavafy, *Collected Poems*, edited by George Savidis (Princeton, N.J.: Princeton University Press, 1975), p. 45.
4. Ibid., p. 51.
5. Charles Dickens, *David Copperfield* (New York: Dodd, Mead & Co., 1943), pp. 169–70.
6. Soren Kierkegaard, "The Sickness unto Death," quoted in Gaylin, *Feelings*, p. 102 note.

CHAPTER 13

1. P. McMannell, founder of the Safety and Fitness Exchange in Manhattan, as quoted by L. Walker in *The New York Times*, Feb. 2, 1984, p. C1.
2. This quote from Allan Stone, *Law, Psychiatry and Morality: Essays in Analysis*, published by American Psychiatric Press, refers to the study by S. and R. Shinnar, "The Effects of the Criminal Justice System on the Control of Crime: A Quantitative Approach," *Law and Psychiatry Review*, 9 (1979).

INDEX

Aaron, William, 114, 199
Abraham, Karl, 238
action figures, 184, 185
Adam, 135–36, 139, 143
adolescents, 8–9, 50, 57, 62, 93–99,
    130–31, 197–98, 209, 213–14, 229,
    241, 249–50
    aggressive, 102–3
    games of, 83, 92, 99
    masturbation by, 121, 131
    personal immortality of, 94
    social approval sought by, 94–95
    see also rites of passage
adornment, 140, 158–60, 164, 165, 189–
    190
    see also male jewelry
advertising, cigarette, 59–60
affairs, sexual, 41, 127–28, 173–74
affection, feelings of, 199, 201, 209, 213–
    214
Africa, 61, 141, 190, 224
aggression, 5–6, 32, 33, 69, 119, 181,
    186–88, 202, 211–13
    adolescent, 102–3
    androgens in, xxvi, 35, 56, 101
    as fostered by automobiles, 84–85
    gender differences in, 32, 33, 101,
        186–87, 211–12
    passive, 5, 84–85, 230
    rechanneling of, 187–88
    survival value of, 5, 101
    see also war
aging, 37, 43, 71, 174–76, 179, 188, 229,
    253

dependency in, 230–31
health in, 147
paranoia increased by, 219
power and, 134, 231
in primitive societies, 42, 146–47
retirement and, 135, 146–48, 153,
    231
sexuality and, 134, 174–75, 230–
    231
agriculture, 75, 141–42, 143, 145, 164
    gardening, 136, 139–40
AIDS, 212
Allport, Gordon, xviii, 170
Alzheimer's disease, 219
"Analysis of a Phobia in a Five-Year-Old
    Boy" ("Little Hans" case) (Freud),
    129
Andalusia, 118–19
androgens, xxvi, 35, 56, 101
"anesthetic" penis, 124, 130
anger, 4–6, 43–44, 122–23, 195, 211,
    221, 249–50
    survival value of, 4, 103, 104, 240
    see also rage
anhedonia, 237
animals, 3, 7, 17, 81, 87, 88, 101, 136
    caretaking among, 42–43, 112
    domestication of, 142
    labor of, 136, 137–38, 140, 142
    play of, 186
    pleasure in, 138, 139
    sexuality of, 105–6, 108–10, 111, 112,
        113, 114, 115–16, 142
    see also hunters; hunting

261